CONTENTS

D0118391

At Home With Houseplants

People have been bringing beautiful plants indoors ever since the Victorians first dared to put palm trees in the parlor and ferns on pedestals in the foyer. Today's contemporary home, with its larger windows, skylights, and climate control, provides an even better environment for growing houseplants. Add to that the wide availability of supplemental lighting and humidifiers to improve indoor conditions, and anyone can create optimal conditions for houseplants.

A collection of vigorous plants transforms any room into an oasis of visual appeal and fresh air. When you choose plants compatible with your home and lifestyle, growing them to perfection can transform you too. As your simple regime of care is reflected in their healthy beauty, the results are tangible, rewarding, and sometimes literally delicious. With an investment of only an hour or so each week, more than a dozen different houseplants can thrive in your home. If you are passionate about plants and have more time to tend them, a much greater diversity can be yours. No matter how many or which types of plants you grow, the experience of indoor gardening will bring nature into your home and enrich your life. This book will show you how.

An overview

This introductory chapter explains how to fit indoor plants comfortably into your personal style. You'll learn about designing with plants and why they benefit both physical and psychological health. Important information includes how to select plants and how best to acclimate them to your home.

In "Plant Care Basics" (pages 11–45) you'll learn how to meet the needs of indoor plants, from light, water, and humidity to soils and fertilizer. A section on special care goes beyond indoor gardening tips and into the realm of specialty plants. You'll learn about the particular growing needs of orchids and how to create terrariums, force bulbs, and grow herbs indoors. Cultural care—how to groom, prune, stake, and propagate plants—completes this chapter.

Turn to "Troubleshooting" (pages 46–51) for help diagnosing and treating a specific plant problem. This chapter identifies and discusses insect pests and diseases as well as the symptoms of poor culture and how to alleviate them.

You may be tempted to jump straight into the largest chapter in this book, "Gallery of Houseplants" (pages 52–121), where you'll find more than 150 foliage and flowering plants appropriate for tables, floors, countertops, trellises, hanging baskets, and container gardens. The accompanying photos and easy-to-read descriptions will help you choose the best plants for your home and understand how to keep them healthy.

So read on! Soon you'll be at home with houseplants.

▼ **Many lush foliage and colorful blooming plants are adaptable to indoor environments. You can find just the right combination that will thrive in your home.**

MAKING THE MATCH

Even if you have never grown houseplants before, most of the plants in this broad category are easy to grow and care for. Success lies in selecting plants that are compatible with your lifestyle and home.

Location, location, location

When choosing a home or apartment to live in, you consider factors such as size, cost, and location. Selecting houseplants demands the same considerations, and location is paramount. Matching a plant you like to conditions within your home where it can thrive makes success a simple matter of routine maintenance.

Take careful note of your home's microclimates—the differences in light, humidity, and temperature from room to room and even from one area to another within a room. They often differ widely and thus can host diverse plants. For example, thick-leaved succulents and drought-tolerant cactus do best in bright, south-facing windows. The same plants will soon die in a humid, windowless bathroom where shade-loving ferns thrive. A drafty room is no place for a prayer plant or a weeping fig but can be nearly ideal for a Norfolk Island pine, a cyclamen, or a primrose. Check the temperature in the cellar or an unheated porch. It may be perfect for resting amaryllis bulbs or florist's gloxinia tubers.

The variety of available houseplants is stunning, and your home likely has more than one microclimate ready to welcome an assortment of blooming and foliage plants. Making the match makes the difference, and the "Gallery of Houseplants" on pages 52–121 describes plants for every combination of conditions and personal taste.

◀ Give plants in hanging baskets room to climb or trail to best effect.

Complement your style

Although there are many reasons for acquiring houseplants, one of the most common is to complement a home's decor. Some plants naturally fit well with a particular style or season, such as poinsettias in December. Others make a strong design statement. An orchid seems at home on a glass coffee table in a contemporary room, and a spiky dracaena provides contrast in a country kitchen. You can express your personal style and set the mood for a room with the right plants. A little planning before you shop will help you make the best decorating statement.

Sometimes a substitution is in order, as when the plant you want is too big for the space you have. Dwarf citrus trees and tabletop palms, for example, deliver the look you love without crowding the room as their larger relatives would. By using the design strengths of your plant choices, the creative statement you make becomes entirely your own.

▼ Choose plant colors and textures that complement the scale and style of a room.

DESIGNING WITH HOUSEPLANTS

As beautiful as indoor gardens can be, you will enjoy them more when you arrange them compatibly in a pleasing design. Here are some basic design concepts to help you achieve the look you want.

Style basics

Houseplants easily become the focal point of any room. Depending on your style and space, that center of attention might be a group of tall palms behind the sofa, a zebra plant blooming in the center of the dining table, a basket garden of firecracker flowers by the window, or a single bromeliad in a handpainted pot.

Point of view: You determine point of view by choosing where the plants will be seen. An island grouping on a coffee table will have many points of view, while a spectacular solo pot may be located so it is seen only from one angle.

Formal or informal: Express your essential style to create the most comfortable environment for yourself and your plants. Formal style tends toward neat symmetry, employing geometric patterns and complementary colors. Informal designs freely use contrasting placements, colors, textures, and shapes. The effect is visually mixed but not chaotic.

Combining plants: Select plants with a mix of forms, heights, textures, and colors that need the same cultural care. Large plants make good anchors in a group, while small plants create intimacy.

Form: The three-dimensional profile, or outline, of a plant is called form. Arrange tall and short as well as upright and climbing shapes together so the diversity of their forms can be appreciated.

Height: Place plants so that large species do not overwhelm smaller ones. If plants are too short to be seen, display them separately or elevate them on a plant stand or table.

Texture: The appearance of a plant's leaves adds to its visual interest, and a combination of contrasting textures is more appealing than a single type. Coarse-textured plants give depth and energy to a display. Fine leaf texture adds soft, airy movement and draws the viewer in. Small, finely textured leaves are best seen at the front of a group of plants.

Color: Flowering houseplants come in every color to match or contrast with your decor. Bright reds and purples catch the eye immediately, while white and silver

▲ A handpainted ceramic cachepot complements the orchid it holds and blends well with other formal decorative elements in this tabletop grouping.

blend well with other colors and lighten the mood. Blue comforts, pink and yellow convey optimism, and intermediate colors such as peach and magenta provide a trendy contrast to primary hues. Soul-soothing green is, fortunately, the primary color of houseplants. Using it to create a more welcoming, comforting home is a natural choice.

IMPROVING HEALTH WITH HOUSEPLANTS

> ➤ Scientific studies indicate that houseplants reduce indoor air pollution, increase worker productivity, and contribute to the health and well-being of people who live, work or study near them.

THE BEST AIR FILTERS

The following 12 houseplants, in approximate order of efficiency, are generally considered the best plants for reducing air pollution.

Boston fern
Florist's mum
Pygmy date palm
'Janet Craig'
  dracaena
'Kimberley
  Queen' fern
Bamboo palm
Rubber tree
English ivy
Weeping fig
Peace lily
Areca palm
Corn plant

If you have ever enjoyed their company, you know that plants make people happy. At home and in public spaces, plants enhance mental, physical, and social health. Scientific research shows that interacting with plants has measurable benefits as well. Working with or near plants and flowers lowers blood pressure, eases stress, and actually makes people feel better. People who care for plants derive pleasure from their well-being. Such a nurturing relationship fulfills human emotional needs.

Members of the American Horticultural Therapy Association (AHTA) develop indoor and outdoor gardening programs designed to feature the therapeutic, vocational, and wellness benefits of people-plant relationships. Horticultural therapy programs are found in group settings such as nursing homes, assisted-living communities, hospitals, and prisons. Therapy programs rely on the fact that plants appeal to human beings' senses, even when those senses are somewhat diminished. Plants can elicit a peaceful and serene feeling or even evoke pleasant memories helpful to healing. Regular garden walks can help to focus attention and recover strength, and they may reduce depression and negative thoughts.

Positive effects also are evident in industrial settings where the presence of plants raises humidity levels, making the workplace more comfortable. Such oxygen-rich working environments also may suppress airborne microbes that carry disease. Because improved mood and lowered blood pressure can be attributed to working around plants, it is no surprise that productivity increases.

Pollution fighters

Houseplants are a first line of defense against indoor air pollution, one of the fastest growing environmental problems, according to U.S. Environmental Protection Agency studies. Energy-efficient houses, apartments, schools, and office buildings are sealed against the elements, trapping pollutants in indoor spaces. Copy machines and printers, rug pads and carpeting, insulation and other synthetic materials, veneer furniture, products made of pressed wood and plywood, smoke, and detergents all give off volatile organic chemicals, such as xylene, benzene, trichloroethylene, ammonia, and formaldehyde.

You can reduce these toxic substances by growing plants indoors to act as natural filters, as the National Aeronautics and Space Administration does. Researchers at the National Space Technology Lab found that houseplants reduced pollutants, particularly nitrogen and formaldehyde. In fact, just a single spider plant in an enclosed chamber filled with formaldehyde removed 85 percent of the pollutant in a day. As few as 15 houseplants can significantly reduce the pollutants in an average home. Besides breaking down toxic chemicals in the atmosphere, plant leaves clean the air by trapping dust and other particulate matter. And in their natural process of respiration, plants absorb our respiratory waste product—carbon dioxide—and give us oxygen and moisture in return.

BUYING HOUSEPLANTS

Some houseplants are given to us as leaf or stem cuttings to start, and a few are dug up from the garden to extend their season indoors. Most often, though, you'll select and purchase your own. These ideas will help you make smart shopping choices.

Look closely

Healthy houseplants are lush and colorful but not unnaturally shiny. They should be full and bushy with only small spaces between leaves on the stems. Foliage should have no brown tips or signs of recent pruning. Flowering plants are best purchased with buds just beginning to open. Be wary if some plants in a display look good and others do not, especially if some are wilted. Undersized or yellowing leaves can indicate stress, fertility, or pest problems and are best avoided.

Inspect the leaves and stems of apparently healthy plants for any sign of insects or disease. Look for dark spots or holes in leaves and cottony masses, webs, or sticky residue in leaf axils. If plants look dry or rusty, tap a leaf over a piece of white paper. Moving dust could be spider mites, which will infest other plants in your home. Ask about any insects you don't recognize. Some nurseries release beneficial predators to eat the problem pests.

Pick up the container. If it is extremely lightweight, the plant may be drought stressed. If roots are growing through the drainage hole, the plant may be pot-bound; choose another. Avoid plants with algae, slime, or a dry white chalky crust on the potting mix or the pot. Plants with unusual odors, such as rotten milk or chemicals, may have serious disease or infestation problems. In extreme cold weather, use paper wrapping, plastic sleeves, or a covered box to protect plants during transport from the store to your home.

Shop carefully

Houseplants are available for sale almost everywhere, and high-quality plants can be found in everyday places, such as at county fairs and grocery stores, as well as on the Internet. Mail order sources often can provide plants and supplies not available locally. The convenience of home delivery and access to rare plants make these sources attractive but mature specimens can be expensive. The plants themselves are valuable and their heavy weight can

make them costly to ship. Smaller plants are less expensive and often complete the journey with less stress than larger ones. If your new plants are coming from another country, you'll also be charged fees for inspection and a phytosanitary certificate.

▲ Protect newly purchased plants from sun and drafts on the trip home.

◄ Like many houseplants, ponytail palm *(Beaucarnea recurvata)* grows slowly. This combination illustrates three different sizes of the plant. Always purchase a plant large enough for your current needs.

▲ Plant production specialists are a good source for healthy plants.

► Check plants carefully for signs of disease, pests, or cultural problems before purchasing them.

For the best selection and the easiest access to information, look in your own locale for plant specialists at a retail greenhouse, garden center, nursery, plant center in a home supply store, florist's shop, or botanic garden that sells plants. Specialty sources, such as orchid, bonsai, or hydroculture suppliers, are an invaluable source of plants and tools not readily available elsewhere. Ask about return policies and whether a horticulturist is on staff to answer questions year-round. Find out how plants are cared for, and if the answers are unsatisfactory, look elsewhere.

Be prepared

When you have ordered a shipment of plants, check your schedule. If you won't be home, make arrangements with a willing friend, neighbor, or building manager to accept and inspect them. Always get any tracking numbers available in case a box becomes lost in transit, and notify the company right away if a shipment is late or damaged. Most will reimburse you or give credit toward future purchases only if you call about problems immediately.

When the box arrives, open it and take out the plants right away. Inspect the plants closely for any damage or insect problems. Water plants if they are dry and pot up bare-root plants and cuttings without delay. Plan to repot small plants

into larger containers within a few weeks. Allow all new houseplants time to adjust to your indoor garden.

Ease the transition

Take newly purchased plants home right away and remove any wrapping as soon as the plant is inside. In almost every case, new plants are in a sort of shock when you bring them home. The rigors of shipping and environmental changes are stressful but can be overcome.

Acclimatization can take several weeks but also gives you time to be sure no pests have arrived with the plant. Even a new plant that will eventually tolerate low light was likely grown under bright light. Ease the plant through the transition by moving it to a series of interim locations with decreasing light intensity before placing it in its final site. Take special care not to overwater plants during this process.

Trust your instincts

Garden centers receive new plants regularly all year, and plant societies often schedule benefit sales in spring and summer. Get to know the delivery days at seasonal garden centers and supermarkets. Their plants are often inexpensive but quite healthy when they first arrive. Avoid the temptation to buy sick plants at a bargain price.

PLASTIC BAG ACCLIMATING

One way to acclimate a plant while keeping it isolated is to place it in a large, transparent plastic bag (a dry-cleaning bag, for example) and set it in the brightest light possible, but not direct sun. The high humidity inside the bag is just what the plant needs to help it adapt to the lower light of the average home, and the plastic keeps any insects trapped. After two weeks, if no insects are discovered, move the plant to a light level closer to what it will ultimately require and punch holes in the bag, one or two per day, so the plant can slowly adjust to the lower humidity of your home. When the bag is in tatters, remove it. You'll find your plant is now thoroughly acclimated to its new growing conditions. Even if you move it into lower light, it probably won't drop a leaf.

PLANT CARE BASICS

Houseplants are wild plants cultivated and bred to flourish in an indoor environment. They have one essential feature in common with their untamed cousins: adaptability. They can endure filtered light, widely varying temperatures, and the low humidity found in most offices, stores, and homes.

▼ **Most common houseplants need only minimal care beyond adequate light, water, and humidity.**

Today you can select from a wide range of houseplants, from familiar favorites to countless new hybrids. Providing the right amount of light is the key to success. Most homes, even the smallest apartments, offer a variety of light conditions. You can find plants in this book to suit almost any indoor environment.

Watering is the only task you'll need to repeat with any regularity. With just a little practice, you'll learn how to anticipate a plant's watering needs and quickly discover how meeting them can become a natural part of your household routine.

This chapter will also help you understand the importance of proper temperature, air circulation, and humidity. In most cases, you can meet the requirements simply by locating your plants in a specific part of your home. In some special situations, you can grow healthy plants by making a few easy adjustments, such as running a humidifier when the indoor air is exceptionally dry.

Most plants are already in pots and thriving when you buy them, but all will eventually outgrow their original containers. These pages show you when and how to repot as well as how to choose the correct size and type of pot and the best potting medium. The tips on plant division and propagation will help you share your favorite specimens with friends and family. You'll also learn how to fertilize according to your plants' needs and how to prune, stake, or train plants for optimum growth and attractive appearance.

Some houseplants do best when planted in containers that can be moved outdoors during the summer. This chapter also explains the special care needed for orchids, bromeliads, cacti, and succulents as well as how to create bonsai and terrariums. You'll learn how to force flowering bulbs, grow edible herbs indoors, and enjoy the best blooms from florist gift plants.

Most houseplants are simple to grow. Their needs are few and usually easy to meet with just a moderate amount of care. You'll find all the basics here.

HOW PLANTS SURVIVE

Although the to-do list of watering, lighting, fertilizing, grooming, and propagating may be bewildering at first, these tasks become easy and natural once you understand the basic processes of plant growth.

■ **Plant parts:** There are four parts to most plants: roots, stems, leaves, and flowers. All are crucial to plant growth and health.

Roots anchor the plant and absorb the water and minerals that nourish it. Most of the absorption occurs through the root tips and the tiny hairs on young roots. Roots send water and nutrients to the stem, which carries the nourishment to other parts of the plant. The thickened roots of some plants also store food.

▼ **Intensity, quality, and duration of light must be in balance to maintain good plant health.**

The stem transports water, minerals, and manufactured food produced in other parts of the plant to the leaves, buds, and flowers. It also physically supports the plant. In some cases, stems store food during a plant's dormant period; in others, the stems manufacture food. In some plants, stems grow as runners that creep aboveground (stolons) or belowground (rhizomes).

The vast majority of plants have clearly defined leaves. Each leaf manufactures food for the plant through photosynthesis, absorbing light over its thin surface area. Its pores absorb and diffuse gases and water vapor during photosynthesis, respiration, and transpiration.

The flower is the sexual reproductive organ of the plant. Most plants flower in their natural environments, but only some plants will bloom indoors.

■ **Photosynthesis:** Like all other living things, plants need food for energy. The basic food element for all living things is sugar or other carbohydrates. Unlike animals, however, plants are able to harness the energy of the sun to manufacture their own sugar.

In photosynthesis, light energy, carbon dioxide, and water interact with the green plant pigment chlorophyll to produce plant sugars and oxygen, which is released into the atmosphere. (Houseplants get light from the sun, filtered through windows, or from artificial lights.) The carbon dioxide is drawn in from the atmosphere by the leaves, and the roots supply the water. Plant photosynthesis supplies most of the oxygen on our planet.

Photosynthesis requires an environment that provides adequate light, warmth, and humidity for plants. No amount of fertilizer can compensate for an unfavorable growing environment.

■ **Respiration:** The sugar created by photosynthesis combines with oxygen to release energy used for growth and survival. Respiration produces carbon dioxide, water, and a small amount of heat, which are released into the atmosphere.

■ **Transpiration:** Sunlight falling on a leaf can heat it well above the temperature of the surrounding air. As water vapor leaves the plant through leaf pores (stomata), the leaf cools. The higher the temperature and the lower the humidity, the faster a plant transpires. If it loses more water than it can absorb through its roots, it wilts—which is why proper watering is so essential to the survival of a houseplant.

LIGHT

Consider light availability first when choosing a location for a plant. Plants need light for photosynthesis, which produces the food and energy necessary to keep them alive, as well as for hormone production, which induces flowering. Plants are affected by the amount of light (intensity), the color of light (quality), how long it lasts (duration and photoperiodism), and the direction it comes from (bending of plants toward light through phototropism).

Intensity: Depending on geographic location and time of year, east and west windows receive a few hours of direct sun each day, the western exposure being the hotter of the two. South windows can receive five or more hours of direct sun even in winter, yet sometimes only indirect (but intense) light in summer. North windows receive minimal direct light in northern regions. The amount of indirect light received depends on any reflective surfaces nearby.

As the seasons change, so does the angle at which the sun hits a window. In summer the sun is high in the sky, and an overhanging roof may block its rays. In winter, when the sun is lower in the sky, its rays may directly enter south windows. Outdoor elements, such as awnings, nearby buildings, and trees, reduce light coming in; reflective surfaces (indoors and out) increase it.

The amount of light a plant receives varies widely depending on its distance from the primary light source. A plant that requires moderate light will do well close to an east window or a few feet away from a hotter west window.

Quality: Sunlight is the best source of light because it has the greatest range of spectrum colors and the greatest intensity. The intensity of reflected light is reduced and therefore less beneficial to plants. You may need to add supplemental lighting to provide plants with the quality of light they need to thrive.

Duration: Most houseplants require 8 to 16 hours of light every day. Plants given too many hours tend to have slowed growth. Too few hours causes elongated shoots and thin, easily damaged leaves. Add supplemental light to lengthen the day or turn off the lights to give more dark hours.

Photoperiodism: The cycle of light and dark is particularly important for blooming plants because it helps trigger flower production. Some plants flower when daylight lasts 14 hours or more. Other plants, known as short-day plants, flower when they receive at least 14 hours of darkness while their flower buds are forming. Most plants, however, bloom regardless of day length as long as there is a cycle of day and night.

▲ In frost-free climates, put short-day plants such as Christmas cacti and poinsettias outdoors in the fall, in a protected spot where they won't receive any other light but daylight. Or in colder regions, put them in a dark closet or cover them with a cardboard box in the evening, then expose them to bright light again in the morning. This effort wil help them bloom in time for the holidays.

THE FULL SPECTRUM

Plants have spent millions of years adapting to sunlight, a complete source of light that gives off rays (or wavelengths) crossing the entire spectrum. In contrast, artificial lights have a narrower range and give off light in only a limited part of the spectrum. Although plants use primarily blue-violet and red colors for growth, they grow best when the entire rainbow plus ultraviolet light rays (the full spectrum) are provided.

The intensity of direct light coming in your windows varies as the seasons change. When the sun is higher in the sky (summer in the Northern Hemisphere), the light is hotter and more intense but reaches a shorter distance into the room. In winter the sun is lower in the sky, providing direct but less intense light farther into the room because of its lower angle.

Watch for signs of improper light. Spindly, pale growth that seems to stretch toward the light source is suffering from a lack of light; move the plant to a spot where it will receive better illumination. Rapid wilting and yellow or whitish leaf color indicates too much light; move the plant away from the light source. Healthy green leaves but few flowers on blooming plants indicates a need for slightly more direct light.

LIGHT *(continued)*

▶ **Outdoor structures or trees may reduce the amount of sunlight that reaches plants inside windows.**

◀ **As light intensity increases in summer, low- to medium-light plants, such as *Dieffenbachia*, may need to be moved back from south or west windows in order to avoid sunburned leaves.**

▶ **Some flowering plants, such as the Hindu rope plant *(Hoya carnosa)*, may thrive in low light but won't bloom unless placed where they can receive brighter light.**

Light requirements

Plants in this book are described as needing low, medium, bright, or intense light, although some plants thrive in a range of light levels. Plants may tolerate slightly more or less light than is optimal; however, too much direct sun causes damage by scorching foliage, and too little light causes plants to become spindly.

■ **Low light:** Light shade, a position well back from the nearest window. It provides enough light to read by without too much strain but little or no direct sunlight.

■ **Medium light:** An all-purpose level at which both foliage and flowering plants thrive. Medium light is found in a northeast or west window that receives a few hours of early morning or late afternoon sun.

■ **Bright light:** Direct sunlight for several hours in the morning or afternoon, but not the full strength of midday sun. Usually this light is found directly in front of an east or west window or a few feet back from a south window. It is ideal for many flowering plants, herbs, vegetables, cacti, and succulents, but too bright for most foliage plants.

■ **Intense light:** Four or more hours of direct sunlight daily. An unshaded window facing due south during the summer months receives intense light. It is usually accompanied by high heat, so few plants thrive there. Install sheer curtains or move plants back several feet from the window to reduce the impact.

Increasing light

Most indoor settings are darker than they seem to the human eye. In many homes, it's difficult to read a newspaper even at midday without extra light. Bright light is often attainable only directly in front of windows. Here are some strategies for increasing the light plants receive:

■ Keep the windows clean. Dust and grime reduce light considerably.

■ Remove window screens when they're not needed. They will cut light by up to 30 percent.

■ Paint walls flat white or pastel shades and use pale furniture and floor coverings to reflect light. Dark colors absorb light.

■ Hang mirrors strategically to reflect light.

■ Add artificial lighting.

■ Keep the foliage clean. Dust blocks light from reaching chlorophyll in leaves.

■ Replace small windows with larger ones,

or add a greenhouse window, bay window, or solarium.

Supplementing light

If you don't have the right amount of light for what you want to grow, supplement with artificial lighting. Good supplemental sources provide more light than heat. Plants respond best to the full spectrum of sunlight. There are several ways to get it.

■ **Incandescent:** Bulbs commonly found in lamps and ceiling fixtures are not appropriate as the sole source of light for houseplants. Not only are they hot, but they also emit only the red and far-red part of the spectrum, which is too narrow for plants to thrive. Although inefficient, they can be used to supplement natural light if placed far enough away from the plants to avoid overheating the leaves.

■ **Halogen:** Popular in contemporary interior design, these lights produce a nearly perfect spectrum. However, their narrow beams and their extreme heat make them inappropriate for houseplants.

■ **Fluorescent:** These lights remain cool to the touch, allowing plants to grow much closer to the tubes without damage. They also cost less and use less electricity than other lights. Cool white tubes have an enhanced blue range, and warm white tubes have an enhanced red range. A combination of the two provides a wide, although not full, spectrum that's usually sufficient for most plants. Costlier full-spectrum grow lights are best for plants that require full sun. To be effective, fluorescent lights must be close to the plants. Rotate plants regularly because the ends of the bulbs provide less intense light than the centers. Or put low-light plants toward the ends and bright-light plants in the middle.

■ **High-intensity:** By far the most efficient supplemental lighting, high-intensity lamps work best in large areas. They are more expensive than fluorescent lights but are worth it if you need a great deal of supplemental lighting.

■ **Metal halide lamps** offer the best spectrum for the largest number of plants and are intense enough to work in areas with limited or no natural light.

■ **High-pressure sodium lamps** are good for flowering plants that need extremely bright light.

■ **Low-pressure sodium lamps and mercury discharge lamps** are generally used for commercial purposes only.

All types of lights lose effectiveness over time, so replace bulbs regularly, especially fluorescent tubes. Fixtures should have white reflectors to make best use of light.

▲ A fluorescent fixture attached to a kitchen cabinet provides adequate light for growing African violets.

Controlling day length

When almost enough natural light is available, turning on supplementary lighting only a few hours each day—often early in the morning or late in the afternoon to extend the day length in northern areas during the winter months—is usually sufficient.

Plants grown under lights alone, however, need 8 to 16 hours of lighting every day. Studies have shown that most plants grow best with 12 to 16 hours of light per day. Put short-day plants such as poinsettia under 10- to 14-hour days for a few months each year, though, or they won't bloom.

Using a timer ensures plants get the right amount of light. Watch your plants for a few weeks and adjust the timer cycle as needed. Also adjust it as the sun's intensity and duration change over the year. Many indoor gardeners give their plants 14- to 16-hour days during much of the year, then cut back to 12 hours or less to simulate the shorter days of winter.

WATER

When to water

How do you know when to water? It's simple. Give plants water when they need it. Look at your plant. A well-watered plant looks healthy. Its tissues are firm because all the cells are filled with water, and its leaves are glossy. Many plants show signs of decline before wilting entirely: Their leaves have lost their sheen and are slightly limp and pale. Such flagging is a sure sign that a plant needs water. If you catch a plant at this point, before it actually wilts, you can prevent permanent damage.

Underwatering and overwatering can cause the same symptoms. Consistently overwatering plants saturates the soil, which causes the plant's tiny root hairs to rot and die. And a plant without root hairs can't absorb water, so it wilts even though the soil is saturated. More water will not reverse the wilting or save the plant.

To know when plants are ready for water, check the moisture level of the soil by inserting a finger (down to the second knuckle in the case of plants in large pots) into the mix. If a plant needs moist soil, the surface should be damp. If a plant should dry somewhat between waterings, the top inch or two of soil can be dry, but if it's dry below that point, water the plant. Letting a plant completely dry out damages the roots, sometimes beyond repair.

You may eventually know your plants well enough to lift a pot and judge from its weight whether to water. You will learn which plants dry out most quickly, such as those in clay pots, south windows, or some potting mixes. Over time, adjusting your watering to accommodate your plants will become second nature.

A plant's water requirements vary as the seasons change. Watering according to a set schedule—for example, once a week—doesn't take into account these variations. Instead, check your houseplants frequently and keep in mind all the factors that affect their watering needs.

Plants absorb more water when humidity is low. If your skin is dry, your plants are probably dry too. However, plants grow more slowly in the cooler, shorter days of winter, a sign that they're using less water. So if you compensate for dry air by watering on a schedule suited to the warm days of summer, you'll end up overwatering your plants.

High humidity slows transpiration, which reduces moisture uptake by roots. Unless the plant is in a breezy area where wind moves moisture away from the leaves, you'll need to water less often.

Light affects water uptake too. Overcast skies in spring and fall slow plant growth and reduce water requirements. Plants exposed to bright light use more water than those in low light.

▲ **Potting mix may feel dry on top but still be soaking wet at the bottom. An inexpensive moisture meter makes it easy to tell when it's time to water a plant.**

The best way to water

For most plants, the easiest watering method is to pour water on the soil surface. Pour until water runs out the drainage holes, an action that also leaches

---

HINT

Get into the habit of checking your plants every four or five days, and then water only those plants with soil that is dry to the touch. Some plants, such as tender ferns or plants too large for their pots, may be dry only a few days after a thorough watering, while a cactus or succulent might need watering only once a month or so during winter.

adequate air circulation but makes watering more challenging. You can water by spraying the plant but may need to do it frequently. It is far easier to soak the slab in tepid water for 20 to 30 minutes.

Hanging baskets may need more frequent watering than pots set on the ground or windowsill. Exposed to air on all sides, they can quickly lose water to evaporation. Give the soil a thorough soaking whenever you water, or water sparingly several times in one day until the mix is evenly moist. Even better, take down a hanging basket and submerge it in a bucket or sink of tepid water for half an hour, then drain carefully before hanging it up again.

Showering is also an effective way to water plants thoroughly and, at the same time, to rinse dust and dirt from the leaves and leach the soil of excess mineral salts. Use lukewarm water and a gentle flow so the soil does not wash out of the container. This is usually done in the bathtub or shower, but if weather permits and your water is not too cold, take plants outside and rinse them with a garden hose.

What kind of water?

To avoid shock and possible root damage from extreme temperatures, use tepid water when watering. Many gardeners let water stand overnight to reach room temperature, but standing water actually can be considerably colder than that.

excess salts from the soil. The goal is to thoroughly moisten the growing mix.

If dry soil has pulled away from the sides of the pot so that water runs down the sides without wetting the soil, immerse the entire pot in a bucket of lukewarm water. Let it sit for about 30 minutes, then drain. This technique, called submerging, is also useful for plants that need massive amounts of water, such as blooming plants or florist's hydrangea and other gift plants that dry out quickly.

A few plants, such as African violets, benefit from bottom watering. Simply set the pot in a saucer of room temperature water and capillary action draws the water into the soil. This method takes longer than top watering, but it keeps water off the leaves. Empty excess water from the saucer after 20 minutes.

Semiaquatic plants, such as umbrella plant, actually prefer to sit in water at all times. Place pots in larger cachepots and keep adding water as the moisture level drops. You can even submerge the entire root ball under an inch or so of water.

Some plants, such as staghorn ferns, bromeliads, some orchids, and other plants that take moisture from the atmosphere, are frequently grown fixed to slabs of wood, cork, or osmunda fiber. This allows

▲ A tray of pebbles catches any spills from plants that need watering from the bottom and increases air humidity too.

▶ Thorough watering from a gentle spray washes away dust and grease that block light and leaches excess mineral salts from the potting mix.

WATER *(continued)*

◄ A watering hose attached to an indoor faucet is a timesaver for a homeowner with many houseplants.

► Double-potting reduces the need to water often. Excelsior wood fibers help the soil retain moisture.

Tap water is fine for houseplants unless the species you are growing is known to be sensitive to fluoride or softened water. Unless your municipal water supplier issues a treatment warning, there is no need to let tap water stand for 24 hours before using it. The small amount of chlorine it normally contains is not dangerous to most plants.

If your tap water is hard (alkaline) and you're growing plants that like an acid soil, such as pot azaleas *(Rhododendron)*, you'll need to amend the soil. For example, regularly repotting in a lime-free mix with added acid soil amendments such as peat moss will provide what these plants need. You can also use fertilizers designed specifically to retain soil acidity.

Alkaline conditions make it difficult for plants to absorb iron and other trace elements. Regular applications of iron chelate, included in some fertilizers, help keep foliage green. When the new foliage on acid-loving plants is yellow, it's a sign that the plant may need extra iron chelate.

Softened water contains sodium that may accumulate in the soil and harm plants. If your home has a water softener, use an outdoor tap for plant water or install a bypass tap in the water line before it enters the softener so you'll have a source of hard water for plants. If this is not possible, draw water just before the softener cycle, when sodium is at the lowest level.

Reducing watering needs

If watering every four or five days is too frequent for your schedule, there are a few ways you can keep plants moist a bit longer.

▉ **Larger pots:** Repot plants that dry out too quickly into larger pots. The increased potting mix will hold more water.

▉ **Double pots:** Place a pot inside a larger cachepot, adding peat moss, sphagnum moss, Spanish moss, or perlite to fill the void around the inner pot. When you water, moisten the filler material as well as the soil. Double potting also reduces the soil temperature, thus further reducing watering needs and humidifying the air.

▉ **Self-watering pots:** These special containers have a water reservoir that needs attention only when it gets low, usually every couple of weeks. Fertilizer is typically added to the water at the same time. Plants that need to dry out between waterings don't grow well in self-watering pots.

WHEN YOU TRAVEL

If you're going to be away for a few days and can't find someone to care for your plants, you can easily set up a self-watering system. Simply line a sink or bathtub with old towels, newspapers, or any thick, absorbent material. Set pots with drainage holes directly on the matting. Soak the matting well and leave the faucet dripping on it. The plants will draw up moisture as needed.

Another temporary self-watering method: Make a wick out of a nylon stocking and put one end into the drainage hole of the plant you want to water, making sure it is in contact with the potting mix. Run the other end into a bowl of water.

Moisture will soak slowly from bowl to plant. Cover the bowl with a plate if you have pets that might drink the water. Several plants can share the same water source this way, but make certain there is enough water in the bowl to last your entire absence.

As an option, you can clean up your plants, removing dead and fading leaves and flowers, water them well, and seal them inside large transparent plastic bags. Place them well back from full sun or they will cook. Inside the plastic bags air still circulates, yet water can't escape, so your plants can go for weeks without added water.

TEMPERATURE, AIR CIRCULATION, AND HUMIDITY

You know your home and its idiosyncrasies better than anyone else, so you are the perfect person to find the best places for your indoor garden. Once you know your home's microclimates, you can map out areas in your home where houseplants will thrive.

When choosing a location, consider humidity, temperature, and air circulation as well as light. Avoid extremely hot, intensely sunny areas or dark locations where success with most plants will be limited. Indoor microclimates change with the season and the weather, so plants may be ideally situated in winter but need relocation in summer. Move plants as needed to find the best growing conditions. You'll know in a week or so whether a change has improved a plant's health.

Temperature

Most homes maintain a year-round temperature perfect for the average houseplant, between 65°F and 75°F. Turn the thermostat lower at night if possible; a 10°F drop triggers blooms in orchids, flowering maples, and other plants.

Indoor temperatures vary somewhat from season to season, from room to room, and even within a single room. Take advantage of these differences by choosing plants that can profit from them. Since cool air sinks, the air near the floor is cooler than the air in the rest of the room. This is a great place to put plants such as ferns that do not need much heat. Hot air rises, so watch for signs of overdrying in plants on top of bookshelves or cabinets.

▲ Plants grouped closely create a higher humidity level than those spaced far apart.

▼ A ceiling fan circulates the air, helping to inhibit plant diseases.

In the warmest areas around fireplaces, heat vents, incandescent lights, and windows in the summer, grow cacti and succulents that can best use warmth and low humidity. Where conditions are both hot and humid—near a dishwasher, clothes dryer, or humidifier—try thin-leaved species, such as false aralia and bougainvillea. Avoid areas where rapid temperature changes may occur. Cold drafts or hot air blasts near windows and entrances can make some plants wilt.

Use a minimum/maximum thermometer to determine cool spots and warm corners in your home. Leave it in one place for 24 hours to record the low and high temperatures during the period. Do this in several rooms in your house, make a note of the temperature variations, and place plants accordingly.

Air circulation

Plants grouped together look attractive but overcrowding can harm plant health. Air movement around each plant is necessary to remove moisture from the leaves and can help prevent disease problems. Regular air movement around leaves produces sturdier, denser plants that grow continuously at a steady rate. Open a window in mild weather to increase air movement. A ceiling or table fan also keeps the air moving.

TEMPERATURE, AIR CIRCULATION, AND HUMIDITY *(continued)*

▲ **A room humidifier adds moisture during winter.**

furnace. Alternatively, a room humidifier provides localized moisture control in the air around the indoor garden.

Grouping plants helps raise humidity because each gives off moisture through transpiration. You can increase the humidity around plants by placing the pots on a tray of pebbles kept wet. That water simply evaporates, adding humidity to the air. When adding more water to the humidity tray, make sure the top pebbles remain partially exposed so the plants aren't sitting directly in water. Mulching also increases the humidity in the air around the plants. Misting plants is inefficient in raising humidity, as the spray evaporates too quickly. Misting causes wet leaves, which invite disease.

Home microclimates

■ **Windows:** South windows give a room extra warmth in winter and are a good place to put tropical plants, especially since light is brightest there. In summer a south window can become too hot for

▼ **Plants kept in the kitchen accumulate grime. Spray or sponge greasy dirt off the leaves.**

Humidity

Humidity level describes the degree of moisture in the atmosphere—that is, the percentage of water in the air. Generally, the colder the air outside, the drier the air indoors. Humidity tends to be lowest in winter, when home heating systems are in use, but air-conditioning lowers indoor humidity almost as much. Most homes range from 20 percent humidity in winter to 65 percent in summer in some climates.

Although many plants have adapted to drier air indoors, most grow best when the air humidity is at least 50 percent, which is difficult to achieve in a home. When humidity is too low, plants exhibit a variety of symptoms, most often brown leaf tips and edges. Low-humidity problems are intensified if the soil is allowed to dry out, if the plant's location is drafty, or if it is in full sun. High humidity is seldom a problem except in rooms devoted to indoor pools or hot tubs. In those circumstances, consider rotating plants out of the humid area for short periods.

The most efficient way to increase humidity is to install a humidifier on your

most plants. Unless the window has blinds or sheer drapes, use southern exposures only for plants that can take heat, such as hibiscus or succulents.

A north-facing room stays quite cool in winter, making it the perfect spot for plants such as florist's gloxinia that need a cool dormant period. The same north room in summer provides a cool spot for low-light plants that don't tolerate high heat. Move cold-sensitive plants such as crotons away from cold windows in winter.

■ Vents: The areas around heat registers and air-conditioning vents often are too dry or drafty. Plants native to arid climates tolerate these conditions but many tropical plants cannot. Good air circulation is better achieved with a fan.

■ Fireplaces: The space above a fireplace is hotter and drier than it looks. A beautifully draped English ivy gracing the mantel may turn crisp and brown with the first fire of the season.

■ Bathrooms and kitchens: Rooms with running water naturally are more humid than the rest of the house. You can take advantage of these locations with plants that need the almost constant humidity of the rain forest, such as ferns. Remember, however, that bathrooms often lack adequate light, and plants in the kitchen may accumulate greasy dust on their leaves. Allow time in your plant-grooming schedule to wash them occasionally, spraying or sponging the leaves with a weak soapy solution (a teaspoon of mild dish detergent per gallon of water).

To maintain correct temperature, air circulation, and humidity, watch your plants carefully. Raise the humidity if plants show signs of drying out, and increase the air circulation if you see insects or fungal infections.

▲ **Plants native to arid climates should be spaced well apart to increase air circulation and keep humidity low.**

PLANTS TO MATCH MICROCLIMATES

Steamy Bathroom (With Good Light)
Cape primrose
Coleus
Croton
Fern
Flamingo flower
Hibiscus

Cool Foyer
Cactus
Citrus
Japanese fatsia
Spider plant
Umbrella plant

Dark Corner of Living Room
Cast-iron plant
Chinese evergreen
Dracaena (some)
Philodendron
Pothos
Snake plant

Cool Sunroom (in Winter)
Artillery plant
Asparagus fern
Cactus
Christmas cactus
Clivia
English ivy
Swedish ivy

Warm Sunroom (in Summer)
Bromeliad
Cactus
Crown-of-thorns
Ficus
Grape ivy
Jade plant
Nerve plant
Panda plant
Ponytail palm
Wax plant

PLANTS HARMFUL TO PEOPLE AND PETS

Although most houseplants are perfectly harmless, the following are toxic if ingested or if the sap gets on the skin:

African milk bush
  and other *Euphorbia*
  (except poinsettia)
Amaryllis
Anthurium
Caladium
Chenille plant
Chinese evergreen
Clivia

Crinum lily
Croton
Dumb cane
English ivy
Fern palm
Ficus
Heliotrope
Jerusalem cherry
Mandevilla

Natal plum
Oleander
Ornamental pepper
Peace lily
Philodendron
Pothos
Pregnant onion
Sago palm
Swiss cheese plant

CONTAINERS AND POTTING MIXES

▲ The height and width of a pot should be in scale with the size of the plant it contains.

▲ Soilless potting mixes work well in all types of containers and can be customized according to the pot as well as to the plant.

Every houseplant needs a safe place for its roots to grow and be protected. Although some plant roots thrive in water, most are grown in a sturdy container with a high-quality potting mix.

Potting mixes

Most potting mixes for indoor plants are actually soilless. The best contain peat moss or decomposed bark and vermiculite or perlite in various proportions. Unlike garden soil, they are free of pests, diseases, and weed seeds. Soil pH also is inconsistent in garden soils. Most packaged potting mixes are slightly acid; they have a pH of about 6.5 to 6.8, ideal for most houseplants. They are inexpensive, lightweight, and widely available. Packaged specialty mixes are available for such plants as cacti, African violets, and orchids. However, if you prefer to blend your own mixes, use the following guidelines.

▶ Always use a tray or saucer underneath a pot to catch the moisture that eventually seeps out.

Specialty mix ingredients

African violets and other flowering plants: Mix equal parts sand, peat moss, sterilized topsoil, and leaf mold.
Cacti and succulents: Mix 2 parts sterilized soil, 1 part coarse sand, and 1 part calcined clay. Add 2 tablespoons dolomitic lime and 1/3 cup charcoal to 4 quarts mix.
Ferns: Mix 3 parts peat moss-based potting mix, 2 parts perlite, and 3 parts leaf mold. Add 1 cup charcoal to 2 quarts mix.
Epiphytes, orchids, and bromeliads: Mix equal parts sphagnum moss, coarse bark, and coarse perlite. Add 1 tablespoon dolomitic lime and 1 cup horticultural charcoal to 3 quarts mix.

Individual ingredients

Calcined clay: Clay pulverized by heating, most commonly available as unscented cat litter, adds weight, drainage, and aeration.
Charcoal: Absorbs salts and byproducts of plant decay, keeps the soil sweet, removes acidity. Use only horticultural grade.
Leaf mold: Decayed leaves of all types. Excellent organic additive for moisture retention, some nutrition.
Peat moss: Partially decayed plant material mined from the middle and bottom of peat bogs. It has an acid pH and is highly moisture retentive but adds no nutritive value to the mix.
Perlite: Expanded volcanic rock that is lightweight, and improves drainage and aeration. It holds little moisture and adds little nutritive value.
Sand: Adds drainage and weight. Lime-free

▲ **A decorative basket shows off an artful combination of individual small pots.**

coarse river sand or builder's sharp sand is most desirable.

Shredded bark: Finely shredded or ground hardwood or pine bark. Equivalent in use to peat moss. No nutritive value.

Sphagnum moss: Plant matter harvested from the top of peat bogs, it has fibers longer than those of peat moss and decomposes slowly. Used mainly to line baskets and in orchid mixes; rarely used in regular potting mixes.

Vermiculite: Mica expanded by heating to become moisture- and nutrient-retentive.

Containers

The only two essential considerations when choosing a pot are how it drains and what the shape and size are in relation to the size of the plant and its root system. Otherwise, selection is a matter of personal preference.

Drainage: There is no substitute for a pot that drains well. No matter what type of plant you are growing, the pot must have holes for drainage. If you want to use a decorative pot that doesn't have drainage holes, drill drainage holes in it, or slip the nursery pot into it, creating a cachepot.

Ignore the myth about putting gravel in the bottom of pots for drainage. Water tends to stagnate in the gravel, where roots soak in it and rot.

Size: Make sure your pot is large enough to contain plenty of mix to accommodate a growing root system and to maintain an inch of room above the soil, called head space, for watering.

Containers come in lots of shapes and sizes, and everyone has favorites. Pots also come in a variety of materials, but plastic

and terra-cotta are the most popular and available. Generally, potting mix stays more evenly moist in a pot that is a bit wider than it is deep.

Plastic: Plastic pots are lightweight, break-resistant, and easy to clean and store. They are good for moisture-loving plants.

Clay: Unglazed terra-cotta and clay pots are porous; thus soil dries more quickly than in plastic. Clay is breakable and harder to clean but provides weight for stability. Soak new clay pots in a basin of water for several hours before planting in them.

Self-watering: These pots provide a water reservoir, allowing you to leave them unattended for days. They are perfect for people who travel frequently and for offices and public spaces.

Baskets: Usually made of plastic or wire lined with sphagnum moss, hanging baskets are ideal for trailing and vining plants. Decorative woven baskets hold multiple pots for tabletop combinations.

Saucers and trays: To prevent water damage to household surfaces, a saucer must be at least as wide as the pot's upper diameter and also deep enough to hold any excess water that may flow through the pot during watering. Look for "pot feet"—risers to lift the saucer or pot above surfaces—and saucers with ridges. Both increase air circulation under plants.

Cachepots: Any ornamental container can be used to hide a nursery pot—ceramic bowls, watering cans, baskets, or anything else that suits your style. Use saucers or pot feet under unglazed cachepots to prevent damage from seepage and condensation.

▲ **Most packaged potting mixes are ideally formulated for houseplants. Some also include slow-release fertilizer granules and moisture-control crystals.**

POTTING, REPOTTING, AND DIVIDING

Young plants need to be repotted as soon as they have filled their pots with roots—that might be twice a year or more. Surprisingly, though, many mature houseplants seldom need repotting. Some plants even perform better or bloom better if they are pot-bound. Other plants need repotting if they outgrow their pots, if the soil has become depleted, or if the plant is infested with soil-dwelling pests. A plant needs repotting when you can't seem to water it enough. This is a sign that it has used up all of the soil's water storage capacity.

You can repot anytime, but the prime time occurs right before active growth starts in spring. Avoid repotting plants during a plant's dormant or resting period.

Is it time?

To determine whether a plant needs repotting, tap it out of its pot and look at the root system. If the roots are spread out with few (or none) growing through the drainage holes, repotting may not be necessary. However, if the root ball is such a mass of roots that virtually no soil is left, the time has come to repot.

With a plant that has outgrown its pot, you have the option of putting it into a bigger container or pruning the root ball and putting the plant back into its original pot. If you want the plant to grow bigger, give it a larger pot—but only 1 or 2 inches larger in diameter. If you choose a pot that is too large, it will hold more soil and therefore more water than the plant can use, a situation that could lead to rot.

To maintain the plant's size, tap it out of its pot and slice off about an inch all around the root ball, including underneath, with a sharp knife. When you disturb the root system this way, the plant may drop some of its foliage in response to losing a portion of its roots.

When a plant looks as if it needs feeding but doesn't respond to fertilizer, it's probably time to replace all or part of the soil. For partial replacement, remove the plant from its pot and knock off some of the old soil; tease out the roots a bit to encourage them to grow into the new soil; and then repot the plant. Another option is to top dress the plant or scrape off the top inch or so of soil and add new soil. Topdressing is the easiest way to replace soil for plants that should not have their roots disturbed, such as amaryllis.

▲ To prepare for repotting, loosen the plant from its old pot and slip it out gently, taking care not to injure it.

▲ Gently tease apart any tight or circling roots. Loosen old soil gently from the root ball with your fingers.

▲ Clip any damaged or diseased roots. If you are returning the plant to the same pot, remove part of the root ball too.

▲ Center the plant in its new container, making certain the crown is at the same depth as in the old pot.

▲ Fill in around the root ball with soil, tamping and firming it gently with your fingers.

▲ Water the newly potted plant thoroughly, allowing excess water to drain well into a saucer.

If the soil is completely depleted or infested with insects, remove as much of the soil around the roots as possible. Tap off loose soil, and then wash the roots with warm water. Examine the roots for any problems, prune out diseased or damaged areas, and repot.

It is never necessary to add a "drainage layer" of gravel or potsherds when repotting. Studies have shown that such layers actually hinder proper drainage and waste valuable root space. If you're worried that the potting mix will run out the drainage hole or holes, place a piece of newspaper, paper towel, or a used dryer sheet across the bottom of the empty pot.

Steps for potting or repotting

1. Thoroughly water the plant several hours before repotting.
2. Gather needed supplies such as a pot and saucer, material to cover drainage holes, newspaper to cover your work surface, and potting mix.
3. Moisten the potting mix by adding warm water and mixing it in with a spoon to make it easier to handle. Potting soil is hard to wet once it's in the pot.
4. Loosen the plant by running a knife around the inside edge of the pot or tapping the pot on a table. Slip out the plant. Hold the top of a small plant between your fingers, supporting the root ball in your palm. Remove a larger plant by laying the pot on its side and sliding out the plant.
5. Unwind circling roots and cut off any that look rotted. If the plant is pot-bound, make shallow cuts from the top to the bottom of the root ball with a sharp knife. Cut off an inch or so of the root ball if you intend to put the plant back into the same container.
6. Pour some potting mix into the new pot and center the plant at the same depth as it was planted before. Then fill in more mix around the roots.
7. Tamp the soil lightly with your fingers as you work; pressing too hard will compact the growing mix. Water the plant well.
8. If you pruned the roots substantially, cut back the top of the plant accordingly.

Dividing

While you're repotting, you can divide overgrown plants that have multiple stems or crowns (the base of the plant where the roots and stems join). Doing so rejuvenates

▶ To divide a plant, remove it from its pot and separate or unwind roots circling around the edge of the root ball.

◀ Pull or cut apart some stems from the root ball, keeping some roots and soil attached.

▶ Center the plant division in a new pot, then fill with potting mix and water thoroughly.

plants that have outgrown their pots and provides you with new plants.

Remove the plant from its pot and slice through the root ball with a sharp knife or spade. You may need to saw some plants apart, but others gently break apart by hand. Make sure each division includes some of the main root and stem system. Plant the divisions immediately in potting mix in permanent containers, and then water thoroughly. Keep the pots in bright light but out of direct sun, watering frequently until the plants root. You also can put the potted divisions inside clear plastic bags to reduce moisture loss. When they appear upright and healthy, place them in a permanent location and care for them as you would mature plants.

PROPAGATING

Starting new plants from old ones is fun and rewarding. It's neither difficult nor time-consuming in most cases. Propagation is a great way to develop healthy new plants from an aging specimen and allows you to have beautiful gift plants to share with friends and relatives.

Propagation is best done when plants are in active growth but can be carried out any time of the year.

Cuttings

Growing houseplants from cuttings is the most popular method of vegetative propagation. It is an easy way to duplicate the attractive features of the original plant—the new plant is a genetic copy of the original.

Depending on the plant, you can take cuttings from stems, leaves, or roots. Cuttings will root in a variety of media: in a commercial rooting medium, in vermiculite, in soilless potting mix, or in water. Plants rooted in water will need some form of support to hold them upright. In addition few root hairs develop on cuttings rooted in water.

Although some gardeners routinely dip all cuttings in powdered rooting hormone before planting them, this step is not

STEM CUTTINGS

1 Select a healthy stem and take a 3- to 5-inch cutting with several nodes (the point where the leaf attaches to the stem).

2 Pinch or cut off all but the top two or three sets of leaves. If leaves are quite large, cut them in half widthwise to prevent excess transpiration.

3 Dip the cut end of slow-rooting plants into rooting hormone and tap off the excess.

4 Make a hole in the potting mix with a pencil or your finger, and then insert the cutting in the hole and firm the potting mix around the stem.

5 Water gently and cover the cutting with a plastic bag to retain moisture. Check to see if the cutting has rooted after a few weeks by tugging lightly (a rooted cutting resists). Do not water or cover cuttings of cacti and succulents. Water them only after new roots have formed.

necessary for all plants and may actually inhibit fast-rooting plants, such as coleus and Swedish ivy. Plants with slightly woody stems, such as miniature rose, are more likely to benefit from use of a rooting hormone. You can buy extra-strong rooting hormones for woody cuttings that are especially difficult to root, and adding bottom heat from heating cables may be useful for some cuttings.

Stem cuttings: This is the most common type of cutting, good for most plants that have stems.

Leaf cuttings: Only a few plants reproduce from leaf cuttings, including African violets, some begonias and peperomias, florist's gloxinia, sedum, kalanchoe, echeveria, and jade plant. Certain plants, such as snake plant, also produce a new plant from just a section of leaf. Cape primrose and some begonias also root from leaf segments.

Root cuttings: A few plants propagate from latent buds in their roots, such as the ti plant. To propagate from a root cutting, simply set 2-inch sections of thick root horizontally in rooting medium. When a plantlet forms, transplant it as you would other cuttings that have rooted.

LEAF-SECTION CUTTINGS

1 Cut a snake plant into 3-inch sections, making sure to keep them oriented upright. Make a small notch in the top of each piece to help you identify which end is the top.

2 Stick the leaf cuttings into the potting mix, notched side up. Firm the soil around the cuttings and then water thoroughly. Cover each pot with a plastic bag until the cuttings root.

LEAF CUTTINGS

1 Remove an African violet leaf with its petiole (leaf stem) attached by clipping close to the crown of the plant. Rooting hormone speeds development of new plants.

2 Poke a hole in the potting mix and insert the leaf into the hole, burying the petiole. Firm the soil and then water gently but thoroughly from the top, taking care not to splash the leaf. Cover the pot with a plastic bag and check every few days for new plants to form at the base of the leaf.

Layering

Layering is a technique similar to rooting cuttings, except that the part of the plant (usually a branch) to be rooted remains attached to the parent plant. The great advantage of layering is that the parent plant supplies the new plant with water and nutrients while its roots form. Daily maintenance is therefore unnecessary. For plants slow to root this is a distinct advantage. There is one disadvantage: New plants develop more slowly from layering than from cuttings.

A suitable plant for soil layering has a branch that's low enough for you to bend into contact with the growing mix. Creeping and trailing plants are ideal subjects for the technique. Note that many plants self-layer wherever they touch the soil. In this case, simply detach the rooted branch and transplant it into a new pot.

Air layering—rooting from a notch in a stem—works well for some plants, such as dieffenbachia, dracaena, and rubber trees, that lack branches conveniently close to the ground. It is especially useful for salvaging leggy plants or mature specimens that have lost their lower leaves.

LAYERING

1 Move the parent plant to a stable location and place a pot with fresh potting mix next to it. Pin a trailing stem to the potting mix, but leave the growing tip free.

2 When roots develop at the node (this can take months), cut the new plant free of the parent plant.

AIR LAYERING

1 Make a notch in the stem, removing a tiny sliver of growth.

2 Dust the notch with rooting hormone powder.

3 Loosely wrap plastic around the stem, holding it at the base with tape or twist tie. Fill the plastic with dampened sphagnum moss.

4 Close the top of the plastic with electrical tape or twist ties. Check weekly for moistness, opening slightly to add water if needed.

5 After roots develop, cut the stem of the plant below the plastic. Remove the plastic and the moss.

6 Plant in fresh potting soil. New stems should sprout below the cut on the parent plant.

Plantlets

Several common houseplants reproduce by sending out miniature new plants on runners or shoots. These include spider plant, flame violet, strawberry begonia, and many varieties of Boston fern. Some even produce plantlets on leaves, such as piggyback plant and several kalanchoes. After roots develop on the plantlets, the young plant can be cut away from the parent plant and repotted. Or plantlets can be removed from the parent plant and rooted, similar to cuttings.

Offsets

Small new plants that form at the base of an old plant and remain attached to it are known as offsets. You can break them off and plant them just as you would with divisions. Detach offsets only when they are mature enough to survive on their own—usually when they have taken on the look of the mature plant and have an established root system. You can propagate the screwpine and many bromeliads using this method.

PLANTLETS

▲ Peg the plantlets of stoloniferous plants, such as strawberry begonia, into adjacent pots.

▲ Plantlets will propagate easily if they are well developed and have healthy roots.

OFFSETS

1 Gently separate an offset from the parent, using a knife if necessary. You may have to remove the parent plant from its pot for easier access.

2 Plant the offset in growing mix at the same depth it grew in the original pot. Tamp the soil lightly, then water it. Give the offset the same care as you give the parent plant.

Seeds

Although most houseplants are propagated from cuttings, some can be grown only from seed, such as single-trunk palms and an array of annuals perfect for hanging baskets. When you venture into seed growing, you have more choices. You decide what color and kind of ixoras and begonias you want to grow, and you can try unusual geraniums or flowering maples at modest prices. Ferns and bromeliads have many more family members than the market offers, but with patience you can start even the rare ones from seed.

Houseplant seeds are available from many garden centers and mail-order nurseries. Look for seed packets with descriptions of cultural needs. Check the fine print for special instructions on light and sowing depth.

To get seeds started, fill a tray or shallow pot with sterile seed-starting mix made for this purpose. Put the tray or pot in a warm (70°F to 75°F) room with strong light and readily available water. Bottom heat from cables or mats will speed germination.

For greater success with seeds, remember that large, hard seeds (including those of palms if they appear dry) should be soaked in tepid water overnight before sowing. Cover large seeds to a depth twice their diameter, firming the growing mix around each seed by pressing gently.

Scatter tiny seeds such as those of primrose and cyclamen on top of moist growing mix and leave them uncovered. Sow medium-size seeds such as those of ornamental pepper and coleus on the growing mix and cover them with a thin layer of seedling mix or milled sphagnum moss. Water lightly, and then slip the seed tray or pot into a plastic bag or cover it with paper, glass, or the clear lid of a starting kit.

When seedlings emerge, remove the covering and move the containers into brighter light. When true leaves appear, thin the plants or pot individual seedlings. Keep the seedlings moist and begin fertilizing when they are two to three weeks old. Fertilize at half strength for a few weeks and then at full strength as recommended for mature plants.

Once they sprout, seedlings require full-spectrum light above them, but the light must be raised gradually as they grow in order to produce sturdy plants. An adjustable grow light or fluorescent shop light is often a wise, low-cost investment.

▲ **When two to four true leaves develop, transplant the seedlings to small containers.**

Fern spores

You will need plenty of patience to propagate ferns from their spores, but the reward can be stunning and unusual plants for low-light, humid indoor spaces. Spores are similar to seeds but smaller and much slower to sprout and grow. Sow as you would other fine seeds, by pressing them into damp seeding mix. Keep spores routinely moist and don't give up; they can take months to sprout.

Dividing bulbs, corms, tubers, and rhizomes

The word "bulb" describes one of a group of plants distinguished by their ability to form underground water storage structures. Most bulbous plants, including true bulbs, such as daffodil and tulip, and plants that grow from corms, such as crocuses, reproduce naturally by forming young bulblets called offsets. When they first emerge around the mother bulb after flowering, the offsets are tiny. Let them grow just large enough to handle, then unpot the whole plant, separate the offsets, and plant them in new pots. Many bulbs, such as amaryllis, can be cut into pieces for propagation. Each piece needs to include a portion of the flat basal plate of the bulb, and must be allowed to air dry until the surface heals. It will form a callous in about a week and should be repotted right away.

▲ When spore cases on the back of a fern frond have turned dark, lay the frond on a piece of white paper in a protected area. Spores will fall on the paper when they are ripe.

▶ To divide tubers, cut carefully between two growing points. Pot the sections after they have had time to heal.

"Tuber" comes from the Latin word for lump, well illustrated in caladium. The lumpy, swollen underground stems develop distinct growing points that can be separated easily. Use a sharp knife to cut carefully between two points on a tuber to produce two potential plants. Let the cuts heal for a week, and then pot the sections as you would intact adult tubers.

Like tubers, rhizomes such as those of elephant's ear grow differently from true bulbs and corms. Also like tubers, rhizomes (also called rootstocks) are swollen underground stems. By nature, rhizomes grow at or below the soil surface, dividing at the tips. You can simply cut the rhizome so each piece has its own growing point and pot the pieces immediately. You can also break apart scaly rhizomes, such as those produced by eyelash begonias, into individual scales. They are tiny, but treat them like seeds and they will quickly sprout, producing full-size blooming plants the same year.

New bulbs, tubers, and rhizomes (but not scales) benefit from a potting mix that includes ample ground bark to provide good drainage.

FERTILIZING

Photosynthesis provides plants with the sugar and other carbohydrates they need for energy. Fertilizers provide the nourishing minerals that plants need to sustain healthy growth. Most purchased plants are in good nutritional health, and fertilizer is often premixed into potting soils, but over time plant roots absorb the fertilizer or watering rinses it out of the pot. Many easy-to-use products are available to suit your plants and your schedule.

Read the label

Fertilizers come in many different formulations for many different types of plants. Some work quickly, and others become available over time. Product labels list three important numbers that represent the percentages of nitrogen, phosphorus, and potassium (N-P-K). Phosphorus and potassium are usually expressed as percentage of phosphate and potash.

▼ It is possible to give plants too much fertilizer, which burns roots and leaves. Choose a product formulated for the types of plants you have and follow the label directions.

Nitrogen enriches the greenness of the foliage and promotes stem growth. Phosphorus encourages flowering and root growth. Potassium contributes to stem strength and disease resistance. Trace elements also are needed but in much smaller amounts: sulfur, calcium, and magnesium, plus minute quantities of iron, zinc, manganese, copper, chlorine, boron, and molybdenum.

If the formula is balanced, the N-P-K numbers are the same, such as 12-12-12. Most houseplants, even blooming ones, can thrive on a balanced formula, but you may want to alternate that with one made for blooming plants, such as 5-20-10.

Product types

■ **Soluble fertilizers:** Most houseplant fertilizers are water soluble; that is, concentrates designed to be diluted in water. They work quickly and are depleted in about a month.

■ **Slow-release fertilizers:** These tablets, sticks, or granular formulas are placed in the pot to release their nutrients over time as water is applied. They are easy to use and last several months.

Timing

When to fertilize depends on the plant and its health but generally, apply soluble fertilizers monthly whenever plants are in active growth. Many indoor gardeners apply a slow-release formula twice a year, and then supplement with soluble forms of plant food every six to eight weeks or at half strength monthly.

Wilted or sickly plants do not benefit from fertilizing, and even healthy plants can be damaged by incorrectly mixed or too-frequent applications. Leaves can look burned or contorted, and a white crust may appear on the soil or pot if overfertilized.

If you accidentally overfertilize a plant, leach it thoroughly by pouring lukewarm water through the pot several times in a row. Leaching improves pH and oxygen content and removes excess fertilizer and mineral salts from the pot.

Miracle-Gro® Water Soluble
All Purpose Plant Food 24 -8-16

GUARANTEED ANALYSIS

Total Nitrogen (N)	24%
3.5% Ammoniacal Nitrogen	
20.5% Urea Nitrogen	
Available Phosphate (P₂O₅)	8%
Soluble Potash (K₂O)	16%
Boron (B)	0.02%
Copper (Cu)	0.07%
0.07% Water Soluble Copper (Cu)	
Iron (Fe)	0.15%
0.15% Chelated Iron (Fe)	
Manganese (Mn)	0.05%
0.05% Chelated Manganese (Mn)	
Molybdenum (Mo)	0.0005%
Zinc (Zn)	0.06%
0.06% Water Soluble Zinc (Zn)	

Derived from Ammonium Sulfate, Potassium Phosphate, Potassium Chloride, Urea, Urea Ph Boric Acid, Copper Sulfate, Iron EDTA, Manga EDTA, Sodium Molybdate, and Zinc Sulfate.

Information regarding the contents and leve metals in this product is available on the inte http://www.regulatory-info-sc.com

KEEP OUT OF REACH OF CHILDR

Scotts Miracle-Gro Products, Inc.
14111 Scottslawn Road
Marysville, OH 43041

New & Improved!
The Fast Way to Bigger, More Beautiful Plants!

New and Improved
Miracle-Gro® Plant
was developed by the truste
experts of Miracle-Gro® branded pro
to provide plants with the ideal mix of nutri
thrive. Plants grow bigger and more beautiful,

PRUNING

Not all plants benefit from pruning, but many need pinching and cutting back to stay shrubby and full. Pruning encourages and directs growth, and corrects structural problems so a plant becomes a prime specimen. In some cases, pruning is essential to remove diseased or damaged wood and nonflowering stems. It also limits a plant's height and width.

Tools

Invest in sharp high-quality bypass pruning shears. They will pay for themselves many times over by giving you clean cuts. Anvil-type pruners tend to crush the stem rather than slice it off. You also can use sturdy scissors, but make sure they are very sharp.

Goals

The main reason for pruning is to make the plant look better. Always think carefully before making any cuts. Lop off a major stem accidentally and you may have to wait a long time for another stem to replace it. To remove diseased tissue, prune back into healthy tissue, always keeping in mind the overall shape of the plant. Dispose of the prunings immediately (don't leave them near the plant) and sterilize your pruners with rubbing alcohol or a solution of 1 part household bleach to 9 parts water between cuts to avoid spreading disease.

Some plants, such as African violet and peperomia, send up leaves from a flat crown in a symmetrical shape called a rosette. Prune them only to maintain an even shape. Remove older leaves from the underside of the rosette, pinching off the leaf and petiole close to the base.

Trailing plants, such as Swedish ivy and pothos, produce new leaves on the ends of long stems. Regular snipping will force new leaves to grow along the stem. Cut a stem just above a node, or leaf joint. Try to clip the stems at different lengths to keep the plant looking natural.

Other plants, such as ming aralia and fishtail palm, have naturally irregular shapes, so you need only remove an occasional unhealthy leaf. Stemmy plants, such as fibrous begonia and Swedish ivy, benefit from periodic severe pruning to force healthy new growth.

Pinching

Pinching is often done with the fingernails rather than pruners. Pinch out the tip of a stem and its topmost few leaves to promote growth of the side buds. Pinching is a great way to keep shrubby plants full at the center. In some plants, such as coleus, pinching out flower spikes encourages development of the more attractive foliage.

Root pruning

Deliberately pruned roots and the broken roots that occur during repotting stimulate new growth. Severe root pruning is done to keep a plant in a small pot, although there are limits to how much of the root system you can remove without hurting the plant. A reduction in the number of roots means less nutrient uptake, so when you root-prune a plant, remove some foliage at the same time.

▼ To keep plants bushy, regularly pinch off the stems just above a leaf. Also pinch off the flower spikes of plants grown only for their foliage.

GROOMING

Houseplant care includes grooming plants to remove old flowers and leaves. Working closely on each plant also provides the opportunity to check for signs of insects or disease symptoms. The earlier you detect problems, the easier they are to remedy. Routine grooming keeps plants looking and growing their best.

◄ **Remove faded or damaged leaves at their base using sharp scissors or handheld pruners.**

▼ **Dust on leaves blocks light and transpiration. Gently wipe off dust with a soft, damp cloth while supporting the leaves from underneath.**

Leaves

First examine the leaves. A yellow, brown, or withered leaf won't green up again and should be removed. Take off the entire leaf instead of trimming off brown parts. Use narrow-bladed hand pruners or sharp scissors to make a clean cut without tearing the plant. Leaves that are pale green or yellow may green up again after fertilizing, so hold off on trimming them.

While you are grooming the leaves, rotate each pot a quarter turn. This lets all parts of the plant have equal access to the light and assures even growth.

Flowers

Unless the plant develops attractive fruits, such as citrus, Jerusalem cherry, or ornamental pepper, keep fading flowers and stems clipped off to maintain plant health and promote rebloom. Even ornamental seedpods are an energy drain and should be removed.

Dusting and washing

Dust buildup on leaves not only looks bad but also clogs leaf pores (stomata), preventing transpiration, and can even block light. Spray small-leaved plants with water or gently shake off the dust. To dust large-leaved plants, carefully wipe with a soft cloth while you support each leaf with your other hand. If the dust is greasy, use a solution of ½ teaspoon of dish detergent to 1 gallon of water to clean the leaf. Use a damp cloth to wipe off any white mineral deposits. Plants with small and ridged leaves, like some peperomias, benefit from a quick rinse with tepid water.

Avoid "shine" products containing wax that can build up. Once you clear away the dust, a leaf's natural shine will come through on its own.

Mulching

Houseplant soil mix looks great when the plant is first potted, and adding mulch keeps it looking good. More important, mulch reduces evaporation from the soil surface. Mulch can be organic, such as bark or sphagnum moss, but pebbles and glass rock keep the surface neat and colorful. Living groundcover plants make superb mulches and add another shape and texture to the container.

STAKING AND TRAINING

You may decide to stake or train a young plant temporarily to correct its growth habit or create an interesting form. However, if an improperly grown plant requires such support, prune it back drastically or start over with a new plant.

Choose a black or bright red temporary stake so you will remember to remove it as soon as possible. If you are training a vine to hold its flowers up permanently, use a strong material such as bamboo or metal in tan or green that will soon be camouflaged by stems and leaves.

When you tie a plant stem or vine to a stake, make the shape of a figure eight, with one loop around the stake and one loop around the plant. This allows the plant a little movement, which may prevent breakage. Tie the plant in several places, and check the ties often to be sure they are not cutting into the growing stem. Such girdling can be fatal.

Ties for stakes and forms need to be flexible; the wider or softer a tie, the less chance it will injure the plant stem. Ties can be made of jute, raffia, plastic-coated wire, florist's or other tape, or even recycled nylon stocking, but choose green or brown whenever possible so the support is invisible. If you cannot hide the ties, use ones made of a natural fiber such as grapevine tendrils or raffia and make them a part of the plant's design.

You can use plant pins to train sturdy vines such as philodendron to climb a tall pole. Always pin loosely around the vine or stem, without puncturing or binding it, so plant growth is not hampered.

All types and sizes of poles, trellises, hoops, obelisks, globes, and elegant stakes are available commercially. Some plants

▲ Pin climbing vines loosely to their support to encourage growth.

can be trained to grow directly onto some structures, while others must be tied or pinned in place. Wire and wood forms enable you to grow topiaries with nearly unlimited shapes, from geometric designs to bunnies and frogs. Use several small plants instead of one large one to surround a form and cover it more quickly. To maintain a thick, mature topiary, trim it regularly. As new growth emerges, train that onto the form.

► Stakes made of natural materials and colors will disappear within mature foliage.

TRAINING A STANDARD

A standard is a plant trained to a single stem—usually in a lollipop form. Indoor plants that lend themselves well to this type of training are those with strong or woody stems, such as coleus, flowering maple, geranium, lemon, ming aralia, and herbs such as rosemary.

1. Choose a well-rooted cutting or seedling with a single sturdy stem. Pot the plant in a heavy pot in well-drained potting mix. Tie the stem loosely at several intervals to a firmly seated stake, taking care not to bind the stem.

2. Pinch off side shoots, letting leaves remain along the main stem to sustain the plant. When the plant has reached the desired height, pinch out the growing tip to force side shoots. As side shoots develop, prune them to achieve the shape you want.

3. As the plant gains size and becomes more top-heavy, repot it into a larger, heavier pot. Remove the stake if the plant stem can stand on its own.

SPECIAL CARE

Moving plants outside and indoors

After a long, dark winter, many houseplants enjoy a dose of fresh air, filtered sunlight, and rainwater. This treatment rejuvenates them and adds a bright touch of greenery to porch, patio, or yard.

Outside for the summer: Take only the toughest plants—those that can withstand unexpected wind and cold—outdoors. Wait until all threat of frost has passed and temperatures remain above 45°F at night. Keep the plants in a protected, well-shaded spot for at least a week. Then move them to a spot where they'll get a few hours of filtered sunlight each day and protection from the wind. Some houseplants, such as many cacti and succulents, eventually tolerate full sun outdoors.

Keep a close watch for evidence of excessive dryness, pest infestation, or shock. Houseplants growing outdoors for the summer are susceptible to damage from heat, hail, and wind.

Display houseplants outdoors in their pots, insert the pots into flower boxes,

▲ Move your houseplants outside in containers that will allow rain to drain away. Group them in a spot protected from direct sun.

or plant the pots directly in the garden, sinking them just below ground level if the site has good drainage.

Indoors for the winter: Bring plants back indoors before temperatures begin to dip in autumn. That way the plants need only adapt to a drop in light when they move inside; the temperature and humidity will remain essentially the same. A plant left outdoors during cool evenings will begin to slow down for winter and may suffer in the drier air of a heated interior. Plants that prefer cool weather, such as pot azaleas, Japanese aralia, and holiday cacti, can be kept outside late into fall, until the first frost threatens.

Before moving plants indoors, clip off yellowed leaves, spent flowers, and seedpods. If the plant has grown too large for its pot, reshape it with some careful pruning or repot it into a larger container. Clean both the plant and the outside of the pot with warm water. Examine the foliage carefully for insect pests and diseases, and treat infested or infected plants with the appropriate control (see pages 46–49), following label directions.

Container gardening

Container gardens display strong style in small spaces and make houseplants movable with the seasons or your decorating moods. Container gardening allows you to showcase a jasmine in full bloom or hide a tired orchid. Plants that need to be stored during dormancy can easily be relocated to a closet or basement until the next growing season begins. Garden annuals can be dug and combined in one large pot to extend the look of summer indoors when the outdoor growing season ends.

Containers may be small enough to hold one plant apiece or large enough to display a jungle of foliage and flowers. Two kinds of container gardens are most popular: individual pots grouped together inside larger cachepots or baskets, and combination pots, where different types of plants grow together in the same soil. Each brings advantages to your collection.

Houseplants moved outdoors in warm weather may wilt and topple over after just a day, even in shade, unless you water them daily. Arrange a handsome display in a large basket, window box, or jardinière using pots of varying sizes. Use inverted empty pots or bricks to elevate small pots,

and then spread sphagnum moss mulch across the tops of all the pots to retain moisture and unify the look. So long as each pot drains well, the plants will thrive. Pull back the moss to water and fertilize each plant as needed. Grouping them into one container increases humidity, reducing the drying effects of wind and heat.

Combine upright, trailing, and filler plants in large clay pots, planter boxes, or oversized hanging baskets to make a bold statement indoors as well as on the deck or patio. Vary the textures, heights, and forms to create an appealing focal point. Make a container garden that doubles as a holiday decoration. Add a strand of twinkling lights to a Norfolk Island pine encircled by ornamental pepper plants for a colorful alternative. Or tuck miniature pumpkins and florist's mums among the coleus and English ivy at the base of a weeping ficus.

Arrange small cacti and succulents in a dish garden for a brightly lit windowsill. A large nursery pot inside a woven basket or copper bowl can hold an assortment of small ferns, ivies, and palms, or any other combination of plants with similar cultural requirements. Use your imagination to find an unusual or dramatic container to display your favorite plants.

▼ A woven wicker basket makes a decorative container for a dish garden of complementary plant textures and shapes.

Terrariums

Terrariums are miniature landscapes created by combining a collection of plants in a glass container. Suitable containers include fish tanks, bubble bowls, brandy snifters, and bottles. Depending on the choice of plants, the location, and the type of container used, you can create the effect of a woodland dell, a rocky coastline, or a tiny jungle.

Plants do best under clear rather than tinted glass. Wide-necked containers are easiest to plant and maintain because you can reach inside them with your hands.

◄ **Use a plastic funnel or a sheet of rolled-up paper to guide pebbles and potting mix into a bottle terrarium.**

► **Use a chopstick, skewer, or other long tool to position plants and cover their roots with potting mix.**

■ **Planting a terrarium:** Clean and dry the chosen container thoroughly before you start planting. Before you add any plant to a bottle garden or terrarium, inspect it carefully for insects, diseases, and rotted roots. These problems are especially prevalent under glass.

Most containers used for terrarium gardening have no drainage holes. To keep the growing mix sweet smelling and healthy, line the bottom of the container with ½ inch of charcoal chips (available where indoor plants are sold). Then add at least 1½ inches of ordinary commercial soilless mix with a little extra vermiculite or perlite added to improve air circulation to the roots.

Small-necked bottles require delicate, long-handled tools for planting. Use a

rolled-up piece of newspaper or funnel to get the growing medium into such a bottle. To shape the terrain, use a chopstick or bamboo skewer with a small measuring spoon taped to the end. When you are ready to "bottle" the plants, gently remove most of the potting mix from the roots, drop each plant through the neck of the bottle, coax it into the right position with your miniature "spade," and cover the roots with growing media. Use just a few plants: An overstuffed terrarium quickly becomes crowded and difficult to maintain.

Once the plants are in place, a final mulch or ground carpet of moss completes the scene. Mist with clear water to settle the roots and to remove soil particles from the leaves and the sides of the bottle.

■ **Maintaining a terrarium:** The most common misconception people hold about terrarium plantings is that they require no care and will thrive just about anywhere indoors. In fact, they need occasional watering and regular grooming to remove spent growth and to contain fast-growing plants.

Terrariums do best in bright but indirect light. Sunlight shining directly through the glass for more than a few minutes is likely to cook the plants. Terrariums do well under fluorescent tubes lit for 12 to 14 hours a day.

Watering can be tricky, especially in bottle gardens. When the soil appears dry or there are no moisture droplets on the inside of the container, add a tablespoon of water. If the soil is still dry, add another spoonful the next day. If you accidentally add too much water, remove the surplus with a turkey baster or a piece of paper towel on the end of your long stick tool.

Grooming is easy if the container has an opening big enough to insert your hand. To remove yellowing leaves, spent flowers, or excess growth from a narrow-necked bottle garden, tape a single-edge razor blade to a thin stick and use it as a cutting tool. You can remove the clippings with slender pieces of wood or a pair of chopsticks. Remove dying leaves and flowers before they rot. Even a tiny amount of rot quickly infects healthy leaves and shoots.

Bonsai

Bonsai is the Japanese art of growing plants in containers. Over thousands of years, the term has come to mean miniaturized trees and landscapes in a small pot or tray. Although some bonsai specimens are several centuries old, it is quite possible to create an acceptable young bonsai in only a few years. You can buy preformed or partially formed bonsai, or start your own from small plants or cuttings.

Bonsai are not necessarily indoor plants; in fact, most true bonsai are hardy plants

▷ **Maintain a mature bonsai by annual root pruning and regular pinching.**

▽ **Houseplants with naturally small leaves and flowers respond well to pruning as bonsai subjects.**

kept outdoors year-round. However, some interesting tropical and subtropical shrubs make excellent bonsai subjects and can be maintained indoors all year.

If possible, choose plants with naturally small leaves, flowers, and fruits; also look for those that respond well to pruning and produce rough, aged-looking bark from the time they are young. An already formed bonsai is readily maintained by annual root pruning in the spring and regular pinching. You also can form your own bonsai plant in one of many styles, such as formal upright, slanting, cascade, or forest. You'll find a variety of pots on the market, each adapted to a specific style of bonsai.

Caring for a bonsai depends partly on the plant grown. Some need intense light, but others adapt to bright or even moderate light. Since they have little root space, watering must be done with utmost care. When the mix begins to feel slightly dry, set the pot in tepid water and let it soak up what it needs. The frequency of watering depends on many factors, including the light level and the season. Fertilize sparingly with balanced fertilizer to minimize excessive growth.

Keeping gift plants growing

When you receive pretty pots of flowering plants decorated with foil and ribbon, you want them to thrive in your care. The first and most important step is to cut through the bottom or remove the decorative sleeve as soon as possible. If excess water collects in the wrapping, it will be reabsorbed into the soil, waterlogging the roots. That can result in leaf tip burn or other problems, including stains on your furniture.

The three most common kinds of gift plants are perennials, shrubs, and annuals. Varieties grown as gift plants often are different from those grown in the garden, and may not perform well outdoors. A potted chrysanthemum, for example, is a perennial plant. Enjoy its flowers, and then prune them off and grow the mum as a high-light houseplant until you can plant it outdoors in the spring. Oleander, gardenia, and pot azalea are shrubs that will last longer indoors if night temperatures are cool. Put them on the floor of a sunroom or a greenhouse but not in a hot window.

Tropical gift plants such as holiday cactus and poinsettia are annuals everywhere but Zone 10. The cactus needs a rest period after blooming, but otherwise you grow tropicals indoors as you do annual plants dug from the garden: water when the top of the soil feels dry, fertilize monthly, and pinch the tips to encourage new growth until it's time to let the plants flower.

▲ **A greenhouse window in the kitchen extends the outdoor herb-growing season.**

◀ **Remove the wrapping from gift plants as soon as they arrive so that water does not accumulate and rot the roots.**

Bringing annuals indoors

Impatiens and angelonia are often blooming wildly and herbs are at their peak just as the first frost approaches, and it's natural to want to prolong their season. To make them part of the indoor garden, groom, dig, and pot them. Leave some of the garden soil attached to the roots but plant in a good potting mix. Water and fertilize the potted plants right away, and then move them indoors.

Extending the growing season

Many annuals and gift plants need more sunlight and humidity than the average foliage houseplant. Indoor gardeners often turn to greenhouse windows, sunrooms, or greenhouses to provide the right growing conditions. Their investment results in year-round blooms and edible herbs. If you decide to install a greenhouse window, glassed-in porch, or add a greenhouse to your home, its location should allow maximum winter sunlight in from the south and west. Glass expanses focus sunlight, however, intensifying its effects, so plants may dry out more quickly. If you live where summers are extremely hot, plan to use blinds, shade cloth, drapes, or strategically planted trees to keep plants indoors from burning up. If you find you are watering more frequently and the plants are actively growing, you may need to fertilize more often too.

Forcing bulbs and corms

Bulbs of all sorts can be easily coaxed to flower outside their natural season. Good choices for forcing include hyacinth, tender narcissus, tulip, crocus, Dutch iris, grape hyacinth, squill, ornithogalum, freesia, amaryllis, and gladiolus. Select early blooming varieties and always buy large, firm bulbs. Because most take 8 to 12 weeks to force, start planting in September to have blooming pots from Thanksgiving through New Year's Day.

Narcissus, such as 'Paperwhite' and 'Soleil d'Or', can be forced in shallow containers filled with rocks or gravel. Choose heavy containers twice as deep as the narcissus bulb is tall, at least 4 inches. Look for vases made especially for forcing narcissus, hyacinth, and crocus in water. Fill and maintain the water level in these vases so the base of the bulb or corm is just above it. Keep these containers in a dark, cool place until roots form, and then move them into bright light.

Other narcissus, crocus, and hyacinths also can be forced in standard pots filled with soil. Begin by filling the pot two-thirds to three-quarters full with moist potting mix. Place the bulbs or corms so they do not touch each other, with pointy tops just below the rim. Cover them loosely with moist potting mix; don't firm the soil around them. Label each pot and place it in a cool, frost-free place such as a garage, basement, or anywhere temperatures range from 35°F to 50°F. Water just enough to keep the soil moist, and watch for roots to emerge from the drainage holes. By then, sprouts will be showing and the pots can be moved to a warmer, sunny location (55°F to 65°F) to trigger flowering. Narcissus stems naturally elongate but will not be as spindly if grown in a cool, dark environment until they are 4 inches tall.

Forced plants will not bloom in the pot again, but cut off the flower stalks and

▽ **Hyacinths forced indoors can be planted outdoors but may take several years to recuperate and bloom again.**

maintain the leaves until they fade if you want to add the plants to your outdoor garden. Amaryllis bulbs need slightly different care after blooming because they can be forced again indoors for many years. The leaves will grow steadily for several months to replenish the bulb. By late summer, the foliar nutrients have been absorbed into the bulb and the leaves may begin to decline. If this happens, stop watering, cut off the yellow leaves, and wait while the plant goes through dormancy. Keep the soil barely moist until new growth starts up again, then resume watering to force again. Repot rarely because crowded amaryllis roots, like those of clivia and bougainvillea, promote flowering.

▲ **Herbs need less water and fertilizer than other plants indoors, so group them together for ease of care.**

Growing herbs indoors

Herbs belong in your houseplant collection for many reasons. They are healthful, providing savory tastes to tempt your palate without added fat or salt. Their leaves are often as aromatic as they are eyecatching and as useful in potpourri as they are in salads and stews. Many of these attractive plants grow well in warm, bright kitchens, bringing the pleasure and ease of herb gardening indoors. Provide herbs with bright light such as in a sunny window.

Herbs will grow in any container, but grouping them together is wise for two reasons. Because you are growing herbs to eat, keeping them isolated from other plants helps prevent exposure to insect pests and thus eliminates the need for insecticides. In addition, herbs are tastier when watered and fertilized sparingly, so having them in a separate space reminds you to treat them differently. Use a potting mix that drains well.

A long narrow basket can hold several small pots of individual herbs handy for easy care and culinary use. But a wide shallow bowl filled with several herbs also works well, requires watering less often, and makes a quick transition outdoors in warm weather, doubling as a living centerpiece.

Growing herbs indoors successfully requires consistent clipping to promote compact growth. You may find that freezing the excess harvest of most herbs is easier than drying them. Strip the leaves off the stems, rinse and dry them well, then tear or chop them into small pieces. Mixing in just enough light vegetable oil, such as canola or grapeseed, to coat the leaves helps to prevent oxidation. Fill ice cube trays two-thirds full with the leaf mixture and freeze. Store the frozen cubes in freezer-safe bags.

The top 10 herbs for indoor growing are:

■ **Basil (*Ocimum basilicum*):** Keep basil pinched for compact growth to season tomato soups and Cajun and Italian dishes. Replace plants or reseed annually in spring.

■ **Chives (*Allium schoenoprasum*):** To clip delicious onion or garlic chives all winter, leave the pot outdoors through the first frost. Then bring it indoors to start tender new growth.

■ **Cilantro (*Coriandrum sativum*):** Cut stems and leaves as needed for Asian, Latin, and Middle Eastern dishes. Reseed regularly for a fresh supply.

■ **Marjoram (*Origanum majorana*):** A substitute for stronger-flavored oregano, sweet marjoram can last several years indoors. If it becomes leggy or less tasty, start new seeds in spring.

■ **Mint (*Mentha* spp.):** Mints tolerate lower light than other herbs. Pinch frequently to keep compact. Enjoy mint as tea or in Mediterranean cuisine.

■ **Parsley (*Petroselinum crispum*):** Parsley tastes best when clipped from young plants, such as those grown from seed sown in fall and then replaced in spring. Flat-leaved (Italian) parsley has a stronger but less bitter flavor than curly varieties.

■ **Rosemary (*Rosmarinus officinalis*):** Not hardy below Zone 7 or 8, rosemary can be grown successfully indoors in bright light. Popular as a topiary, it can be clipped regularly. Cut above woody stems to promote new growth.

■ **Summer savory (*Satureja hortensis*):** Annual summer savory has a sweet, peppery flavor that goes well with beans and other vegetables. Reseed periodically for a continuous supply.

■ **Tarragon (*Artemisia dracunculus* 'Sativa'):** French tarragon is the most flavorful type and grows well in medium to bright light. Use the leaves in cream sauces.

■ **Thyme (*Thymus vulgaris*):** Many varieties of thyme are among the easiest herbs to grow indoors, and they blend well with most meats and vegetables.

Bromeliads

Few plant groups can draw a crowd the way blooming bromeliads do, yet still look completely presentable once the flowers fade. More than 2,700 species and hundreds of bromeliad hybrids make up three basic groups: tank (or vase) plants, terrestrial types, and air plants. Each group has members that make dramatic, easy-to-grow houseplants when you provide medium to bright light plus moderate temperatures and humidity. If you like strong colors and textures from bold to fine, grow bromeliads.

Bromeliad flowers are discreet—small and tucked into the center of the plant or along a stalk. The colorful centers and stunning, sometimes rainbow-striped spikes are bracts, leaves that modify themselves to attract pollinators to the otherwise nondescript flowers. The coloration often lasts for months.

Bromeliads bloom only once, then slowly—sometimes over several years reproduce and finally die. Little plants, offsets called pups, emerge on the sides of the mother bromeliad. Cut them free and pot them to begin the next generation.

The terrestrial group includes pineapple (*Ananas*) and earth star (*Cryptanthus*), believed to be relics from millions of years ago when all bromeliads grew in soil. These still do and are particularly interesting because of their ancient history and distinctive looks. To grow your own pineapple, simply slice the crown off a ripe one and root it in a shallow dish of water. Put the rooted top in a relatively large pot and keep it watered and fertilized. It will bloom in about a year and may grow a pineapple at the top of the flower spike, as it does in the field.

The largest group of bromeliads, the tank types, are mostly epiphytic, growing best on driftwood or bark slabs, although some thrive in pots. *Neoregelia* 'Tricolor' may be the best known of this latter type that blooms deep in a vase of pointed leaves, while *Guzmania* has sharply pointed leaves that lift the flowers high above the foliage. If you buy a tank bromeliad mounted on a board, keep its vase filled with water and submerge it occasionally. Water potted bromeliads when the top of the soil feels dry to the touch, and keep their tanks full too. Add a balanced soluble fertilizer every three months.

The air plants are pure epiphytes, often native to climates where intense

▲ **Some bromeliads have central "tanks" that collect and store water. Pour water directly into the tank, allowing it to cascade down into the soil.**

evaporation and scarce water challenged their evolution. This group adapted to produce scurf, the thick grayish scales that cover their leaves, but includes some that developed cups or vases to hold water. You can recognize the vase-type air plants, such as flaming sword (*Vriesea*) by their flattened bract spikes. The most popular of the scurf types, *Tillandsia*, are often grown glued to small ceramic ornaments, shells, or pieces of driftwood. Their skinny gray leaves spring out as gracefully as a ballerina's tutu. A quick plunge into tepid water once a week keeps air plants hydrated, and a mist of fertilizer solution once a month provides plenty of nutrients.

For more information on growing bromeliads, see pages 62 and 63 in the "Gallery of Houseplants."

Orchids

Exotic as the plants and flowers may look, growing conditions for many orchids are quite average and similar to those for many other houseplants. For example, this gigantic family (some 600 genera, including 250,000 species, and 100,000 hybrids) divides into two basic light preferences. While some need very intense light to bloom, many, including colorful moth orchid *(Phalaenopsis)* and the small comet orchid *(Angraecum),* thrive in an east or west window or under fluorescent lights

▼ **Some orchids, such as this *Dendrobium aggregatum*, are grown on wood or osmunda fiber slabs to increase air circulation.**

and can be grown successfully in the majority of indoor environments.

At least eight orchid types grow well in average to slightly increased humidity and temperature conditions, although many benefit from a cool, dry environment for several weeks in fall to trigger flowering. Others, such as *Rodriguezia* and moth orchids, bloom reliably once or more each year with regular maintenance.

Some orchids, such as slipper orchid *(Paphiopedilum),* accommodate varying microclimates in your home by having selections with different needs. Greener slipper orchids need cool conditions, while those with variegated leaves adapt well to a wider range of temperatures.

The watering routine for any orchid depends on its form, particularly whether it has the swollen, sometimes wrinkled stems called pseudobulbs, as pansy orchids do *(Miltonia).* The thinner-leafed types, such as *Cymbidium,* should be watered as soon as the potting mix begins to dry. Allow those with pseudobulbs and thick stems or canes, such as buttonhole orchid *(Epidendrum)* to dry out between waterings.

Orchids exhibit two primary growth habits, monopodial (upright) and sympodial (sideways, by way of rhizomes). Upright types, such as moth orchids, lose lower leaves as they gain upper foliage and flowers. They multiply by forming offsets at the soil surface and on the stems. Called keikis ("children" in Hawaiian), the offsets soon develop aerial roots and can be moved to their own pots. Sympodial orchids, such as dancing lady *(Oncidium),* bloom on the new stems that arise from their rhizomes. Many form pseudobulbs, which should be left on the plant until the stems become leafless and yellow.

Orchid roots require particularly good air circulation, readily achieved by using a potting mix containing plenty of ground bark, perlite, peat moss, or other bulky matter. Repot only when the plants cease to grow well, usually long after aerial roots form. Slatted wood boxes, clay pots with extra drainage holes, and slabs of wood, cork, or tree fern further improve air circulation, drainage, and potting media options. Jewel orchids *(Ludisia)* are the exception to all these rules, best grown in ordinary potting mix for their velvety, veined leaves as much as their spiky white flower stalks.

For more information on growing orchids, see pages 96–98 in the "Gallery of Houseplants."

Lift a spiny cactus for repotting by wrapping a 3-inch-wide strip of folded newspaper around the plant and using the two ends as a handle.

Cacti and succulents

One reason cacti and succulents are popular houseplants is because they are so easy to grow. Many people find that these plants withstand considerable neglect a definite plus if you're very busy. Benign neglect is actually the secret to their successful culture.

Cacti and succulents exhibit a wide variety of colors, shapes, textures, and sizes. These are the camels of the plant kingdom: Their well-developed water conservation techniques can carry them through periods of drought.

During their growing season, cacti and succulents need water whenever the potting mix begins to dry out. During dormancy, however, water sparingly (just enough to keep the roots alive). Never let them get dehydrated; water before the foliage and stems go limp and shrivel. In springtime, when plants show signs of fresh growth, begin thorough watering again. Set the pots in a pan of water and allow them to "drink" until the soil is just moist on top.

Clay and other porous containers make it easier to control the moisture level because they allow excess water to evaporate. (You also can use plastic pots for these plants if you water less frequently.) Clay pots stabilize taller plants that tend to become top-heavy. Bonsai containers are splendid for displaying succulents because the larger-than-usual drainage holes allow unabsorbed water to drain freely.

Provide a potting mix that drains well. You'll find a recipe for such a mix on page 22. Fertilize cacti at half or one-quarter of the recommended strength and only during the growing period. When plants cease seasonal growth, stop fertilizing.

Place cacti and succulents where they will get as much light as possible. Many will adapt to bright or even medium light, although their growth may slow drastically. Thin, elongated, or pale growth indicates a need for more light.

Cacti and succulents are predictably heat-resistant but do best when the evenings are cool. During the fall and winter, cacti generally need cool to cold night temperatures, or they may not bloom.

Both cacti and succulents are usually propagated by stem cuttings. Unlike other plants, though, their cuttings should be potted in a dry mix, not a moist one, and should not be covered with a plastic bag. Watering before the cut ends have healed over may lead to rot. Begin to water only when you see new growth or when the plant resists when you tug on it (a sign that it is rooted).

For specific details on growing these plants, see cacti on pages 64–67 and succulents on pages 117–119 in the "Gallery of Houseplants."

TROUBLESHOOTING

Check your plants for signs of insects or disease every time you water them. Move infected or infested plants away from others and check nearby plants to make sure the problem has not already spread. Then use the information provided here to diagnose and fix the problem. If you use an insecticide or fungicide, always check the label to make sure your pest or plant is listed, and follow the instructions carefully.

INSECTS

Aphids

Problem: New leaves are curled, discolored, and smaller than normal. A shiny or sticky substance may coat them. Small (1/16 to 3/8 inch), wingless, soft-bodied green, pink, yellow, black, brown, or gray insects cluster on buds, young stems, and leaves. Aphids are extremely prolific and reproduce rapidly. Damage results when they suck sap from leaves and stems. They excrete excess sugar in a fluid called honeydew, which often drops onto leaves or surfaces below.
Solution: Wipe off aphids with cotton swabs dipped in rubbing alcohol, rinse the foliage under the faucet two or three days in a row, or take infested plants outdoors and knock off the aphids with a strong stream of water. Spray weekly with insecticidal soap or an insecticide if necessary.

Cyclamen mites

Problem: The stem tips or new growth in the plant center becomes severely stunted. Leaves become brittle, stay very small, and may be cupped or curved; their color may change to bronze, gray, or tan. Flower buds fail to develop properly and do not open.
Solution: Spray infested plants several times with an insecticidal soap or a miticide, and then isolate them. Discard heavily infested plants. Scour the pots and wash the area where the pots were sitting with a solution

Cyclamen mites destroy flowers.

Fungus gnats cause little damage.

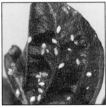

Aphids suck sap and spread viruses.

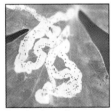

Leaf miner larvae bore inside leaves.

Wipe off mealybug egg sacs.

of 1 part household bleach to 9 parts water. Observe nearby plants so you can spray if symptoms appear. Avoid touching infested plants and then touching healthy plants.

Fungus gnats

Problem: Small (1/8 inch), slender, dark insects fly around when plants are disturbed. They frequently run across the foliage and soil and may also be found on windows. Fungus gnats and their close relatives, shore flies, are small flies that do little damage. They lay their eggs in soil that contains organic material. After a week, the eggs hatch and the larvae crawl through the upper layer of the soil. The larvae are white, 1/4 inch long, and have black heads. When present in large numbers, larvae may feed on the roots of some plants, killing seedlings.
Solution: Place yellow sticky traps directly on potting soil to catch adults. Let potting mix dry slightly between waterings: Larvae cannot survive in dry soil. Apply *Bacillus thuringiensis israelensis* to the soil.

Leaf miners

Problem: Irregular winding white to brown tunnels or patches appear on upper leaf surfaces. Small dark-headed white grubs sometimes are seen in the tunnels. Leaf miners are minuscule flies (1/10 inch) that lay white eggs in clusters on the undersides of leaves. The larvae bore inside the leaves of susceptible species and spread through contact with other plants.
Solution: Damage from leaf miners is unattractive but not fatal to a mature plant. Remove infested leaves. Isolate infested plants. Foliar sprays are ineffective but a systemic insecticide may be helpful.

Mealybugs

Problem: White cottony or waxy insects 1/10 inch long cluster on the undersides of leaves, on stems, and in the leaf joints. Egg masses also may be present. Honeydew, a sticky excretion, may cover the leaves or drop onto surfaces below. Leaves may be spotted or deformed. Infested plants are unsightly, do not grow well, and may die.
Solution: Control is difficult. Wipe off pests with a damp cloth or use cotton swabs

dipped in rubbing alcohol. Also wipe off any egg sacs under the rims or on the bottoms of pots. For serious infestations, thoroughly spray the soil, stems, and both sides of the leaves with an insecticide or insecticidal soap.

Narcissus flies

Problem: Amaryllis bulbs fail to produce new leaves after their dormant period. When squeezed, they feel soft. Upon inspection, frass (brownish insect excrement) may be found near a hole at the bulb's base. When cut open, the bulb contains a single (rarely more) large (½ to ¾ inch) brown larva inside and substantial rotting material. You may see a black-and-yellow-striped adult flying near the plants.
Solution: Carefully extract the larva with a piece of wire. If the center of the bulb is intact, dust the opening with powdered sulfur. Don't repot until the wound is healing. If the bulb is gutted, cut it open and remove rotted material. Lay the bulb in vermiculite in a cool spot. New bulblets may appear from intact bulb scales. Avoid putting amaryllis plants outdoors, where narcissus fly infestation occurs.

Scale insects

Problem: Nodes, stems, and leaves or fronds are covered with cottony white masses, brown crusty bumps, or clusters of flattened reddish gray or brown scaly bumps that scrape off easily. Leaves or fronds turn yellow and may drop. A sticky excretion called honeydew may cover the plant parts and drip on surfaces below. The young, called crawlers, are small (about ¹⁄₁₀ inch) and soft bodied. They feed on the sap. Eventually their legs disappear, but the scales remain in place.
Solution: Pick off scales by hand or use a soft toothbrush dipped in soapy water. The young can hide under adult shells, so remove all scales as soon as possible. Insecticidal soap or indoor horticultural oil is most effective on crawlers.

Spider mites

Problem: Leaves are stippled, yellow, and dirty; they may dry out and drop. There may be webbing over flower buds, between leaves, or on the lower surfaces of the leaves. Tap a leaf or stem sharply over a sheet of white paper. Minute green, red, or yellow specks will drop to the paper

Narcissus flies gut amaryllis bulbs.

Springtails mostly threaten seedlings.

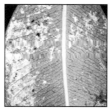

Use insecticide to control thrips.

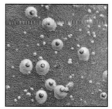

Pick or brush off scale insects.

Spider mites thrive in dry air.

Vacuum whiteflies or use insecticide.

and crawl around. Spider mites multiply rapidly and cause damage by sucking sap from the undersides of leaves.
Solution: Rinse infested plants in the shower or with a hose, or spray them weekly with insecticide or insecticidal soap. Increased humidity discourages reproduction.

Springtails

Problem: Small white to black insects up to ⅛ inch long jump when plants are watered. Springtails prefer potting mixtures rich in peat moss. They do little damage to mature plants but are harmful to seedlings.
Solution: Let the potting mix dry slightly between waterings. Use a pasteurized mix when sowing seeds, and cover seed containers to prevent infestation. Soak the plants in water to bring larvae to the surface, and then spray them with an insecticide containing pyrethrins.

Thrips

Problem: Flowers and leaves are abnormally mottled or streaked with silver. Young leaves and flowers may be distorted. Pollen sacs on African violets spill open, leaving yellow powder on the flowers. Dusty black droppings collect on leaves or flowers. Tiny (up to ¹⁄₁₆ inch) dark insects scuttle away when you breathe on the plant. Both adult and immature thrips damage plant surfaces with their rasping mouth apparatus. They hide in crevices between stems and flowers and lay their eggs inside plant tissues or in the potting mix.
Solution: Thrips reproduce many times each year, so remove heavily damaged leaves and flowers to reduce infestation. Apply an insecticide or insecticidal soap to affected plants and potting mix weekly.

Whiteflies

Problem: Tiny (¹⁄₂₀ inch) winged white insects flutter around the plant when you touch it. Translucent scalelike larvae are present under leaves. Leaves may be mottled and yellow. Whiteflies excrete excess sap, which coats the leaves and may drop from the plant.
Solution: Isolate heavily infested plants. Use yellow sticky traps to catch adults. Wipe off larvae with a damp cloth or cotton swab soaked in rubbing alcohol, or shake the plant and vacuum up the cloud of flies. Spray severe infestations weekly with insecticidal soap or insecticide.

DISEASES

Bacterial spot

Problem: Leaves, stems, or both develop many spots that look dark and wet and are sometimes circled by yellow halos. Wet and crowded conditions cause bacterial spot.
Solution: Remove the diseased plant parts, dipping your shears in a solution of 1 part household bleach to 9 parts water or wiping the blades with rubbing alcohol after each cut. Water slightly less frequently until plants recover and begin new growth. To prevent recurrence, put the plants in a warmer location, increase air circulation around each pot, and do not mist susceptible plants.

Bacterial stem blight

Problem: Soft, sunken areas with water-soaked margins appear on the stems. Affected areas sometimes crack. Lower leaves may turn yellow and wilt. The stem may rot through so the top of the plant breaks off. Inner stem tissue is brown. Bacterial stem blight is caused by the bacterium *Erwinia chrysanthemi*.
Solution: No cure exists. Discard severely infected plants. If some stems are still healthy, cut them off above the diseased area and reroot them. Do not reroot any stems that have brown streaks. To prevent bacterial stem blight, use a well-draining potting mix and avoid splashing leaves with water. Water from the bottom and discard excess water after 20 minutes. Increase air circulation around the plant.

Botrytis

Problem: Light brown patches on leaves, stems, or flowers gradually darken and turn soft and moist. A grayish mold covers the affected surfaces. Infected plant parts curl up and fall off. Botrytis, or gray mold, is a common airborne fungal disease that spreads quickly and is common during periods of high humidity and inside closed containers, such as terrariums. When the plant stem is infected, the entire plant may rot away.
Solution: Remove infected plant parts. Spray the rest of the plant with a fungicide or fungicidal soap. Improve air circulation around the plants to keep humidity low. Do not mist susceptible plants.

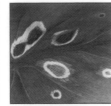

Bacterial spot

Crown, stem, and root rot

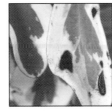

Leaf spot

Bacterial stem blight

Botrytis

Powdery mildew

Crown, stem, and root rot

Problem: Plants fail to grow. Leaves appear dull, then turn black. Lower ones may turn yellow and drop. Leaves in the center of the plant turn dark green, then black. When the condition is severe, all the roots are rotted and the plant may wilt and die. Rot is caused by soil-dwelling fungi (*Pythium*), or water molds, that attack the roots, and it usually indicates that the plant has been watered too frequently or that the soil mix does not drain well.
Solution: Let the soil dry between waterings or transplant into a fast-draining potting mix in a container that drains freely. Discard severely infected plants and soil. Soak empty pots in a mixture of 1 part household bleach to 9 parts water for 30 minutes. Then rinse with water and dry thoroughly before reuse. Wash your hands before touching healthy plants.

Leaf spot

Problem: Circular reddish brown spots surrounded by yellow margins appear on the leaves. Several spots may form a blotch. Badly spotted leaves may turn yellow and die. Leaf spot is caused by one of several fungi including *Septoria*. Spotting is unsightly but not always fatal.
Solution: Clip off badly spotted leaves. Water carefully to avoid leaf splash, and keep the foliage dry to prevent the spread of the fungus. If spotting continues, spray the plant with a fungicide or fungicidal soap.

Powdery mildew

Problem: White or gray powdery patches develop on the leaves, stems, and flowers, usually appearing first on older leaves and the upper surfaces of leaves. Tissue under the powdery growth may turn yellow or brown. Affected leaves may drop. The powdery patches are fungus strands and spores. The windborne spores can reach nearby plants and infect them. The disease favors low light, dry soil, and warm days with cool nights.
Solution: Remove infected leaves, and then spray plants with a fungicide or fungicidal soap weekly until the disease is gone. Move plants to locations with more light and better air circulation but keep them out of cool drafts.

Rust

Problem: Concentric circular rings of brownish spores appear on the undersides of fuzzy-leaved plants, such as geraniums. Calla lilies may erupt in orangey brown spots or streaks along their leaves.
Solution: Remove all the damaged leaves, and then spray the plant with fungicide or fungicidal soap. When new growth appears, spray again and repeat weekly until new leaves are healthy and there is no recurrence of the disease. Increase the space between pots and use a small fan to improve ventilation.

Sooty mold

Problem: This black coating on leaf surfaces can easily be rubbed or washed off. Several different fungi present in air and water produce sooty mold, which often reappears a few weeks after it is removed. The coating blocks the leaf pores and slows down or stops photosynthesis.
Solution: Physically removing sooty mold is the first step, but it is a sign of a serious insect infestation. Aphids, whiteflies, mealybugs, and scale insects are the most common houseplant insects that excrete a sticky fluid called honeydew after they pierce and suck plant tissues. This creates an ideal environment for the growth of sooty mold. Identify and control the insects and the mold will not return.

Virus

Problem: Plants grow slowly and without vigor. Leaves are lightly mottled or streaked with yellow; they also may show ringed yellow spots. Leaves can be distorted. Viruses are carried from plant to plant by insects or on infected tools.
Solution: No cure exists for infected plants. Destroy them. To prevent viruses, control insects through preventive treatment. When pruning, dip tools into rubbing alcohol or a solution of 1 part household bleach to 9 parts water between each cut.

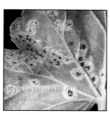

Rust

Bud blast

Sooty mold

Edema

Virus

Guttation

CULTURAL PROBLEMS

Bud blast

Problem: Flower buds form but fail to open. They may turn brown shortly after forming or attain nearly full size before brown patches appear. Sometimes they simply drop off. Dry air is the most common cause. Other causes are air pollution, excessive heat or cold, too much fertilizer, too little or too much water, and fungal disease. Bud blast is normal in young houseplants and others, such as gardenia.
Solution: As flowering approaches, place plants on a humidity tray (see page 20) or in a room with a humidifier to increase humidity. Move plants out of direct sunlight and away from air-conditioning and heating vents.

Edema

Problem: Brown, corky patches appear on stems or leaves. Scratching off the patches reveals underlying, healthy cells. Too much water, especially during humid weather, is usually the cause of edema. Cells swell up with moisture and burst, then scab tissue forms as the plant heals, leading to a corky appearance. Sucking insects, such as spider mites, may also cause edema on some plants, notably succulents.
Solution: Cut away badly damaged tissues. Prevent edema by watering less frequently, especially when the air is humid and light levels are low. Also check for and control spider mites.

Guttation

Problem: Drops of water or sap collect on the tips or the undersides of leaves. They may blacken or form translucent crystals as they dry. Too much soil moisture is the most common cause of guttation. The plant absorbs more water than it can use, causing it to secrete the excess through its leaves. A small amount of guttation is normal in some plants such as dieffenbachia.
Solution: Reduce watering so the plant does not absorb excessive amounts of moisture. Increase light and air circulation and lower humidity so any moisture exuded evaporates rapidly.

High temperature

Problem: Outer leaves turn yellow, then brown, and then may die. Stems become soft. The plant stops flowering. High temperatures cause problems for cool-weather plants, which tolerate warm days as long as nights are cool (below 60°F).
Solution: Grow cool-weather plants in a cool room with as much light as possible. If a cool room is not available, put the plants near a window at night. When temperatures are not below freezing, putting the plants outside at night will promote flowering. Keep plants adequately watered and fertilized.

Insufficient water

Problem: Leaves are small; the plant fails to grow well and may be stunted. Plant parts or the whole plant wilts. The edges of broad leaves or the tips of narrow leaves may dry out and become brittle, but they still retain a dull green color. Bleached areas may occur between the veins. Leaf tissues may die and remain bleached or turn tan or brown. The plant may die.
Solution: Water the plant thoroughly. If the soil is completely dry, soak the entire pot in water for a couple of hours.

Iron deficiency

Problem: The newest leaves are yellow at the edges. The yellowing progresses inward; in advanced stages, the last tissues to lose their green color are the veins. In severe cases the entire leaf is yellow and small, and the plant may be stunted. Iron deficiency is a common problem in acid-loving plants. When the pH is 7.5 or higher (alkaline), iron is chemically unavailable to some plants.
Solution: Spray the foliage with a solution containing chelated iron and also drench the soil in the pot. Or spray a fertilizer containing chelated iron and drench the soil with it too. Use an acid-based plant food for the plant's regular fertilizing. When planting or transplanting acid-loving plants, use an acidic growing mix that contains at least 50 percent peat moss. Do not add lime or dolomite.

High temperature

Lack of bloom

Insufficient water

Lack of light

Iron deficiency

Low humidity

Lack of bloom

Problem: The plant fails to flower during its blooming season. No signs of insects or diseases are visible.
Solution: The plant may be too immature to flower. The three most common causes of failure to bloom in mature plants are lack of light, insufficient humidity, and improper temperature. Move the plant to a brighter spot, place it on a humidity tray (see page 20), and check its temperature requirements. A lack of minerals or an excess of nitrogen could be the cause; give the plant a flowering plant fertilizer. Double-check for insect infestation.

Lack of light

Problem: The plant fails to grow well. Leaves may be lighter green and smaller than normal. Lobes and splits normal in mature leaves may not develop. Lower leaves may yellow and drop. Stems and leafstalks may elongate and grow spindly and weak. The plant bends toward a light source. A flowering plant fails to produce flowers, and a plant with colorful foliage becomes pale. A variegated plant may lose its variegation.
Solution: Gradually move the plant to a brighter location. Close sheer curtains when the sun shines directly on the plant. If necessary, provide supplemental lighting.

Low humidity

Problem: Growth is slow and leaves tend to curl downward. The plant wilts rapidly and needs frequent watering. Flower buds and new leaves wither or fail to develop properly. Leaf edges and tips may turn brown and dry up.
Solution: Place the plant on a humidity tray (see page 20) or keep it in a room with a humidifier. Water as soon as the potting mix is dry just below the top inch. Group plants so the moisture given off by transpiration increases the air humidity around them all. Moving the affected plant to a cooler, less sunny spot also helps.

Nitrogen deficiency

Problem: The oldest leaves, usually the lower ones, turn yellow and may drop. Yellowing starts at the leaf edges and progresses inward. Growth is slow, new leaves are small, and the whole plant may be stunted. Nitrogen is easily leached from soil during regular watering.
Solution: Spray the leaves with a foliar fertilizer. Then fertilize the plant with a soluble plant fertilizer rich in nitrogen. If there is room in the pot, topdress the soil with pasteurized organic material.

Salt damage

Problem: Leaf edges of plants with broad leaves or the leaf tips of plants with long, narrow leaves turn brown and brittle. This browning occurs on the older leaves first; when the condition is severe, new leaves also are affected. On some plants the older leaves may yellow and die. Salt damage is a common problem found on container-grown plants.
Solution: Leach excess salts from the soil by flushing with water. Never let a plant stand in the drainage water. If the plant is too large to lift, empty the saucer with a turkey baster. Do not overfertilize. Trim off dead stem tips with sharp scissors.

Sudden leaf drop

Problem: After you move the plant to a new location, leaves first turn yellow, and then they drop off.
Solution: Purchase plants that have been preacclimated to local conditions rather than shipped directly from a field to the store. Put plants in the brightest light possible and increase humidity. Cover newly arrived plants with clear plastic bags to temporarily increase humidity while the plants adjust to lower light, as described on page 10. Keep plants away from cold drafts.

Nitrogen deficiency

Sunburn or leaf scorch

Salt damage

Too much water or poor drainage

Sudden leaf drop

Water spots

Sunburn or leaf scorch

Problem: White, tan or brown dead patches develop on leaves exposed to direct sunlight. Leaf tissues may lighten or turn gray. In some cases the plant remains green but growth is stunted. Damage is most severe when the plant is allowed to dry out. Sunburn or leaf scorch occurs when a plant is exposed to more intense sunlight than it can tolerate. A plant that is grown in low light burns easily if it is suddenly moved to a sunny location.
Solution: Move the plant to a shaded spot or close the curtains when the plant is exposed to direct sunlight. Prune off badly damaged leaves or trim away damaged leaf areas to improve the appearance of the plant. Keep the plant properly watered.

Too much water or poor drainage

Problem: The plant fails to grow and may wilt. Leaves lose their glossiness and may become light green or yellow. Roots are mushy and brown. The soil in the bottom of the pot may be soggy and have a foul odor. The plant may die.
Solution: Discard a severely wilted plant or one without white root tips. For a plant that is less severely affected, do not water again until the soil is almost dry (barely moist). Prevent the problem by using a lightweight potting mix with good drainage.

Water spots

Problem: White, yellow or tan blotches in various patterns occur on older leaves. Small islands of green may be left between the discolored areas. Brown spots sometimes appear within the discolored areas. Water spots are a common problem on fuzzy-leaved plants. They occur most commonly when cold water is splashed on the leaves while the plant is being watered.
Solution: Avoid getting cold water on leaves when watering. Use tepid water, which will not cause spotting if it touches the leaves. Spotted leaves will not recover. Remove them if they are unsightly.

GALLERY OF HOUSEPLANTS

ouseplants with fabulous foliage and amazing flowers, many that are easy to grow and some that are a bit of a challenge—you'll find them all in this chapter.

More than 200 plants for indoor gardens are featured, listed alphabetically by individual botanic name or in plant groups such as succulents, orchids, and cacti. (Use the index on pages 123–127 to look up common names.) Plants included here are easily obtained and have great potential to

▼ **With such a great variety of plants to choose from, you'll find some that are just right for your indoor garden.**

thrive indoors and to deliver outstanding blossoms, leaves, and silhouettes. Use this chapter to assemble a collection that best fits your style preferences or to make smart choices for particular microclimates within your home.

Although many plants adapt to a variety of indoor conditions, this chapter gives you specific information about each one's ideal environment and care. You will find practical advice about cultural needs and how to identify potential problems. The following definitions will help you understand the requirements listed.

Light

■ **Low light** means an interior location away from a window or light source.
■ **Medium light** is common in most homes, where there is indirect light all day, with direct sunlight available for a few hours in either early morning (east window) or afternoon (west window). Medium light levels are also found several feet inside a room with a sunny window, and from two-tube light fixtures with complete-spectrum bulbs.
■ **Bright light** corresponds to south and west exposures where plants get at least two hours of direct sunlight and indirect sunlight during the hottest part of the day. It also describes the light generated by four-tube fluorescent fixtures.
■ **Intense light** is available in a southern exposure that receives full sun for much of the day or in a sunroom or greenhouse that receives bright light all day.

Humidity

■ **Average humidity** is typical in most homes and is usually lower than optimal for houseplants, especially when heating or air-conditioning systems are in use.
■ **High humidity** means that air moisture must be consistently elevated all year, usually requiring the use of a humidifier or humidity tray.
■ **Very high humidity** is the province of greenhouses and terrariums and difficult to achieve in living areas except bathrooms and spas.

Temperature

■ **Cold:** 35°F to 50°F.
■ **Cool:** 50°F to 65°F.
■ **Average:** 65°F to 80°F.
■ **High:** above 80°F.

Abutilon
uh-BYEW-tih-lahn

Flowering maple

- **Light:** Medium to bright
- **Water:** Keep evenly moist
- **Humidity:** Average to high
- **Temperature:** Average, but cooler in winter
- **Fertilizer:** High phosphorus
- **Size:** 1-6'H×1-3'W

A. ×hybridum cultivars have upright blooms on compact plants.

Old-fashioned flowering maples are tall with an open habit and hanging flowers, such as *A. pictum*. Modern types (mostly *A. ×hybridum*) are shorter, denser plants with outward-facing cup-shaped flowers in white, pink, yellow, orange, or red. Blooming occurs all year long when light is good but is often most intense in spring and summer. The slightly fuzzy leaves range from deeply cut and maple-like to nearly rounded and can be solid green or splotched with white or yellow. *A. megapoticum* cultivars are trailing plants.

Repotting: Annually.
Propagation: Stem cuttings or seed.
Problems: Repot or leach soil salts frequently. Watch for whiteflies, mealybugs, and scale insects.
Tips: Prune occasionally throughout the year to prevent legginess, or cut back severely in midwinter. Grow cultivars with white variegation as foliage plants; they rarely bloom.

Acalypha
ak-uh-LY-fuh

Chenille plant

- **Light:** Medium to bright
- **Water:** Keep evenly moist
- **Humidity:** Average to high
- **Temperature:** Average, avoid cold drafts
- **Fertilizer:** All-purpose
- **Size:** 2-6'H×2-3'W

The chenille plant, or red-hot cat's tail, is an indoor shrub with shiny, oval, lightly toothed green leaves and pendent spikes of downy, red flowers. Prune to keep it small and dense. It flowers in spring and summer, sometimes all year. The flying foxtail (*A. repens*) is similar but has much smaller leaves, stems that spread out and downward, and shorter red chenille-like flower spikes. It is generally used in hanging baskets.

Copperleaf or Jacob's coat (*A. wilkesiana*) has insignificant flower spikes but brightly colored foliage, often coppery red or splotched pink, orange, white, and other shades.

Repotting: As needed.
Propagation: Stem cuttings.
Problems: Spider mites, whiteflies, mealybugs, and fungal diseases are possible.
Tips: Small plants adapt better to new environments. Keep the plant away from children and pets; its sap may irritate sensitive skin and is also slightly poisonous.

Flying foxtail *(Acalypha repens)* is named for its flower spikes.

Aeschynanthus lobbianus
eh-skih-NAN-thus lo-bee-AN-us

Lipstick plant

- **Light:** Medium to bright
- **Water:** Allow to dry slightly between waterings
- **Humidity:** Average to high
- **Temperature:** Average
- **Fertilizer:** High phosphorus
- **Size:** 8-24"H×10-36"W

Lipstick plant *(Aeschynanthus lobbianus)* blooms in the fall.

The lipstick plant is named for its dark purple tubular cups, which appear at the tips of the branches, each one encircling a bright scarlet flower bud. Lipstick plant produces branches that arch outward, then downward (perfect for hanging baskets) and waxy-looking dark green leaves, often with a reddish margin. It sometimes blooms sporadically throughout the year.

A. longicaulis (also known as *A. marmoratus*) 'Black Pagoda' is a semitrailer with dark green mottled leaves and bright red-orange flowers.

Repotting: Infrequently.
Propagation: Stem cuttings.
Problems: May need some full sun or supplementary light to bloom. Mealybugs, scale insects, aphids, and thrips are possible pests.
Tips: Prune after flowering if necessary. Plants placed outside in summer attract hummingbirds.

Aglaonema commutatum
ag-lay-o-NEE-muh kah-myew-TAY-tum
Chinese evergreen

- **Light: Low to medium**
- **Water: Keep evenly moist**
- **Humidity: Average to high**
- **Temperature: Average to high, avoid cold drafts**
- **Fertilizer: All-purpose**
- **Size: 10-36"H×12-30"W**

Chinese evergreen grows slowly and tolerates low light.

A foliage plant appreciated for its slow, regular growth even under low-light conditions, Chinese evergreen is essentially an upright plant with thick, nonbranching stems and long, leathery, often silver-mottled dark green leaves. Three or more plants are usually grown per pot for a bushier appearance. Older plants may lose their lower leaves over time, exposing bare stems.

Chinese evergreens occasionally bloom indoors, but the blooms are insignificant. Long-lasting, bright red berries follow; they yield seeds that can be sown.

Repotting: Infrequently, in any season. Keep the root ball intact.
Propagation: Stem cuttings, air layering, division, or seed when available.
Problems: Watch for mealybugs, scale insects, and aphids.
Tips: Keep the leaves dry to avoid leaf spots. Chinese evergreen grows slowly, so buy the size you want. The sap contains oxalic acid, which can be toxic.

Alocasia
al-o-KAY-zhuh
Alocasia

- **Light: Medium**
- **Water: Let dry slightly between waterings**
- **Humidity: High**
- **Temperature: Average to high, avoid cold drafts**
- **Fertilizer: All-purpose**
- **Size: 1-4'H×1-4'W**

The striking foliage of alocasia, also known as elephant's ear (see also *Caladium*), is its claim to fame, as it rarely blooms indoors and its flowers are not striking. The leaves are usually arrow- or heart-shaped, sometimes with lobed or wavy margins, and are often a shiny dark green very close to black, with contrasting silvery veins.

Dozens of species exist but only a few alocasias are offered as houseplants. Perhaps the most common is A. ×*amazonica* because it combines beautiful leaves with a relatively sturdy constitution. Similar plants include A. *lowii*, A. *korthalsii*, and an ever-increasing list of hybrids.
Repotting: Infrequently.
Propagation: Division.
Problems: Spider mites, mealybugs, and scale insects are possible pests.
Tips: Leave the top of the rhizome or tuber exposed when repotting to help prevent rot.

Elephant's ear rarely blooms indoors; enjoy it for its dramatic foliage.

Alpinia zerumbet 'Variegata'
al-PIN-ee-uh ZER-um-bet vair-ee-uh-GAHT-uh
Variegated ginger

- **Light: Medium to bright**
- **Water: Keep evenly moist**
- **Humidity: Average**
- **Temperature: Average**
- **Fertilizer: All-purpose**
- **Size: 3-4'H×3-4'W**

Variegated ginger isn't edible but offers graceful leaves and flowers.

V ariegated ginger lacks culinary usefulness, but its vivid colors and strong lines make it a standout in any brightly lit room. Upright canes hold graceful, sword-shaped foliage striped like dizzy zebras. Golden yellow and traffic-signal-green leaves curve out gently, then narrow to sharp-looking points. That curve is repeated in the shape of the white flowers that hang like smooth shells in sumptuous clusters. The best of its genus for growing indoors, variegated ginger has shorter stems and more tolerance of home humidity conditions than its relatives. Group it with croton, lipstick plant, and sago palm for color and compatibility.
Repotting: When pot is crowded.
Propagation: Division of rhizomes.
Problems: Control height and spread by root pruning and repotting into the same container.
Tips: Individual stems may bloom after two or three years, then decline and should be pruned out.

Anthurium
an-THUR-ee-um
Anthurium

- **Light:** Low to bright
- **Water:** Let dry slightly between waterings
- **Humidity:** Average to high
- **Temperature:** Average to high
- **Fertilizer:** All-purpose
- **Size:** 8-36"H×8-36"W

Pigtail anthurium *(A. scherzerianum)* tolerates dry air.

Few plants offer such possibilities as anthuriums. Among the hundreds of species are flowering and foliage plants as well as terrestrial plants, epiphytes, and climbing plants, all in a huge range of shapes and forms. Most adapt readily to the low light and less-than-perfect humidity of the average home.

Many in the largest group, epiphytic anthuriums, produce thick aerial roots much like those of orchids, used to capture and absorb water and nutrients and to affix themselves to their support. Anthuriums, however, adapt readily to regular potting mixes, so these aerial roots can be seen simply as curious appendages.

The best-known anthuriums are those grown as flowering plants. They produce a spike of tiny, insignificant flowers, sometimes scented, called a spadix, but the main attraction is a large colorful leaflike bract, often leathery, called the spathe. Each single inflorescence often lasts a month or more, and since many anthuriums are repeat bloomers, they can be attractive for months on end. Many of the species have bright red blooms, but hybrids are now more common and come in a wider range of colors.

Flamingo flower

(A. andraeanum) is popular for use in cut arrangements, but the plant requires the high humidity of a greenhouse to thrive indoors.

Pigtail anthurium

(A. scherzerianum) is easy to grow indoors. Its thick, lance-shaped leaves and twisting spadices are usually the same orange-red as the bracts, although some cultivars have white-speckled bracts. Its greater tolerance of dry air makes it a long-lasting, yet slow-growing, flowering plant.

Hybrid flowering anthuriums

have been developed specifically for use indoors. They bloom abundantly all year long (even under low light) and are not difficult to maintain. Popular cultivars include the Lady Series in shades of red, pink, and white, and 'Southern Blush' with lavender blooms. New releases are introduced every year.

Crystal anthurium

(A. crystallinum) is one of the most striking foliage anthuriums, with long-stemmed, heart-shaped, emerald green leaves to 12 inches across and 20 inches long and overlaid with silver veins.

***Anthurium* hybrid 'Red Hot' blooms year-round indoors.**

Bird's nest anthurium

(A. hookeri) is so-called because its nearly stemless, leathery, paddle-

Crystal anthurium *(A. crystallinum)* is grown for its striking foliage.

shape dark green leaves form a dense rosette vaguely resembling a bird's nest. *A.* 'Fuch's Ruffle' is similar to *A. hookeri*, but with wavy leaf margins.

Repotting: Every two years.

Propagation: Offsets or stem cuttings.

Problems: Excess mineral salts cause leaf-tip burn and stem dieback. Overwatering causes crown rot. Low light or dry air causes poor blooms. Mealybugs, thrips, and scale insects are possible. Avoid spraying leaves to prevent leaf spots.

Tips: Thin-leaved anthuriums need high humidity; leathery-leaved anthuriums can cope with drier air. Pot into a well-aerated growing mix, perhaps half orchid mix and half regular potting mix, leaving the upper roots exposed; cover those with sphagnum moss to replicate the treetop growing conditions of most species. As plants age and produce abundant aerial roots, repot into deeper containers, again covering the upper roots with moss. Or prune out the oldest stems and leaves and reroot the cuttings. New offsets will form at the base.

Aphelandra squarrosa
aff-el-AN-druh skwar-OH-suh

Zebra plant

- **Light: Medium to bright**
- **Water: Keep evenly moist**
- **Humidity: High**
- **Temperature: Average, but cool in winter**
- **Fertilizer: High phosphorus**
- **Size: 10-24"H×10-24"W**

Zebra plant *(Aphelandra squarrosa)* needs high humidity to rebloom.

Zebra plant's bright golden bracts last for months and bear shorter-lived tubular flowers in a similar shade. After blooming, the plant is a spectacular foliage specimen until the following fall, when it reblooms.

Modern cultivars are compact plants that rarely exceed 15 inches tall. The most commonly available are 'Dania' and 'Apollo'.
Repotting: If needed, in late winter or early spring.
Propagation: Stem cuttings.
Problems: Dry air and cold drafts cause leaf scorch. Soil kept too wet or too dry and mineral salt buildup cause leaf drop. Aphids, thrips, whiteflies, mealybugs, and scale insects are possible pests.
Tips: Best considered a one-season wonder, to be bought and enjoyed in bloom, then composted. Simple enough to keep in good shape once it is in bloom but not as easy to rebloom without high humidity and careful watering. Easier to grow in a greenhouse.

Araucaria heterophylla
air-ah-KAIR-ee-uh heh-teh-ROH-fil-luh

Norfolk Island pine

- **Light: Medium**
- **Water: Keep evenly moist**
- **Humidity: Average**
- **Temperature: Average, but cool in winter**
- **Fertilizer: All-purpose**
- **Size: 1-8'H×1-4'W**

Actually a conifer that originated on Norfolk Island, off Australia, this tree produces one new whorl of symmetrical branches each year. Its formal appearance makes it a hit indoors, where it can serve as a replacement for a Christmas tree. The shiny green needles are short and borne all around the branches. For a fuller look, growers usually plant several seedlings to a pot.
Repotting: Infrequently.
Propagation: Not feasible indoors.
Problems: Dry soil, overwatering, excess mineral salts, insufficient light, and hot, dry air all cause lower branches to drop off. Spider mites, mealybugs, and scale insects are possible. The plant reacts badly to pruning.
Tips: Under poor conditions or when watered erratically, Norfolk Island pine loses lower branches and looks bare; hide its "bare legs" behind other houseplants. It grows slowly, so buy one large enough for your immediate needs.

Norfolk Island pine *(Araucaria heterophylla)* is actually a conifer.

Ardisia crenata
ar-DEE-zhuh cre-NAH-ta

Coralberry

- **Light: Medium to bright**
- **Water: Keep evenly moist**
- **Humidity: Average to high**
- **Temperature: Cool to average**
- **Fertilizer: All-purpose**
- **Size: 12"H×18"W**

Coralberry *(Ardisia crenata)* has colorful fruit that last for months.

Coralberry is both woodsy and primly formal. It spreads rampantly underground as it would in the forest floor, but aboveground, coralberry looks too shy to venture anywhere. No more than a foot tall, crooked gray stems soon shed their lower foliage to form a neat tuft of oblong evergreen leaves with toothy edges. New growth forms a jaunty copper cap on top, but coralberry's most charming feature hangs below the leaves on special lateral stems. That's where pinkish white, ¼-inch flowers bloom, followed by shiny berries that last for months.
Repotting: When pot is crowded.
Propagation: Seeds or division.
Problems: Young plants grow slowly and may take two years to produce berries.
Tips: Look for varieties with white and pink berries as well as traditional red. Protect plants from direct summer sun.

Asparagus
uh-SPAIR-uh-gus
Asparagus fern

- **Light: Medium to bright**
- **Water: Let dry slightly between waterings**
- **Humidity: Average**
- **Temperature: Average, tolerates cool winters**
- **Fertilizer: All-purpose**
- **Size: 18-60"H×18-36"W**

Asparagus fern *(Asparagus setaceus)* looks best in a hanging basket.

Not ferns at all, but rather subtropical relatives of the asparagus, these plants get their name from their fernlike appearance: light and airy with plentiful medium green "needles" (actually modified leaves called cladodes). The only true leaves are the prickly scales hidden along the stems. Asparagus grows from thick, knobby roots, sending shoots upward and outward, which creates an attractive appearance in hanging baskets.

Of the more than 300 species, two are commonly grown indoors: *A. densiflorus* and *A. setaceus*. Emerald feather, or emerald fern (*A. densiflorus*), has two popular cultivars, both with small white flowers, half-hidden among the needles, that turn into bright red berries.

A. d. 'Sprengeri' is the most widely available asparagus fern. It bears 18- to 36-inch arching stems with flat, l-inch dark green needles. Give the plant a regular quarter turn to keep the branches from all growing to the same side. Foxtail fern (*A. d.* 'Myers') has a more upright habit that looks best on a tabletop plan.

The stems of asparagus fern (*A. setaceus*, also sold as *A. plumosa*) bend at right angles at the tip and, covered with tiny needles, look much like fern fronds. When young, it is a bushy plant less than 2 feet tall and looks best in a hanging basket. It becomes a climber when mature; keep it pruned for denser growth or train it on a trellis or other support for stems up to 10 feet long. Its tiny white flowers give way to shiny black berries.
Repotting: Annually.
Propagation: Division (use a saw or sharp spade) or seed.
Problems: Needles turn yellow and drop if the plant is kept too wet or too dry or moved suddenly to low light. Spider mites are possible.
Tips: Massive root systems quickly crush growing mixes and fill up all available space, so watering from above is ineffective (water runs around the root ball without moistening the soil). Either repot into increasingly larger pots or soak the pot in a sinkful of tepid water at each watering. Pruning long, ungainly growth stimulates shorter stems. Asparagus fern is an excellent basket plant for hanging outdoors.

Emerald feather *(A. densiflorus)* has airy stems similar to a true fern's.

Aspidistra elatior
as-pih-DEE-struh eh-LAY-tee-or
Cast-iron plant

- **Light: Low to bright**
- **Water: Let dry slightly between waterings**
- **Humidity: Average to high**
- **Temperature: Cold to high**
- **Fertilizer: All-purpose**
- **Size: 2-3'H×2-3'W**

Cast-iron plant *(Aspidistra elatior)* is a great choice for forgetful gardeners.

Very few houseplants are as easy to grow as cast-iron plant. Its common name refers to its cast-iron constitution: It tolerates almost any growing condition, from scorching sun to deep shade and from burning heat to near frost as long as its root ball is protected from overwatering.

Were it not for its tough nature, this plain-looking plant probably never would have become popular. The somewhat arching, oblong, leathery dark green leaves are borne on 6-inch stalks from a rhizome. Insignificant dark purple bell-shaped flowers appear at the soil surface. Several variegated cultivars are also offered.
Repotting: Infrequently.
Propagation: Division.
Problems: Spider mites, mealybugs, and scale insects are possible pests. Soggy soil causes rot.
Tips: Buy a large plant for an instant effect, as it is extremely slow growing, especially in low light. It can remain in the same pot for decades.

Aucuba japonica
aw-KYEW-buh juh-PAHN-ih-kuh

Japanese aucuba, gold-dust plant

- **Light:** Bright
- **Water:** Let dry slightly between waterings
- **Humidity:** Average
- **Temperature:** Average, but cool in winter
- **Fertilizer:** All-purpose
- **Size:** 1-3'H×1-3'W

Japanese aucuba *(Aucuba japonica)* **has dark leaves dusted with gold.**

This broad-leaved evergreen shrub is commonly grown outdoors but also makes an attractive houseplant. It produces numerous branches covered with leathery shiny dark green leaves. Most cultivars are variegated, with small yellow spots over the leaf surface. The small purplish flowers and bright red berries are rarely produced indoors.

'Variegata' is the classic gold-dust plant and the one most readily available. Modern selections, such as 'Crotonifolia', has larger, more abundant spots. 'Picturata' has yellow-centered leaves with small spots.
Repotting: As needed.
Propagation: Stem cuttings.
Problems: None significant.
Tips: Place in a cold spot during winter dormancy, or at least avoid night temperatures above 65°F. Prune regularly for dense growth.

Bamboos

- **Light:** Medium to bright
- **Water:** Keep evenly moist
- **Humidity:** High
- **Temperature:** Average, but cold to cool in winter
- **Fertilizer:** All-purpose if needed
- **Size:** 1-15'H×spreading W

The hollow, woody stems (culms) of bamboo sprout new leaves every year. The narrow evergreen leaves are borne on slender branches from knots along the culms.

Hedge bamboo (*B. multiplex,* syn. *B. glaucesens*) grows to 50 feet tall and so needs pruning for use indoors. The thick green to yellow culms provide a distinct bamboo appearance. Pot-bound Buddha's belly bamboo (*B. ventricosa*) has curiously swollen stems. It can grow over 8 feet tall, so it needs pruning for most indoor uses. Pygmy bamboo (*Pleioblastus pygmaeus,* syn. *Arundinaria pygmaea* and *Sasa pygmaea*) is probably the best choice for growing indoors. It is rarely more than 16 inches tall, with thin culms and medium-green leaves.
Repotting: Infrequently.
Propagation: By division.
Problems: None significant.
Tips: It may be necessary to break the pot to remove a pot-bound bamboo for division or repotting.

Pygmy bamboo *(Pleioblastus pygmaeus)* **is easy to maintain indoors.**

Beaucarnea recurvata
bo-KAR-nee-uh ray-kur-VAH-tuh

Ponytail palm, elephant-foot tree

- **Light:** Medium to intense
- **Water:** Let dry thoroughly between waterings
- **Humidity:** Low, tolerates high humidity
- **Temperature:** Average
- **Fertilizer:** All-purpose
- **Size:** 1-8'H×1-4'W

Ponytail palm *(Beaucarnea recurvata)* **can go without water for long periods.**

This popular plant's long narrow dark green leaves arch downward like an upswept ponytail. Its thick trunk's swollen base resembles a pachyderm's foot, reaching 3 feet or more in diameter. The plant is actually an Agave family member. Some plant specialists call it *Nolina recurvata*.

It thrives in almost all indoor conditions, rarely needs repotting or fertilizing, and has few disease or insect problems. Because it stores water in its trunk, it can go without water (and most other care) for long periods. It rarely blooms indoors.
Repotting: Infrequently.
Propagation: Seed (very slow), stem cuttings, or offsets.
Problems: Spider mites, scale insects, and mealybugs are potential pests.
Tips: Purchase a specimen large enough for your current needs.

Begonia
buh-GOHN-yuh

Begonia

- **Light: Medium for foliage species, bright for flowering ones**
- **Water: Let dry slightly between waterings**
- **Humidity: Average to high**
- **Temperature: Average, avoid cold drafts**
- **Fertilizer: All-purpose**
- **Size: 3-48"H×3-40"W**

Angel wing begonia 'Sophie Cecile' has eyecatching leaf shape and colors.

Begonias have many different growth habits, ranging from tall and upright to bushy, creeping, climbing, tuberous, or trailing. Some are grown for their foliage, others for their flowers, and some for both. The distinctive flowers, with separate male and female blooms appearing on the same plant, may bloom year-round, at least intermittently, although some species are seasonal. Likewise, most plants remain in growth all year, while others have a dormant or semidormant period.

Three main groups exist: rhizomatous begonias, with creeping stems called rhizomes that root as they grow; tuberous and semituberous begonias, with a bulblike structure at their base; and fibrous-rooted begonias, which includes plants that have only ordinary roots. These groups subdivide into the following seven categories.

■ **Cane-stemmed begonias** (*Begonia* spp.) are fibrous-rooted, with erect, smooth stems bearing swollen leaf nodes somewhat like those of bamboo. The leaves are asymmetrical and diverse in color, size, and spotting. Although grown primarily for their foliage, the plants bloom intermittently throughout the year if given enough light. Generally they are tough, easy-to-grow plants. Propagate from stem cuttings.

Angel wing begonias (*B. coccinea*) have large leaves, silver spotted on top and red underneath. The plant grows to 3 feet tall and wide. Some, such as *B.* 'Orange Rubra', are pendulous in habit, making them good choices for hanging baskets. The old-fashioned hybrid *B.* ×*corallina* 'Lucerna' (or 'Corallina de Lucerna') is the most common. It bears coral flowers and can reach 4 feet at maturity.

■ **Rex begonias** (*B. rex-cultorum* hybrids) are grown primarily for their foliage but will produce tiny pink or white blooms if given good light. The leaves of most cultivars are large and have asymmetrical blades with diverse, brilliant coloration and textures. Most rex begonias spread by rhizomes that root where they touch soil. Keep them warm and

Iron cross begonia *(B. masoniana)* has unusual leaf texture and markings.

don't overwater. Fertilize lightly. They need humid air at all times. Propagate them from rhizomes or from leaf cuttings or sections.

■ **Rhizomatous begonias** (*Begonia* spp.) grow along or under the soil surface and sometimes hang over the edge of the pot. The foliage is often attractively mottled and textured. In ample light most bear tall stalks of white, pink,

Rex begonia *(B. rex-cultorum)* is grown for its unusual leaf patterns.

or greenish white flowers in winter. Propagate them from rhizomes or leaf cuttings. Most are fairly to very easy to grow.

Iron cross begonia (*B. masoniana*) produces large, bumpy, heart-shaped leaves in yellow-green with a dark burgundy Maltese-cross pattern in the center. It needs high humidity. Some old-fashioned hybrids with thick rhizomes and extra-large leaves are still popular, such as beefsteak begonia (*B. erythrophylla*) and lettuceleaf begonia (*B.* ×*erythrophylla* 'Bunchii'). More popular are the smaller varieties, such as the tiny eyelash begonia (*B. boweri*), star begonia (*B. heracleifolia*), and numerous intermediate hybrids.

■ **Shrublike begonias** (*Begonia* spp.) are fibrous rooted but branch abundantly, hiding their stems from view. Grown exclusively for their foliage, their bloom is seasonal. They are easy-to-grow, adaptable plants. Propagate them from stem cuttings.

Those with shiny upper leaves, called hairless begonias, need more light than the hairy types. The hairless types have smooth, sometimes metallic-looking leaves. The trout-leaf begonia, *B. ×argenteoguttata*, also falls into

Wax begonias are popular outdoors but thrive in bright light indoors too.

the hairless category, although its silver-spotted leaves resemble those of a miniature angel wing begonia. If given very bright light it produces creamy white flowers from spring to autumn. *B. scharffii* is a hairy-leaf begonia with bronze-green leaves. Fern-leaf begonia (*B. foliosa*) has tiny oval leaves on arching stems and produces tiny white flowers.

Tuberous begonias
(*B. ×tuberhybrida*) can be started indoors and their dormant tubers stored indoors over the winter, but they don't make good houseplants.

Wax begonias (Begonia ×semperflorens-cultorum) are the most popular fibrous-rooted begonias. They are bushy plants with shiny, waxy leaves in green or bronze. Given ample light, they bloom profusely in a variety of colors throughout the year. Flowers can be single or double. Wax begonias are best known as outdoor bedding annuals but will flourish indoors with a little fertilizer, bright light, and sufficient warmth. Propagate from

stem cuttings or seed. Popular series include Lotto, Cocktail, Olympia, and Dragon Wing.

Winter-blooming begonias
result mostly from crosses of semituberous or tuberous begonias. They essentially have fibrous roots but with swollen, tuberlike bases. Bushy dwarf plants frequently used in hanging baskets, Lorraine or Christmas begonias (*B. ×cheimantha*) bear profuse pink or white blooms in winter. Propagate the plants from stem cuttings.

Rieger or elatior begonias (*B. ×hiemalis*) are low growing and bushy, with green or bronze foliage. Many are pendulous and used in hanging baskets. The yellow, red, white, or orange flowers are usually large and often double. Give them cooler temperatures and plenty of light during their winter bloom period.

Repotting: As needed. May need annual repotting.
Propagation: See the individual category descriptions for details.
Problems: Overwatering causes crown rot. Low light results in spindly, weak growth. Dry air and cold drafts result in leaf scorch. Examine plants for powdery mildew and mealybugs.
Tips: Pinch or prune occasionally, but don't prune off flower buds.

Rieger or elatior begonias add bright color to an indoor garden in winter.

Bougainvillea
boo-gan-VIL-ee-uh
Bougainvillea

- **Light:** Intense
- **Water:** Let dry slightly between waterings
- **Humidity:** High
- **Temperature:** Average, but cool in winter.
- **Fertilizer:** All-purpose
- **Size:** 2-8'H×2-8'W

Variegated bougainvillea offers bright foliage along with colorful bracts.

Bougainvillea is probably the most popular of all climbers. You also can prune its often spiny, woody stems into a shrublike form or allow them to cascade from a hanging basket. In summer it produces masses of bracts in shades of pink, purple, red, orange, or white. (It also may bloom in winter under ideal conditions.) Bracts are long-lasting but the tiny tubular white flowers they enclose are ephemeral.

B. glabra and *B. spectabilis* are the most common species. Standard, dwarf, and variegated cultivars are available.
Repotting: Infrequently.
Propagation: Stem cuttings, with rooting hormone.
Problems: Intense light is absolutely needed for bloom. Soggy soil causes rot. Spider mites, whiteflies, and mealybugs are possible pests. Some cultivars may lose their leaves in winter.
Tips: Prune plants, especially older ones, harshly after blooming.

Bromeliads

- **Light: Medium for species with spineless foliage, bright to intense for those with silvery leaves or sharp spines**
- **Water: Let terrestrial types dry slightly between waterings, fill tank bromeliad rosettes with water and moisten the soil, mist the leaves of air plants**
- **Humidity: Low for air plants and terrestrials, high for tank types**
- **Temperature: Average**
- **Fertilizer: All-purpose, avoid applying fertilizers to tanks**
- **Size: 1-60"H×1-48"W**

Living-vase plant *(Aechmea fasciata)* has long-lasting flowers.

Bromeliads are easy to grow but require special care, as explained in more detail on page 43. Most bromeliads are rosette-forming plants with lance-shaped leaves in a wide variety of colors. Their flowers are often short-lived, but they generally have bracts, or modified leaves, that change colors at flowering time, and these may remain colored for months. After flowering, bromeliads usually die but not before producing one or several pups (offsets). You'll find three main types of bromeliads:

- **Terrestrials** have normal root systems and are treated much like ordinary houseplants.
- **Tank bromeliads** are generally epiphytes (they grow on trees in the wild) and catch water in their cup-shaped rosettes. They usually adapt well to pots, especially if an epiphytic growing mix is used, but can be grown on bark slabs.
- **Air plants** are small bromeliads that lack a distinct tank. They are mostly epiphytes and absorb water through their leaves. Often sold glued to ceramic figures or pieces of driftwood, they do not do well in potting mixes because their roots serve strictly as an anchor and do not absorb water.
- **Vase plants** *(Aechmea)* are a mostly epiphytic genus of tank bromeliads with spiny leaves. They need medium to intense light. Among the more than 200 species, the most common is *A. fasciata*, living-vase plant or urn plant. Its broad, thick leaves are mottled with gray and sea green stripes, and its conical rosette of pink bracts and long-lasting, large dark blue flowers create a splendid effect.
- **Pineapple** *(Ananas comosus)* is a sun-loving terrestrial bromeliad with gray-green leaves. Most of the domesticated varieties have been cultivated for their spinelessness.
- **Billbergia** is an epiphytic tank bromeliad with lightly spined leaves. Its upright arching flower stalks last weeks. Plants prefer bright light but tolerate medium light for long periods. Queen's-tears, also called friendship plant *(B. nutans)*, has gray-green leaves

Earth star *(Cryptanthus bivittatus)* is grown for its unusual foliage.

and an arching spray of pink and green flowers. It usually flowers during winter in the Northern Hemisphere, producing pups that bloom the following year. It adapts well to medium light.
- **Earth star** *(Cryptanthus bivittatus)* is a genus of small terrestrial species with broad,

Pineapple plant *(Ananas nanus)* is a dwarf type without spines.

earth-hugging rosettes of wavy, pointed leaves bordered in harmless spines. It bears no colorful bracts nor does it change color at flowering. Offsets appear on runners or from the center of the rosette. Medium light best suits these forest dwellers.
- **Dyckia** is a slow-growing, medium-size terrestrial bromeliad with dark green to silver spiny foliage. Given intense light during summer, dyckias produce orange flowers on spikes. The plants are extremely drought-tolerant and should be watered only when dry.
- **Guzmania** has a vase-shaped, spineless rosette that forms a tank. It blooms from late winter to summer, depending on the species. The true flowers are small but surrounded by long-lasting, large showy bracts in red, yellow, orange, or purple. Pups just separated from the mother plant flower within 18 months. This genus does best in medium light.
- **Blushing bromeliad** *(Neoregelia)* produces large rosettes of thick, shiny leaves with spiny edges. The most common is *N. carolinae*.

It reaches a diameter of 30 inches and produces lavender blue flowers that appear to float on the water in the tank. Just before flowering, the young leaves in the center turn bright red. It bears pups near the mother plant, but some of the smaller cultivars, such as *N*. 'Fireball', produce numerous

Guzmania lingulata blooms reliably indoors even in medium light.

outstretched runners bearing pups at their tips, which look good in a hanging basket. Its leaves turn coppery red in full sun.

■ **Bird's nest bromeliad** (*Nidularium*) is an epiphytic tank bromeliad with spiny-edged leaves. The bracts form in a cluster just above the rosette, which changes color, often to bright red, many weeks before the white flowers appear. Foliage color and patterns vary according to species. All need bright light to bloom.

■ **Air plants** (*Tillandsia*) are the largest and most varied genus of mostly epiphytic species. The spineless leaves may be broad, straplike, and green, forming a tank. More often, the leaves are thick, pointed, and covered with gray scales, giving the whole plant a silvery appearance. Such plants lack a central tank for water storage; they have few roots and absorb all their moisture and nutrients through their leaves. The more silvery the foliage, the more light is required.

Some air plants bear flower stalks composed of sword-shaped bracts, from which peep small violet flowers. Others bear flowers directly from the center of the rosette, which often turns bright red for the occasion.

Tillandsia must have its base exposed to air. It will quickly rot if planted in soil. *T. ionantha*, with miniature silver-gray leaves, is probably the most commonly available. The entire plant turns brilliant red at blooming.

■ **Flaming sword** (*Vriesea*) is a genus of mainly epiphytic species with smooth leaves. The plants are grown for their foliage and flowers. When not in bloom, flaming sword looks much like guzmania, but the flattened flower spikes, often in bright reds or yellows, differentiate them. The blooms will last for several weeks.

Repotting: Repot terrestrials as needed. Tank types rarely need repotting. Air plants can be remounted on wood or bark.

Propagation: Offsets (pot or mount with fishing line or plumber's glue); some types from seed.

Problems: Avoid watering or spraying with hard water or water that contains chemical fertilizers, which can stain the leaves permanently. Soggy soil causes root rot. Scale insects and mealybugs are possible pests.

Tips: Initiate flower buds by bagging the plant and an apple in plastic. You can use bromeliad tanks as living vases for cut flower arrangements.

Neoregelia carolinae center leaves turn red just before the plant flowers.

Browallia speciosa
bro-AH-lee-uh spee-see-OH-suh

Browallia, Sapphire flower

■ **Light:** Medium to bright
■ **Water:** Keep evenly moist
■ **Humidity:** High
■ **Temperature:** Average
■ **Fertilizer:** High phosphorus
■ **Size:** 10-24"H×10-12"W

Sapphire flower (Browallia speciosa) may bloom year-round in bright light.

Browallia is a tropical perennial with a woody base. As a houseplant it blooms heavily under only medium light.

It produces multiple stems covered with small elliptic leaves. The flowers are violet-blue with a white eye, or all-white. Browallia flowers most abundantly spring through fall but will bloom all winter if given adequate light.

Browallia can be used as a table plant with regular pinching and pruning. In winter, keep it watered and continue to fertilize lightly until it has finished flowering.

Repotting: Annually.

Propagation: Seeds or stem cuttings.

Problems: Low light may cause spindly growth and poor bloom. Dry air and cold drafts cause leaf scorch. Browallia is susceptible to whiteflies and aphids.

Tips: Pinch regularly for bushy plants. Start anew from cuttings when it becomes too woody. Move it to shade outdoors in summer.

Cacti

- **Light: Intense**
- **Water: Let dry thoroughly between waterings**
- **Humidity: Low**
- **Temperature: Average to high, cold to cool in winter**
- **Fertilizer: All-purpose**
- **Size: 1-96"H×1-48"W**

The cactus family's more than 2,000 species have evolved to adapt to increasing aridity. As a result, most are succulents, with thickened green stems that have taken over the job of photosynthesis. But not all succulents are cacti. Many different plants have developed succulent growth habits, with thick stems and leaves that store water (*Euphorbia*, *Haworthia*, and *Aloe*, for example). Cacti, however, have specialized growing points, called areoles, usually seen as somewhat fuzzy raised or sunken spots on their stems. It is from these areoles that spines, flowers, and new growth appear.

Desert cacti have thick stems designed for water storage and generally no leaves or only small, short-lived ones. An enormous variety of forms is available, from small and squat to long and rambling to tall and candelabra-like. Most but not all bear plentiful spines, and many are so spiny it is hard to see the stems. Some also have attractive woolly areoles or abundant hairs.

Small desert cacti tend to bloom well indoors as long as they have a distinct dormant period with little or no water and cold conditions. Winter night temperatures of 40°F to 50°F are necessary to stimulate bloom, which usually occurs several months later, in late spring or summer.

Larger desert cacti will usually bloom only at maturity, which can take 20 or more years to attain, so they are grown for their unique forms and interesting spines. They do best with cool to cold, dry winters but adapt well to indoor conditions year-round.

Repotting: Infrequently, in cactus growing mix.

Propagation: Offsets, stem cuttings (set in dry growing mix and withhold water until new growth appears), or seed (some species).

Problems: Poor drainage and too-frequent watering cause rot. Mealybugs, root mealybugs, and scale insects are common.

Tips: Small cacti require little grooming. Cut back taller ones as needed.

Rattail cactus has unusual elongated stems, on which flowers appear.

- **Rattail cactus** (*Aporocactus flagelliformis*) produces narrow stems 1 inch wide and to 6 feet long. Its aerial roots grip rock faces in the wild. Indoors let the plant dangle from a hanging basket, and occasionally remove the old brown stems. Purple-red flowers appear along the stems in summer.
- **Bishop's cap or star cactus** (*Astrophytum*) has thick green to reddish stems. Its globular form varies in shape. Many cultivars are spineless, and most are small. Yellow flowers appear on the top of the plant after a cold winter.
- **Old-man cactus** (*Cephalocereus senilis*) can reach a height of 10 feet and a diameter of 8 to 10 inches. Its upright, cylindrical gray-green body is covered with soft white "wool" while still immature, but beware of the hidden sharp spines. The plant grows slowly and rarely produces its funnel-shaped rose-colored flowers indoors.
- **Peruvian apple or curiosity-plant** (*Cereus*) generally has deeply ribbed blue-green stems and few spines. Its large flowers, which open at night, are rarely produced indoors.
- **Peanut cactus** (*Chamaecereus sylvestri*) has short, clustering green stems to 6 inches long; they are ribbed and covered with short, bristly spines. Vivid scarlet red flowers appear in the summer along the stems after a dormant period of cool temperatures and drought. Even young plants bloom readily.
- **Scarlet-bugler or silver-torch** (*Cleistocactus*) has cylindrical green clustering stems that can grow to 3 inches in diameter and 2 to 3 feet tall. They have many ribs and spines, which vary from white to brown and dense to sparse. Tubular scarlet or orange flowers are borne along the length of the stems of mature plants in summer.
- **Golden barrel** (*Echinocactus grusonii*) is a globe-shaped cactus with yellow spines prominent on its stem ribs. It grows very slowly but can reach 3 feet in diameter. Yellow bell-shaped flowers appear on the top central ring of mature plants in summer.

Golden barrel cactus

Old-man cactus

■ **Hedgehog cactus** (*Echinocereus*) is generally cylindrical and upright with self-branching clumps of stems. Spines and colors vary among the cultivars. The pink, purple, or whitish flowers appear near the tops of the stems in late spring or summer.

Urchin cactus produces fragrant night-blooming flowers.

■ **Urchin cactus or Easter-lily cactus** (*Echinopsis*) is best known for its abundant large night-blooming funnel-shaped flowers, which are intensely fragrant, range from white to pink, and sometimes reach 8 inches long. Its gray-green, globular to oval stems are distinctly ribbed and have clusters of spines along the ribs. For better bloom remove most of the offsets.

■ **Barrel cactus or fishhook cactus** (*Ferocactus*) is big and globular to columnar with blue-green to green stems. It has 10 to 20 ribs, broad spines that range from yellow to red, and yellow to red-purple flowers that appear on mature plants in summer.

Chin cactus (left) and little candles cactus (right).

■ **Chin cactus** (*Gymnocalycium*) has globular 8- to 12-inch-thick stems that grow in clusters or singly, depending on the species. They usually bear thick spines, but some are nearly spineless. The bell-shaped, white to pale rose flowers are borne near the top of the plant in spring and summer. It tends to bloom readily from an early age and doesn't require cool winter conditions.

■ **Lobivia or cob cactus** (*Lobivia*) is small and often grown in clumps in a wide, flat container. It blooms more easily than many other cacti even when not exposed to cool winters. The large yellow, red, or purple flowers appear in spring and summer and generally last a long time.

■ **Pincushion or snowball cactus** (*Mammillaria*), little candles cactus, silver cluster cactus, and rose pincushion, is a diverse genus that includes globular and cylindrical forms. They range from tiny individual heads, only a few inches wide, to massive clumps. The tiny flowers form a

Ball cactus

ring around the top of the plant and are often followed by red berries. They are comparatively easy plants to bloom but prefer cool, dry conditions in winter. Snowball cactus (*M. bocasana*) has hooked, yellowish spines and bell-shaped yellow flowers. Rose pincushion (*M. zeilmanniana*) has a solitary stem topped with a ring of purple flowers.

■ **Ball cactus** (*Notocactus*) has bell-shaped yellow or orange

Bunny ears cactus

flowers. *N. leninghausii* can reach 3 feet tall. This genus is a good choice for beginners, as it blooms while young.

■ **Bunny ears or beavertail cactus** (*Opuntia*) usually bears a flattened stem resembling a pad. It has two types of spines: long visible ones and glochids, small tufts of shorter hooked spines that break off and can penetrate the skin. Bunny ears (*O. microdasys*) has reddish, yellow, or white glochids but no spines. Opuntias require minimal care but rarely bloom indoors.

■ **Crown cactus** (*Rebutia*) is small, globe-shaped, and covered with small, warty tubercles. The short spines range from white to dark brown. Large yellow, orange, red, or purple flowers appear at the base of the plant during summer. It flowers when young.

Crown cactus

(continued)

Cacti *(continued)*

- **Light:** Medium to bright
- **Water:** Let dry slightly between waterings
- **Humidity:** Average
- **Temperature:** Average, but cool in winter.
- **Fertilizer:** All-purpose
- **Size:** 1-3'H×1-6'W

Epiphytic cacti use aerial roots to cling to their support. Although they store water, their stems are much thinner than those of desert cacti. Likewise, they are rarely as spiny. Some have just a few hairs where their ancestors' spines used to develop.

Coming from a more shaded environment, epiphytic cacti require more frequent watering and feeding, humus-rich soil, and protection from harsh sun. They often bloom best when pot-bound. Most need a cool, dry dormant period in winter to promote blooms for the following summer.

Repotting: Infrequently. Use a light growing mix for good drainage.

Propagation: Stem cuttings or division; seed (some species).

Problems: Low light causes spindly growth and poor bloom. Overwatering causes stem rot. Mealybugs are possible pests.

Tips: Prune out damaged stems.

Orchid cactus

Orchid cacti (×*Epicactus*) include a wide variety of plants, mostly complex hybrids among the genera *Epiphyllum, Nopalxochia, Heliocereus,* and others. The typical orchid cactus has flat leaflike

***Epiphyllum* hybrid**

branches that arch outward. It is grown primarily for its large showy flowers, which appear in spring and summer. Hybrids are available in reds, yellows, oranges, or white.

Mistletoe cacti or chain cacti (*Rhipsalis*) have jointed, branching, leafless stems that cascade or climb, making them particularly suitable for hanging pots and baskets. Most have tiny flowers and attractive, long-lasting berries.

Mistletoe cactus

Christmas cactus (*Schlumbergera*), also called Thanksgiving cactus or holiday cactus, has arching spineless bright green stems. *S.* ×*buckleyi* has scalloped stems that bear tubular flowers in a wide range of colors in mid- to late December. *S. truncata* flowers earlier. Its stem joints are longer and narrower. The 3-inch-long flowers, borne at the ends of the stems, are shades of white and red. Hybrids between

Christmas cactus

the two offer the widest range of colors, including white, pink, magenta, red, and yellow.

Christmas cactus requires a rich, porous soil kept moist but not soggy and weekly fertilizer when the plant is growing. It does well in front of a cool, bright window. During the summer, you can move it outdoors into partial shade. Budding is brought on by the short days of autumn or by a cold shock. After it has flowered, keep it drier and withhold fertilizer. It often blooms again later in winter.

Easter cactus (*Rhipsalidopsis gaertneri*) is often confused with Christmas cactus, but its spring blooms distinguish it. The scarlet or pink flowers are more symmetrical and less elongated.

Easter cactus

- **Light:** Bright to intense
- **Water:** Let dry slightly between waterings
- **Humidity:** Average
- **Temperature:** Average
- **Fertilizer:** All-purpose
- **Size:** 3'H×3"W

■ **Primitive cacti** include just a few species, and only one, *Pereskia aculeata*, is commonly grown indoors. This shrubby, treelike, or climbing plant still has the slender stems and broad, thin leaves typical of nonsucculents, and its spines are often hidden by foliage.

Barbados gooseberry (*P. aculeata* 'Godseffiana') is a shrubby climbing plant with

Barbados gooseberry bears little resemblace to other cacti.

vicious spines, so be careful working with or near it. Its new leaves are peach-colored, becoming yellow with a reddish tinge underneath—the plant's main attraction because it rarely blooms indoors.
Repotting: Occasionally.
Propagation: Stem cuttings.
Problems: Overwatering leads to root rot. Low light causes spindly growth. Mealybugs and aphids are possible pests.
Tips: Prune as needed to keep growth under control, or train on a trellis or other support. Primitive cacti need regular watering year-round.

Caladium bicolor
ka-LAY-dee-um BY-kuh-ler
Caladium, elephant's ear

- **Light:** Medium
- **Water:** Keep evenly moist, let dry during winter dormancy
- **Humidity:** High
- **Temperature:** Average
- **Fertilizer:** High phosphorus
- **Size:** 9-24"H×9-24"W

Caladium produces masses of paper-thin leaves, 12 to 24 inches long, borne on long stalks. The leaves are spotted and veined in shades of white, pink, red, green, and mixed colors. Most leaves are heart- or arrow-shaped, but some are lance-shaped. The flowers are of little interest; remove them so as not to drain the tuber's energy.

At the end of the summer or after six or seven months of growth, caladiums begin to look tired. Stop watering and put them in the shade. When the leaves die back, cut them off. Store the tubers either loose, in peat moss or vermiculite, or leave them in their pots. Keep them at room temperature or slightly cooler (never below 60°F) for the winter. When new sprouts appear on the tubers in spring, repot and begin watering again.

Caladium's translucent leaves are especially dramatic in mixed colors.

Repotting: Each spring, at the end of dormancy.
Propagation: Division (tuber nodules) and offsets.
Problems: Low light causes spindly growth. Dry air and cool drafts cause leaf dieback. Aphids and spider mites are possible pests.
Tips: If you plant the tubers upside down, they'll grow larger quantities of much smaller leaves, creating a beautiful effect.

Elephant's ear *(Caladium bicolor)* is named for its huge leaves.

Calathea
kuh-LAY-thee-uh

Calathea, peacock plant, cathedral windows

- **Light: Low to medium**
- **Water: Keep evenly moist**
- **Humidity: High to very high**
- **Temperature: Average to high**
- **Fertilizer: All-purpose**
- **Size: 1-6'H×1-3'W**

Zebra plant *(Calathea zebrina)* at left, and peacock plant *(C. makoyana)*

Mottled dots, curvy lines, marbled sections, and prominently colored veins are featured on calathea leaves in exquisitely complex, layered designs. The bottom of each leaf is sometimes colored in shocking contrast to its top. Shades of green, rose, pink, silver, and white are combined to such great effect that calatheas are often best viewed with light filtering through the leaves. The pale, almost translucent tissue, surrounded by dark veins, is reminiscent of stained glass.

Without high humidity levels, calatheas can be challenging to maintain. Try grouping a few plants together in a bathroom. They thrive in damp conditions and add a decorative touch. The amazing beauty of calatheas may be just the motivation you need to add a humidifier to your home, which will benefit other houseplants too.

Peacock plant *(C. makoyana)* is popular for its pale silvery green leaves decorated with oblong patches and fine dark green lines crossing veins and margins. The dark red on the underneath sides shows through when the plant is lighted from behind. It is a consistent showoff in low-light groupings and needs less water than other species. *C. picturata* 'Argentea' has green-edged silver leaves that are red beneath. Zebra plant *(C. zebrina)* combines a dark green upper surface and yellow-green veins and margins with purplish red underneath. It can reach 5 to 6 feet tall if you increase the size of its pot annually, as can *C. ornata* 'Roseolineata'. Its dark olive green leaves have pinkish red stripes that turn white. An increasing variety of hybrid calatheas, such as *C. burle-marxii* 'Ice Blue', are grown more for their flowers than their foliage.

Repotting: When the pot is crowded.

Propagation: Division.

Problems: Excess mineral salts cause leaf tip burn and stem dieback. Overwatering causes crown rot. Dry air causes leaf dieback. Stressed plants are more susceptible to mealybug, spider mite, and aphid infestations.

Tips: Leach pots occasionally to prevent mineral buildup. Remove yellowing leaves.

C. ornata 'Roseolineata' (left), and *C. picturata* 'Argentea' (right)

Capsicum annuum
KAP-sih-kum AN-yew-um

Ornamental pepper

Light: Bright
Water: Keep evenly moist
Humidity: Average
Temperature: Average
Fertilizer: All-purpose
Size: 6-30"H×6-24"W

Ornamental pepper *(Capsicum annuum)* is related to chile peppers.

Ornamental pepper is simply a showy selection of the same chile pepper that many gardeners grow in their vegetable beds. Ornamental types have denser growth and numerous small fruits in bright colors. The leaves can be green, purple, or variegated. The fruits are edible but fiery hot; even handling them causes a burning sensation. Ornamental pepper is usually sold as a gift plant already in full fruit, so simply compost it after the fruits begin to dry up. Put plants in the brightest light possible; place them outside in full sun during summer. Outdoors, insects pollinate the flowers. Indoors, mist the blooms daily to spread the pollen.

Repotting: As needed.

Propagation: Seed.

Problems: Irregular watering causes leaf drop. Overwatering causes root rot. Whiteflies, aphids, and spider mites are possible pests.

Tips: Keep fruits out of reach of children. Harvest seed from the healthiest plants for sowing the following season.

Carissa grandiflora
kuh-RISS-uh grand-ih-FLOR-uh

Natal plum

- **Light:** Bright
- **Water:** Keep evenly moist
- **Humidity:** Average
- **Temperature:** Average, but cold to cool in winter
- **Fertilizer:** All-purpose
- **Size:** 1-5'H×1-5'W

Natal plum's flowers smell like jasmine. The fruits are poisonous.

Dwarf cultivars of natal plum (syn. *C. macrocarpa*) have twisting, spiny branches and shiny leaves that make nearly perfect bonsai. The taller forms are nice floor plants. In spring both types produce abundant waxy white flowers that look and smell like jasmine. They may bloom sporadically through summer and fall in intense light; plumlike purple to dark red fruits follow. Almost all parts of this plant, including the seeds and leaves, are poisonous.

Standard-size natal plums are large shrubs to 10 feet tall, so they will need regular pruning to maintain them indefinitely at about 2 to 3 feet tall and wide. Dwarf cultivars also are available.
Repotting: As needed in late winter or early spring.
Propagation: Stem cuttings.
Problems: None significant.
Tips: A summer outside helps stimulate bloom. Keep away from children because of spiny branches and poisonous fruits.

Chirita sinensis
kuh-REE-tuh sih-NEN-sis

Chirita

- **Light:** Medium to bright
- **Water:** Let dry thoroughly between waterings
- **Humidity:** Average
- **Temperature:** Average, but cold to cool in winter
- **Fertilizer:** High phosphorus
- **Size:** 5"H×6-14"W

This relative of the African violet (*Saintpaulia*) has thicker, shinier, almost succulent leaves. Its sturdy upright stems bear funnel-shaped lavender flowers flushed orange at the throat. The whorled leaves form a short rosette. It's a low-growing plant, ideal for tables or windowsills.

Some plants have dark green leaves but in most common varieties the veins are heavily marked with silver. Leaves can be almost lance shape or very broad and have nearly smooth edges or deep-cut teeth. *C. sinensis* needs cool growing conditions to bloom indoors but the flowers are not as interesting as the leaf patterns. 'Hisako' and 'Augustifolia' are two popular cultivars.
Repotting: As needed.
Propagation: Leaf cuttings, offsets, or seed.
Problems: Avoid spraying leaves to prevent leaf spots.
Tips: Remove faded flowers and leaves to encourage new growth.

Chirita's small size makes it a perfect fit on windowsills or tabletops.

Chlorophytum comosum
klor-oh-FY-tum kuh-MO-sum

Spider plant

- **Light:** Low to bright
- **Water:** Keep evenly moist
- **Humidity:** Average
- **Temperature:** Cool to average
- **Fertilizer:** All-purpose
- **Size:** 1'H×2-4'W (trailing)

Plantlets from the main spider plant are produced on long wiry stolons.

Spider plants' wiry runners, or stolons, rise from among grassy green arching leaves often striped with yellow or white, and bear plantlets at their tips, making this plant perfect for hanging baskets. The stems also produce small white flowers in bright light.

The plant produces dense masses of carrotlike roots that quickly fill up most pots and make watering difficult. The best method is to soak the pot in tepid water, then drain the excess.

Green-leaved spider plants are comparatively rare. Much more common is 'Vittatum', with white to cream central stripes. 'Variegatum' has the reverse variegation: cream leaves with a green central stripe.
Repotting: As needed.
Propagation: Offsets or soil layering. Seed produces all-green plants.
Problems: Repot or leach frequently if excess mineral salts and fluoride cause leaf tips to brown. Dry soil also causes browning.
Tips: Root plantlets in late spring for use in a shady summer border.

Cissus
SIS-us
Grape ivy, kangaroo ivy

- **Light:** Medium to intense, tolerates low
- **Water:** Let dry slightly between waterings
- **Humidity:** Average to high
- **Temperature:** Average
- **Fertilizer:** All-purpose
- **Size:** 2-6'H×2-6'W

Kangaroo ivy *(Ciccus antarctica)* can be trained to a trellis or other support.

This genus includes more than 350 species of mostly climbing plants and is closely related to the common grape *(Vitis)*, which shares the same vining habit. It climbs by means of tendrils and can reach incredible heights in the wild but is easily kept under control indoors through regularly pinching and pruning. Although young stems of grape ivy are green and pliable, old growth eventually becomes woody. Generally it is grown in hanging baskets or trained up trellises. Plants do not usually bloom or produce fruit indoors.

Grape ivy is popular in commercial settings. The plants also grow rapidly at home and acclimate easily to low light and infrequent watering. With care, you can maintain plants for many months in adverse conditions, but they will not flourish unless they are given medium or bright light and kept moderately moist and well fertilized.

■ **Pink cissus** *(Cissus adenopoda)* is a lesser-known tuberous-rooted species with rapidly growing stems bearing coppery green leaves, each divided into three leaflets and lightly covered with purple hair. Although it is found in nurseries, more often starts are shared with family or friends. Pink cissus thrives under ordinary growing conditions.

■ **Kangaroo ivy or kangaroo vine** *(C. antarctica)* is a vigorous indoor climber. It is usually trained onto a trellis, but you can use it in hanging baskets. The toothed single leaves are large and shiny but may be sparse if the plant is not in good light. Train or wrap several vines together to make the foliage look denser. The common name refers to its Australian origin.

■ **Begonia-treebine** *(C. discolor)* is a vigorous vine with stupendous foliage. The leaves resemble those of a rex begonia, velvety with toothed edges and deep red veins with purple undersides. In ample light, pink and silvery colorations appear. It's an ideal choice for a humid greenhouse but less well-adapted to home culture.

■ **Winged grape or veldt grape** *(C. quadrangularis)* has thick and distinctly winged, jointed green stems. The small, dark green maple-like leaves are generally short-lived, giving the plant a

Grow grape ivy *(C. rhombifolia)* in a hanging basket to let it trail.

Wax cissus *(C. rotundifolia)* is easy to grown in intense light.

cactus-like appearance when they fall. A true succulent, this ivy needs intense light and thorough but infrequent watering.

■ **Grape ivy or oakleaf ivy** *(C. rhombifolia)* grows wild in the West Indies and South America. Its stems and buds are brown and have reddish hairs, and its shiny, three-leaflet leaves are similar in appearance to those of poison ivy. Its two cultivars, 'Mandaiana' and 'Ellen Danica', are more widely available than the species. Plants tolerate a wide range of growing conditions and grow rapidly even in medium light.

■ **Grape cissus or wax cissus** *(C. rotundifolia)* has succulent green stems and round, waxy leaves like lilypads in glossy green to olive. Very easy to grow, it needs intense light and thorough but infrequent watering.

Repotting: As needed.
Propagation: Stem cuttings.
Problems: Low light causes spindly growth. Excess mineral salts cause brown leaf tips, so repot or leach frequently. Plants are susceptible to whiteflies, mealybugs, spider mites, and powdery mildew.
Tips: Pinch and prune regularly to control excess growth. Drops of sap naturally form on the underside of the leaves, a phenomenon called guttation. This is not harmful.

Citrus
SIT-rus
Citrus

- **Light: Bright to intense**
- **Water: Let dry slightly between waterings**
- **Humidity: Average**
- **Temperature: Average**
- **Fertilizer: Acid-based with added trace elements**
- **Size: 1-10'H×1-6'W**

Miniature kumquat produces edible fruit if given bright light.

Citrus plants have something for all seasons: shiny dark green foliage; sweetly scented white flowers that appear intermittently throughout the year; and colorful, long-lasting fruits in green, yellow, or orange, depending on the species and the maturity of the fruit. Fruits at various stages of development and color are often found on the plant at the same time. Many citruses offer variegated forms, which bloom and fruit as readily as the all-green ones. All citruses are shrubby plants that normally become large with time, but you can keep them in check with regular pruning. Avoid trimming off branches with flowers or buds, though, if you want to see fruit. Some citruses bear numerous thorns; others have few or none.

Citrus fruits produced indoors tend to be sour or bitter and aren't eaten fresh. You can, however, use them in marmalades and other foods and as candied fruit. To ensure fruit production indoors, pass pollen from flower to flower with a small paintbrush or a cotton swab.

Growing a citrus plant from store-bought fruit is a popular pastime. Sow the seeds in small pots in a moist growing mix, and cover with plastic wrap. Place the pots in a warm, brightly lit spot. The seedlings will appear in two to three weeks and become attractive, long-lived foliage plants. It is unlikely that plants raised from store-bought fruit will ever flower or produce fruit indoors. For good fruit production, take stem cuttings of selections that bloom well indoors or purchase plants that are already in bloom.

The best choice for indoor growing is the calamondin or miniature orange, a cross between mandarin orange and kumquat. It is widely available and blooms and produces fruit year-round. It also remains compact with only minimal pruning. Another citrus that's fun to grow at home is kumquat, which has small orange-yellow, oblong fruits.

Repotting: Infrequently.
Propagation: Stem cuttings.
Problems: Mealybugs, scale insects, whiteflies, and spider mites are possible pests. Lack of iron causes leaf yellowing.
Tips: Prune as needed to maintain the desired size and shape.

Calamondin or miniature orange blooms and bears fruit year-round.

Clivia miniata
KLY-vee-uh min-ee-AH-tuh
Clivia

- **Light: Medium to bright**
- **Water: Keep evenly moist**
- **Humidity: Average**
- **Temperature: Average, but cold to cool in winter**
- **Fertilizer: All-purpose**
- **Size: 12-36"H×12-24"W**

After clivia's flowers fade, the plant forms red berries.

Thick stems 12 to 18 inches tall emerge from a crown of leathery, strap-shaped dark green leaves and support large clusters of trumpet-shaped orange flowers with yellow throats, while some cultivars flower closer to the center of the plant. A few rare cultivars have yellow flowers and variegated leaves. After the flowers fade in late spring, ornamental red berries form and add a touch of lasting color.

Repotting or dividing clivia can cause it to remain flowerless for a year or two, until its pot fills up with roots again.

Offsets may bloom within only a year or so, but seeds can take seven years or more to bloom. Seeds must be fresh and can take several months to germinate.
Repotting: Infrequently.
Propagation: Offsets or seed.
Problems: Short, stubby flower stems result from excess heat or water during the winter months.
Tips: Purchase a mature plant for flowers the same year.

Codiaeum variegatum pictum
ko-dee-AY-um var-ee-GAYT-um PIK-tum

Croton

- **Light: Bright to intense; young plants can adapt to low**
- **Water: Keep evenly moist**
- **Humidity: High**
- **Temperature: Average to high, avoid cold drafts**
- **Fertilizer: All-purpose**
- **Size: 1-6'H×1-5'W**

Croton shows its colors best when grown in bright light.

The varied leaf shapes and exotic colors of croton make it an especially attractive indoor plant. It produces shiny, leathery leaves from 3 to 18 inches long. Foliage may have spots, splotches, stripes, or irregular bands in red, pink, orange, brown, white, or green. Color markings vary even among leaves on the same plant.

Leaves are often most brightly colored when young, then darken as they mature. Leaves can be elliptic, linear, lobed, or even corkscrew. Mature crotons flower quite readily, with arching stems of fuzzy, ball-shaped flowers appearing mostly in summer.

C. variegatum pictum is a shrub that reaches over 6 feet in height outdoors, but you can prune it to 3 or 4 feet for use indoors. It is usually grown several stems per pot to give it a fuller appearance. Regular pinching (wear gloves, as the sticky white sap is slightly toxic) promotes bushier growth.

Crotons are fairly adaptable when young. You can move them to the most unlikely spots, including into fairly low light or dry air, and they still thrive. Once settled, they reach full height over time. Shade-grown plants are not nearly as colorful as plants grown in sun.

If you buy a full-size specimen, ask for a well-acclimated one that has spent at least two months in a local greenhouse.

Repotting: As needed.
Propagation: Stem cuttings (use rooting hormone) or air layering.
Problems: Low light or dry air causes spindly growth and leaf loss, as does soggy or dry soil. Spider mites, mealybugs, and scale insects are possible pests.
Tips: To prevent spider mites, give the plant a monthly shower, washing off the undersides as well as the tops of leaves. This also keeps leaves shiny and dust free. Pinch occasionally to stimulate branching. Croton is slightly poisonous, so keep it out of reach of children.

Codiaeum 'Super Star' is a green-leaved croton sprinkled with yellow.

Coffea arabica
KOF-ee-uh uh-RAB-ih-kuh

Coffee plant

- **Light: Bright**
- **Water: Let dry slightly between waterings**
- **Humidity: High**
- **Temperature: Average**
- **Fertilizer: All-purpose**
- **Size: 6-36"H×6-24"W**

Grow coffee plant *(Coffee arabica)* from fresh unroasted coffee beans.

Coffee plant makes an attractive, bushy shrub up to 3 feet tall or more. The dark green elliptic leaves with wavy margins are attractive and their growth is slow but steady. Keep the plant pruned for a bushy look.

Most seedlings sold are about six to eight years from blooming. Only at maturity do they begin to produce clusters of highly fragrant white flowers that give way to green berries, which eventually turn bright red and then darken. At this point, you can harvest them, extract the seeds ("coffee beans"), roast them, and make… a few spoonfuls of coffee.

You can also grow your own coffee plants from fresh unroasted coffee beans. They germinate readily and produce fine-looking young plants within a year.

Repotting: Annually.
Propagation: Seed or stem cuttings.
Problems: Dry air causes leaf drop. Spider mites are possible pests.
Tips: If possible, purchase a mature specimen already in flower.

Columnea
kuh-LUM-nee-uh

Columnea, Goldfish plant

- ■ **Light:** Medium to bright
- ■ **Water:** Keep evenly moist
- ■ **Humidity:** Average
- ■ **Temperature:** Average, short period of cold (to 50°F) in fall
- ■ **Fertilizer:** High phosphorous
- ■ **Size:** 6-14"H×12-36"W

Columnea's four-lobed flowers resemble swimming goldfish.

More than 150 different species and numerous hybrids of columnea exist. Because they tend to be trailing or only semiupright, they look especially good in hanging baskets.

The stems can be hairy or smooth and the elliptic leaves range in size from no bigger than a shirt button to over 5 inches. They can be smooth or hairy, thin or thick and waxy, and dark or light green, bronze or variegated.

The small orange, red, or yellow tubular flowers have a fishlike shape. Bloom is usually in spring and summer, but some hybrids, such as 'Early Bird' (yellow with orange tips) and 'Mary Ann' (deep pink), bloom continuously.

Repotting: Infrequently.

Propagation: Stem cuttings or seed.

Problems: Spider mites and aphids are possible pests.

Tips: Remove yellowed leaves and faded flowers. Prune as needed to produce even growth.

Cordyline fruticosa
KOR-duh-line froo-tih-KO-suh

Ti plant

- ■ **Light:** Medium to bright, tolerates low
- ■ **Water:** Let dry slightly between waterings
- ■ **Humidity:** Very high
- ■ **Temperature:** Average to high, avoid cold drafts
- ■ **Fertilizer:** All-purpose
- ■ **Size:** 1-10'H×1-5'W

The ti plant *(C. fruticosa,* syn. *C. terminalis)* is touted as the "good luck plant" and frequently sold as "ti logs" (sections of stem) at flower exhibitions and agricultural shows. The "logs" root quite readily: Simply plant them on their sides and half cover them with potting mix.

Popular cultivars grow to 3 feet or more indoors and have green or red foliage with pink or white variegations or margins. Flowers are rarely produced indoors. In fact, this is a difficult plant to grow to perfection indoors because it needs extremely humid air.

Repotting: As needed.

Propagation: Stem or root cuttings or air layering.

Problems: Dry air causes leaf dieback and invites spider mites. Mealybugs and scale insects also are possible pests.

Tips: Use several plants to a pot for a fuller look.

Ti plant is grown for its foliage; flowers are rarely produced indoors.

Crinum
KRY-num

Crinum lily, Bengal lily

- ■ **Light:** Medium to bright
- ■ **Water:** Keep evenly moist, let dry during winter dormancy
- ■ **Humidity:** Average
- ■ **Temperature:** Average
- ■ **Fertilizer:** High potassium
- ■ **Size:** 3-5'H×3-5'W

Crinum lily blooms best when pot-bound and kept consistently moist.

This relative of amaryllis *(Hippeastrum)* has solid stems and arching, straplike leaves to 4 feet long. The funnel-shaped pink, red, or white flowers are fragrant and sometimes 6 inches across. They are borne in clusters on top of a 3- to 5-foot stalk. Bloom is usually in late spring or summer.

Plant the bulb with its tip exposed in a comparatively small pot. In nature, this plant grows in swamps, so it prefers abundant moisture, although it adapts well to drier conditions.

Most varieties lose their leaves during dry dormancy, then start to grow anew in spring, but a few are evergreen.

Repotting: Blooms best when pot-bound, but pot seedlings into larger pots as they grow.

Propagation: Division or bulblets.

Problems: No significant problems.

Tips: The sap is somewhat toxic, so wear gloves when handling it and keep it out of reach of children.

Crossandra infundibuliformis
kros-AHN-druh in-fun-dib-yew-lih-FORM-is
Firecracker flower

- **Light:** Bright
- **Water:** Keep evenly moist
- **Humidity:** High
- **Temperature:** Average
- **Fertilizer:** High phosphorous
- **Size:** 1-3'H×1-3'W

Clip off firecracker flower's spent spikes to promote new blooms.

This colorful houseplant is almost never without bloom, even in midwinter. Modern hybrids are dense, low-growing plants that branch readily and bear numerous glossy, often wavy-edged medium-green leaves. Four-sided green spikes that bear the fan-shaped flowers appear at the tips of the stems. The original species has salmon red flowers, but many modern cultivars come in orange, yellow, and red. The Florida series is especially popular. They adapt more readily to seasonal changes and cooler temperatures.

After the last flower in any individual spike fades, clip off the spike. This will stimulate branching and more flowers. When bloom becomes sparse, start over with a new plant.
Repotting: Annually.
Propagation: Stem cuttings or seed.
Problems: Aphids, whiteflies, and thrips are possible pests.
Tips: Seed-grown plants produce more flowers.

Ctenanthe
ten-ANTH-ee
Ctenanthe

- **Light:** Medium to bright
- **Water:** Keep evenly moist
- **Humidity:** Average to high
- **Temperature:** Average to high
- **Fertilizer:** All-purpose
- **Size:** 10-24"H×6-24"W

If you enjoy peacock plant *(Calathea makoyana)* and prayer plant *(Maranta leuconeura)*, you may also like species of ctenanthe that offer equally showy leaves on more upright plants, their stems fanning out from a dainty rosette. Bamburanta *(C. lubbersiana)* has club-shaped leaves, some almost entirely green, some largely golden yellow, most variegated. These are remarkably random-looking streaks, each leaf's pattern more striking than the next. *C. setosa* resembles prayer plant, with leaves both narrower and not as thick as bamburanta. A softer-looking plant, its medium green leaves are marked by silvery green veins and red undersides. *C. burle-marxii* has silvery green leaves with featherlike olive markings on the leaf surface.
Repotting: When pot is crowded.
Propagation: Division of rhizomes.
Problems: Cold or hard water and direct sun can damage plants.
Tips: Do not fertilize for six weeks after repotting.

Ctenanthe burle-marxii is grown for its striking foliage.

Cuphea ignea
KOO-fee-uh IG-nee-uh
Cigar plant

- **Light:** Bright
- **Water:** Keep evenly moist
- **Humidity:** Average to high
- **Temperature:** Average
- **Fertilizer:** All-purpose during growing period
- **Size:** 6-24"H×8-22"W

Cigar plant *(Cuphea ignea)* is named for the shape of its blooms.

This small shrub has slender stems, tiny dark green needle-like leaves, and ½-inch flowers. Its numerous red, pink, or white flowers bloom spring through fall and sometimes in winter.

Numerous *Cuphea* species and hybrids exist, few of which have been thoroughly tested as houseplants. One that has, though, is cigar plant *(C. ignea,* syn. *C. platycentra)*. A bushy plant with slender stems and tiny dark green needlelike leaves, it produces an abundance of slim, tubular bright red blooms tipped with a white rim and two tiny black-purple petals. As the name implies, they do look like tiny cigars with ashes at their tips. Cultivars come with pink or white flowers and variegated foliage.
Repotting: Blooms best when slightly pot-bound.
Propagation: Stem cuttings or seed.
Problems: Whiteflies and aphids are possible pests.
Tips: Pinch back as needed.

Curcuma alismatifolia
kur-KYEW-muh al-iss-mat-uh-FOH-lee-uh
Siam tulip

- **Light:** Bright to intense
- **Water:** Keep evenly moist
- **Humidity:** Average to high
- **Temperature:** Average
- **Fertilizer:** All-purpose
- **Size:** 20-35"H×10-14"W

Siam tulip's exotic pink bracts hide its smaller violet true flowers.

Siam tulip is often sold in bloom as a gift plant, but you can save money by purchasing and potting rhizomes in the spring and covering them with an inch or so of growing mix. They sprout quickly in warm soil, producing arching, strap-shaped leaves followed by an 8-inch inflorescence composed of pink bracts, with greenish tips, that last up to three months. Smaller violet flowers appear among the bracts.

During the growing season, keep the soil evenly moist and supply bright to intense light. In fall let the plant dry out gradually, then store the rhizomes in peat moss or vermiculite or in their pot, in a cool (55°F), dry spot. In spring, start anew.

Repotting: In spring, as rhizomes come out of dormancy.
Propagation: Division.
Problems: Low light causes spindly and weak growth. Siam tulip rots in winter unless kept nearly dry. It has few insect problems.
Tips: Remove faded leaves and flowers to promote new growth.

Cycas revoluta
SY-kus rev-oh-LOO-tuh
Sago palm

- **Light:** Medium to bright
- **Water:** Let dry slightly between waterings
- **Humidity:** Average to high
- **Temperature:** Average
- **Fertilizer:** All-purpose, not a heavy feeder
- **Size:** 1-6'H×1-6'W

Although it resembles a palm tree, sago palm is more closely related to modern conifers. Its fronds are shiny and extremely stiff. Although they appear tough, they are actually quite easily damaged, and because the plant produces only one new set of leaves each year, any damage remains visible for a long time. The plant forms a thick, rough trunk like a palm trunk after many years. Offsets are produced only on very mature specimens. Young plants are sometimes used for bonsai.

The huge seeds are sometimes offered for sale but can take a year to germinate, and even then produce only a single leaf the first year. If you want a plant with a visible trunk, buy one that has already reached that stage.
Repotting: Repot infrequently.
Propagation: Offsets or seed.
Problems: Watch for spider mites.
Tips: The plant is toxic and spiny, so keep out of reach of children.

Sago palm looks like a palm tree but is closely related to modern conifers.

Cyclamen persicum
SY-kluh-men PER-sih-kum
Cyclamen

- **Light:** Bright, but intense in winter
- **Water:** Keep evenly moist, watering from below, but let dry during dormancy
- **Humidity:** Average
- **Temperature:** Cold to cool
- **Fertilizer:** All-purpose
- **Size:** 4-12"H×6-24"W

Dwarf cyclamen cultivars tolerate average indoor temperatures.

The heart-shaped dark green, silver-mottled leaves of cyclamen form a rosette topped with upright blossoms from autumn through spring. Cyclamen does best in a cool room with good air circulation but no drafts.

When blooming ceases and the foliage dies back, put the plant in a cool spot and let the soil dry. In midsummer, repot the tuber with new soil in a small pot, and place it in a warm area to encourage root growth. Gradually return the plant to a cool location (55°F) to induce blooming.
Repotting: Keep pot-bound.
Propagation: Division or seed (slow to develop from seed).
Problems: Subject to root and crown rot; always water from below. Spider mites and cyclamen mites are possible pests.
Tips: Miniature cultivars are more heat-resistant than the larger, old-fashioned florist's varieties.

Cyperus alternifolia
SY-per-us al-ter-nih-FOH-lee-uh

Umbrella plant, Dwarf papyrus

- **Light: Bright**
- **Water: Keep continuously moist**
- **Humidity: High**
- **Temperature: Average, avoid cold drafts**
- **Fertilizer: All-purpose, not a heavy feeder**
- **Size: 18-36"H×12-20"W**

Dwarf papyrus *(Cyperus alternifolia)* grows best in standing water.

This plant is ideal for gardeners who love to water. Since it is semiaquatic, it actually prefers to stand in water. You can submerge the entire root ball in up to 1 inch of water.

Umbrella plant forms a spreading clump of upright green stems, each topped by a whorl of narrow leaflike green bracts. In summer small greenish to brown flowers form among the bracts and the plant may even self-sow into surrounding pots.

Plant height is variable and depends on lighting conditions. Tall plants may require staking.
Repotting: As needed.
Propagation: Division, seed, or stem tip cuttings.
Problems: Leaf dieback and spider mites are problems in dry air.
Tips: Cut out dead stems. Prune back the roots of mature plants occasionally, or they can clog their container.

Dieffenbachia
dee-fun-BAHK-ee-uh

Spotted dumb cane

- **Light: Medium, tolerates low**
- **Water: Let dry slightly between waterings**
- **Humidity: Average but looks best with high**
- **Temperature: Average, avoid cold drafts**
- **Fertilizer: All-purpose, infrequently**
- **Size: 1-10'H×1-3'W**

Dieffenbachia usually features a single thick, green, canelike stem marked by the scars of fallen leaves. Arching pointed oblong leaves, 10 to 12 inches long, often marbled white or cream, spiral around the "trunk." Dumb canes are often planted several to a pot to give a denser appearance. Mature plants eventually reach ceiling height, then are cut back or air layered. Even leafless stem sections just 3 inches long will form new plants if they are placed on their sides and half-covered in growing mix.

Plant names can be confusing. Any plants sold as *D. amoena*, *D. maculata*, or *D. picta* are now considered variations of a single species, *D. seguine. D. amoena*

The toxic sap of spotted dumb cane causes temporary speechlessness.

'Hilo', with its large dark green leaves and thick white midrib, resembles a canna. *D. maculata* 'Tropic Snow' has appealing splotches through the center of the leaves, while 'Camille' is ivory. *D. picta* has similar dark green leaves with ivory spots or centers.

Dieffenbachia seguine is recognized by its oblong marbled leaves.

Older cultivars are treelike in habit, but newer hybrids are clump forming. They develop multiple shoots at the base and stay compact longer than the older varieties.

Ingested sap from the cane stems causes temporary speechlessness and much pain, hence the name dumb cane.
Repotting: Infrequently.
Propagation: Stem cuttings or air layering. Dumb cane naturally loses its bottom leaves, giving ample opportunity for starting new plants by air layering.
Problems: Poor drainage, overly frequent watering, and standing in water cause root rot. Spider mites, aphids, mealybugs, and scale insects are possible pests.
Tips: Remove faded leaves. Cut off any inflorescences that appear. Rolled-up "leaves" that don't open may in fact be flowers; if so, prune them out. In summer remove old canes to force new ones. The sap is toxic and irritating to the skin, so keep plants away from children and pets.

Dionaea muscipula
dee-on-EE-a mus-KIP-yew-luh

Venus flytrap

- **Light:** Bright to intense
- **Water:** Keep evenly moist except during dormancy, use only rain or distilled water
- **Humidity:** Very high, grows best indoors in a terrarium
- **Temperature:** Cool to average, but keep cold during dormancy
- **Fertilizer:** Do not fertilize
- **Size:** 4-18"H×6"W

Venus flytrap leaves end in hinged traps that catch insects.

Venus flytrap is a carnivorous plant bearing traps that close on flies and other small insects. It does not need to be fed indoors, but you can supply the occasional insect. The plant dies after only a few meals, so resist the urge to stimulate the traps too often. Never give it red meat of any kind.

Venus flytrap is fairly easy to grow for short periods indoors, preferably in a terrarium. It requires cold conditions during winter dormancy. In summer tall stalks bearing small white flowers appear. Blooms weaken the plant, so pinch them off.

Repotting: Each spring, into pure sphagnum moss.

Propagation: Division or leaf cuttings (not practical except in a greenhouse or nursery).

Problems: Too much warmth can cause crown rot.

Tips: Pick off blackened leaves.

Dracaena
druh-SEE-nuh

Dracaena

- **Light:** Medium to bright, tolerates low light
- **Water:** Let dry slightly between waterings
- **Humidity:** Average
- **Temperature:** Average, keep out of cold drafts
- **Fertilizer:** All-purpose during growing season; do not fertilize plants growing in low light
- **Size:** 1-10'H×1-5'W

Most dracaenas have tall stems like palm trees, with tufts of narrow, swordlike leaves near the top. Many grow into large plants, often 10 feet or more in height. Stems of different heights are often planted together in the same pot to offset their natural tendency for tall, leggy growth. Many indoor gardeners air layer the plants to reduce their height. The canes that are left after the air layers are removed will sprout new leafy growth.

Many dracaena cultivars are selected for their foliage and form, and often are used for large-scale plantings indoors. Some have narrow, spiky foliage; others have wider, more arching leaves. Most of the popular cultivars have striped variegation.

'Janet Craig Compacta' has a shrubbier appearance than other cultivars.

■ **Deremensis dracaena** (*D. deremensis*) comes in a wide range of colors and leaf patterns. All normally grow as single-stemmed plants. Most have long, narrow leaves arching outward all along the stem. Because their leaves are long-lived, they remain attractive for many years, until they lose their lower foliage. When that

'Lemon Lime' is a 'Warneckii' cultivar with bright bands of variegation.

happens, start them over again from cuttings or air layering. They are easily maintained at under 6 feet in height. 'Janet Craig' has very dark green shiny leaves. 'Janet Craig Compacta' is the same color but has much shorter, upward-pointing leaves, creating the impression of a thick green bottlebrush. 'Warneckii' is the most common variety. It has narrower leaves with thin white stripes along the edges. It has given birth to numerous cultivars, all with varying degrees and colors of variegation in the leaves. These include 'Gold Star', with broad yellow bands on each side of the leaf, and others with self-explanatory names such as 'Lemon Lime', 'Yellow Stripe', and 'White Stripe'.

■ **Corn plant** (*D. fragrans*) has leaves that are longer and broader than those of *D. deremensis*. The plant is grown two ways: as a single stem with leaves reaching

(continued)

Dracaena *(continued)*

outward all along the trunk, in which case it truly looks like a corn plant, or as a series of bare, woody stems that have been pruned at the top to produce clusters of foliage on stalks that

The variegated form of corn plant is most widely available.

sprout from just below the cuts. In ample light, cornplant may occasionally produce sprays of white flowers that are extremely fragrant, although only at night. The scent is delicious but overpowering, so you may find it necessary to remove the flower stalks. This plant easily reaches 20 feet tall, so it must be cut back occasionally. 'Massangeana,' with a yellow stripe down the center, is the most common cultivar. Under low light, the stripe turns lime green or may even disappear altogether. 'Victoriae' has the opposite pattern: The center of the leaf is green and the leaf edges are yellow.

■ **Madagascar dragontree,** or red-margined dracaena (*D. marginata*), has red-edged narrow leaves that grow in tufts at the top of gray woody stems. This dracaena is often sold with bent and twisted stems, caused by growing the plant on its side in the greenhouse until its stems bend upward, then setting it upright again. Like most dracaenas, it eventually gets too

tall for indoor use and has to be cut back or rerooted. Several cultivars, such as 'Colorama', with extra wide red bands, and 'Tricolor', the leaves of which are striped lengthwise in pink and cream, are available. They generally need more light and higher humidity than the species to do well indoors.

■ **Pleomele** (*D. reflexa*), until recently classified as *Pleomele reflexa*, grows into a large plant with narrow leaves closely set along canelike stems. Several variegated cultivars exist; the best known is 'Song of India', which has cream-edged leaves. It tends to grow at odd angles and must be pruned to keep it under control. It will grow to the size of a tree if you let it; to keep it within bounds, you'll have to do some artful trimming.

■ **Lucky bamboo,** also called ribbon-plant and Sander's dracaena (*D. sanderiana*), has an upright growth habit with leaves well spaced on lanky stems. It will grow to 5 feet in time, but it is usually sold as a small plant, less than a foot tall. The narrow leathery leaves may be all green or abundantly striped in white. It does well in a dish garden or terrarium. If the plant gets too leggy or spindly, take stem cuttings and replant.

To achieve the visual effect of lucky bamboo, remove all the leaves to reveal the bamboo-like stem, then root the stem in water or in water and stones. The stems can be trained into a corkscrew

Madagascar dragon tree (left), and a braided lucky bamboo (right).

Pleomele 'Song of India' can be cut back to keep it short.

pattern or braided together. Surprisingly, lucky bamboo can survive for years in water alone.

■ **Golddust dracaena** (*D. surculosa*) is small and shrubby, with a very different habit than other dracaenas, featuring broad oval leaves on thin branching stems. The leaves are brilliantly spotted with yellow or cream markings. 'Florida Beauty' is even more abundantly spotted than the species. Golddust dracaena must have good light and constant moisture. It is slow growing and will rarely reach more than 2 feet tall, even in ample light.

Repotting: Repot infrequently.
Propagation: Stem cuttings or air layering.
Problems: Excess mineral salts and fluoride buildup cause brown leaf tips, so leach the potting mix frequently. Soil kept too wet or too dry causes leaf drop. Spider mites, mealybugs, and scale insects are possible pests.
Tips: Pick off yellowed leaves. Trim brown leaf tips.

D. surculosa 'Florida Beauty'

Elatostema
ee-lat-OST-em-uh
Pellionia

- **Light:** Medium to bright
- **Water:** Keep evenly moist
- **Humidity:** High
- **Temperature:** Average to high
- **Fertilizer:** All-purpose
- **Size:** 2-12"H×1-2'W (trailing)

Grow pellionia *(Elatostema repens)* where its stems can trail.

Pellionia could be called inchworm plant for the measured way it spreads across the soil surface. Rose or purple stems emerge and arch downward as a pair of leaves unfurls close to the stem, often rooting at each leaf joint. The heart- to lance-shape leaves are satiny green and marbled gray, with prominent veins in shades of brown and reddish purple. The foliage is dense, grows steadily all year, and trails with little guidance, a tidy choice for hanging baskets or pots placed on columns.

One species, called watermelon begonia, has brown-purple leaves overlaid with a patch of silvery green. The trailing stems are pale pink. Masses of tiny greenish flowers appear in the joints between the leaves and stems.
Repotting: Annually until desired size is reached, then as needed.
Propagation: Stem cuttings.
Problems: Drafts and dry air cause leaf scorch.
Tips: Keep pellionia out of direct sun. It grows well in terrariums.

Epipremnum aureum
eh-pi-PREM-num AUR-ee-um
Pothos, devil's ivy

- **Light:** Low to bright
- **Water:** Keep evenly moist
- **Humidity:** Average
- **Temperature:** Average
- **Fertilizer:** All-purpose, not a heavy feeder
- **Size:** Unlimited height and spread (trailing)

Pothos *(Epipremnum aureum,* syn. *Scindapsus aureus* or *Pothos aureus)* is a common indoor plant, both in homes and commercial buildings. It is generally used as a vining groundcover or a cascading accent plant, often in a hanging basket. It also may grow, as it does in the wild, as a climber. Its aerial roots cling to all but the smoothest surfaces, allowing it to mount interior walls.

Pothos's heart-shaped leathery leaves look somewhat like heart-leaf philodendron's, but they are irregularly marbled yellow, with better color in good light. 'Golden Queen' has more yellow than green in the leaf; 'Marble Queen' is just as heavily mottled but with white and gray-green.
Repotting: As needed.
Propagation: Stem cuttings or soil layering.
Problems: Spider mites and scale insects are possible pests.
Tips: Pinch as needed to maintain the desired size and shape.

Move pothos into bright light to obtain the best leaf marbling.

Episcia
eh-PIS-ee-uh
Episcia, flame violet

- **Light:** Medium to bright
- **Water:** Keep evenly moist
- **Humidity:** High
- **Temperature:** Average, avoid cold drafts
- **Fertilizer:** All-purpose
- **Size:** 6"H×1-4'W (trailing)

Episcia flourishes in a hanging basket where humidity is high.

Episcias resemble the African violet *(Saintpaulia),* with short-stemmed rosettes of large, shiny, slightly downy leaves. Unlike African violets, they also produce numerous trailing or hanging stems, or stolons, along which appear smaller plants (offsets). In a hanging basket, plants can trail 4 feet or more. Episcias are generally used in hanging baskets or as groundcover in well-lit terrariums and dish gardens. They produce small red, yellow, orange, pink, lavender, or white flowers.

Several species and hundreds of cultivars exist, each with distinctive foliage texture and coloration. Leaves can have a green, copper, purple, or pink base overlaid with metallic colors.
Repotting: As needed.
Propagation: Division, offsets, leaf cuttings, or soil layering.
Problems: Leaves roll under at the edges or die back in dry air. Watch for mealybugs and aphids.
Tips: For larger leaves and plentiful flowers, thin out stolons.

Eucomis bicolor
yew-KOH-mis BY-kul-er
Pineapple lily

■ **Light:** Bright
■ **Water:** Let dry slightly between waterings
■ **Humidity:** Average
■ **Temperature:** Average to high
■ **Fertilizer:** High phosphorus
■ **Size:** 10-24"H×18"W

Alternating wet and dry periods will promote pineapple lily blooms.

Pineapple lily has distinctive, gently scalloped light yellow-green leaves that hug the soil and a sturdy stalk that is yellow-green, sometimes spotted in maroon. When the papery flowers bloom at the top, you'll know how the plant got its name. The blossoms do evoke pineapple, clustered in a vase shape of pale green stars below stiff darker green bracts. The flowerhead ages gracefully, forming purple seed capsules that last for weeks.

Plant new bulbs with the pointy ends just sticking out of the soil, but wait to water and fertilize until growth appears. To promote flowering once leaves unfurl, provide alternate wet and dry periods.
Repotting: Every other year in well-drained potting mix.
Propagation: Seed and offsets.
Problems: Overfertilizing may prevent flowering.
Tips: Remove and pot small offsets that form at the plant's base.

Euonymus
yew-ON-ih-mus
Japanese euonymus, wintercreeper

■ **Light:** Bright
■ **Water:** Keep continuously moist
■ **Humidity:** Average
■ **Temperature:** Cold to cool, tolerates average if grown in a terrarium
■ **Fertilizer:** All-purpose, not a heavy feeder
■ **Size:** 6-12"H×6-12"W

Japanese euonymus *(E. japonicus)* is a woody, bushy plant that does fairly well indoors if given ample light, although it grows best in distinctly cool temperatures. The glossy dark green toothed foliage is tiny, only about ½ inch long. Most varieties are variegated.

Wintercreeper *(E. fortunei)* does best in a cool location, such as an entranceway. The trailing stems climb and attach themselves to vertical surfaces. Unless cool temperatures can be maintained year-round, though, wintercreeper is unlikely to live long.
Repotting: Infrequently.
Propagation: Stem cuttings.
Problems: Excess heat causes spindly growth. Spider mites, leaf miners, aphids, mealybugs, and scale insects are possible pests.
Tips: Pick off yellowed leaves. Prune at any time to control size.

Japanese euonymus needs consistent moisture and infrequent repotting.

Euphorbia pulcherrima
yew-FOR-bee-uh pul-KEHR-ih-muh
Poinsettia

■ **Light:** Bright
■ **Water:** Keep evenly moist
■ **Humidity:** Average
■ **Temperature:** Cool to average, avoid cold drafts
■ **Fertilizer:** Not needed if grown as a temporary plant
■ **Size:** 1-3'H×1-3'W

With proper care, poinsettia continues to bloom for several months.

Poinsettia's large white, pink, red, yellow, lime green, or bicolor flowers are actually groups of bracts (colored leaves) that surround clusters of small, inconspicuous true flowers. The leaves on the stems below are usually dark green, sometimes with reddish veins or with various shades of variegation.

Treat poinsettias as short-day plants (see page 13) beginning in September to rebloom them.
Repotting: As needed.
Propagation: Stem cuttings.
Problems: Cold temperatures can cause leaf and flower damage. Overwatering or underwatering leads to rapid leaf drop. Watch for spider mites and mealybugs.
Tips: Remove faded bracts and leaves. Prune as needed to keep plants dense. Unwrap plants as soon as you get them home: Ethylene gas can build up under the wrapper and cause defoliation.

Farfugium japonicum
far-FOO-jee-um juh-PAHN-ih-kum
Ligularia, leopard plant

- ■ **Light:** Medium, no direct sun
- ■ **Water:** Medium to high, but let dry slightly between waterings
- ■ **Humidity:** Medium to high
- ■ **Temperature:** Average to warm
- ■ **Fertilizer:** All-purpose
- ■ **Size:** 1–2'H×1–2'W

Leopard plant is easy to grow in average indoor environments.

Sometimes classified in the genus *Ligularia*, leopard plant is grown outdoors as a perennial in warm climates but also makes a bold statement as a houseplant that tolerates low light. The plant grows in clumps and holds its large round or kidney-shaped leaves aloft. The wavy or serrated leaf margins and yellow spots accent the daisylike yellow-orange flowers that bloom profusely in summer if light is adequate. Most cultivars have variegated leaves marked with ivory or yellow and sometimes pink. If you have limited space, look for shorter cultivars, such as 'Kagami Jishi', with crested leaves, or 'Kin Kan', with creamy white leaf edges.
Repotting: As needed, in spring.
Propagation: Division.
Problems: Relatively pest free. Doesn't tolerate standing water.
Tips: Remove spent flowers to encourage new blooms.

× *Fatshedera lizei*
fats-HED-ur-uh LEE-zee-eye
Fatshedera, tree-ivy

- ■ **Light:** Low to medium
- ■ **Water:** Keep evenly moist
- ■ **Humidity:** Average to high
- ■ **Temperature:** Average to high
- ■ **Fertilizer:** All-purpose
- ■ **Size:** 1–10'H×1'W

Bulky but breathtaking, this plant makes an eyecatching display in a foyer or against a wall. It looks like both its parents, reminiscent of a big English ivy vine (*Hedera helix*) but with thicker leaves, like a fatsia. Fatshedera is shrubby yet vining, with large dark green, subtly patterned, ivylike leaves. It must be tied to a support, such as a lattice trellis, but is easily trained into a stunning living sculpture. Start with a large pot, install the support, and add a small fatshedera, tying its stems to the support with jute string. Tip-prune the stems to encourage new growth and keep the plant tidy.
Repotting: Annually until mature.
Propagation: Stem cuttings.
Problems: Lower leaves will brown and drop if drought stressed. Spider mites are a frequent pest.
Tips: Some stems are more pliable than others; prune out what cannot be tied or trained.

Fatshedera offers the vining habit of English ivy but with larger leaves.

Fatsia japonica
FAT-see-uh juh-PAHN-ih-kuh
Japanese aralia

- ■ **Light:** Bright
- ■ **Water:** Keep evenly moist
- ■ **Humidity:** High
- ■ **Temperature:** Cold to cool, tolerates average
- ■ **Fertilizer:** All-purpose
- ■ **Size:** 1–4'H×1–4'W

Japanese aralia thrives in cool areas where the light is bright.

Japanese aralia is a handsome evergreen plant with bold, lobed leaves of shiny green, occasionally variegated with white. It is fast growing, durable, and tolerant of many environments. It is particularly easy to grow in a cool, well-ventilated location with bright light but adapts to average temperatures. Wash and mist the leaves regularly and feed every two weeks during the growing season; otherwise the leaves may yellow from lack of nitrogen.

In winter move Japanese aralia to a cool spot and water much less frequently than usual. If it begins to look gangly or has misshapen leaves, trim it back hard.
Repotting: As needed.
Propagation: Stem cuttings, seed, or air layering.
Problems: Overwatering leads to root rot. Spider mites, whiteflies, mealybugs, and scale insects are possible pests.
Tips: Prune as needed to keep growth under control.

Ferns

- Light: Medium
- Water: Keep evenly moist
- Humidity: High to very high, a terrarium may be necessary
- Temperature: Cool to average
- Fertilizer: All-purpose, not heavy feeders
- Size: 6-60"H×6-60"W

Maidenhair fern (*Adiantum hispidulum* 'Bronze Venus') needs high humidity.

Ferns are primitive plants, popular in households for their delicate, airy appearance. They produce no flowers or seed but have sporangia (spore-producing organs), usually in the form of dusty bumps on the underside of the fronds.

The most common indoor ferns produce multiple crowns that you can divide. Cuttings can be made of surface rhizomes. Others have solitary crowns but occasionally produce offsets that you can pot. A few, however, can be reproduced only by spores (see page 31).

■ **Maidenhair fern** (*Adiantum pedatum*) has striking black hairlike stalks and leaflets that are broad but frilled. Other maidenhair species include *A. hispidulum*, *A. raddianum*, and *A. tenerum*. All require very high humidity, so a terrarium is ideal.

■ **Bird's-nest fern** (*A. nidus*) has graceful, outward-arching, undivided fronds that emerge from a fuzzy dark crown that looks like a bird's nest. Mother fern (*Asplenium bulbiferum*) has finely divided fronds that arch outward from the crown. The fronds carry tiny plantlets that you can use for propagation, hence the common name. Both plants are easy to grow indoors in high humidity but difficult to propagate.

■ **Brazilian tree fern** (*Blechnum gibbum*) forms a neat, ground-hugging rosette of deeply lobed fronds, reaching 3 feet in diameter. New fronds are an attractive red. As it ages, it forms a black trunk to 3 feet tall. This fern must never dry out entirely.

■ **Tree fern** (*Cyathea*) grows slowly indoors. The finely divided fronds, which emerge from the top of a 3- or 4-foot-high trunk, may reach 10 feet long, although 2 to 4 feet is more likely in the drier atmosphere of the average home. Purchase a fairly large plant so you can enjoy its tree stature without delay. Keep the soil wet. Place the plant in a humid spot that's protected from drafts. Several *Cyathea* species are available, as well as relatives *Cibotium chamissoi* and *Dicksonia squarrosa*.

■ **Japanese holly fern** (*Cyrtomium falcatum*) is perhaps the most

Bird's-nest fern (*Asplenium nidus*) is easy to grow in high humidity.

tolerant of indoor environments. It is a slow-growing plant that in time may reach 2 feet wide. The fronds are divided into large leaflets 3 to 5 inches long and to 2 inches wide. They are a glistening green as if covered in wax: an extra-thick cuticle helps protect them from dry air. The cultivar 'Rochfordianum', with more numerous and more deeply cut leaflets, is the most common.

■ **Rabbit's-foot fern** (*Davallia*), also called squirrel's-foot fern or deer's-foot fern, is noted for its finely divided fronds and furry rhizomes, which creep over and down the sides of the growing container and resemble animal feet. *Davallia* is attractive in a hanging basket as the "feet"

Japanese holly fern has thick leathery fronds similar to holly.

Rabbit's-foot fern (*Davallia*) has feathery fronds and fuzzy rhizomes.

Boston fern is popular because it tolerates average home conditions.

cascade or inch downward. You can cut off surplus rhizomes and root them for fast propagation.

■ **Boston fern** (*Nephrolepis exaltata* 'Bostoniensis'), also called sword fern, is tolerant of indoor conditions. Its arching form and long dangling fronds make it especially useful for hanging baskets. Other cultivars and species exist. Some cultivars, such as 'Fluffy Ruffles', are small plants with finely divided fronds; 'Dallasii' (Dallas fern) tolerates dry air, as does *N. obliterata* 'Kimberley Queen'. All produce thin, snaky,

Staghorn fern is an epiphyte with fronds like an animal's antlers.

fuzzy green stolons, forming new plants at their tips. Cut them off if you find them unattractive.

■ **Button fern** (*Pellaea rotundifolia*) has shiny round leaflets borne on ground-hugging black stems, making the plant look more like a groundcover than a fern. It's ideal for the very high humidity of a terrarium.

■ **Bear's-paw fern** (*Phlebodium aureum* syn. *Polypodium aureum*), also called hare's-foot fern or golden polypody fern, got its common names from the furry golden rhizomes that grow along the surface of the soil. The tough blue-green fronds are divided into a few large lobes. The most popular cultivar of hare's-foot fern is 'Mandaianum', which has more deeply cut fronds than the species. All are easy to grow.

■ **Staghorn fern** (*Platycerium bifurcatum*) is an epiphyte that can grow on a bark slab. Growth is slow, but eventually the plant develops massive fronds that resemble the antlers of a large animal. In time plantlets form at the base of the parent plant and emerge between the large, flat basal fronds. To water staghorn ferns, soak them in a bucket or sink.

■ **Dwarf leatherleaf fern** (*Polystichum tsus-simense*) is a slow-growing plant ideally suited to terrariums and dish gardens. The shiny deep green fronds are deeply cut and tolerant of dry air.

■ **Table fern** (*Pteris*), also called brake fern, fan table fern, or silverleaf fern, comes in a wide variety of frond styles that are variegated and divided in different ways. Variegated table fern (*P. cretica* 'Albo-lineata') bears a broad band of creamy white down each slightly wavy leaflet, and silverleaf fern (*P. ensiformis* 'Victoriae') has finely divided fronds featuring a silver band down the middle.

Repotting: As needed.
Propagation: Division, rhizome cuttings, or spores.
Problems: Leaves may die back in dry air or when exposed to drafts.

Button fern (*Pellaea rotundifolia*) makes a good tabletop plant.

Excess mineral salts cause leaf tip burn and stem dieback, so leach plants frequently. Overwatering leads to root rot. Dry soil can be fatal. Mealybugs and scale insects are possible pests.
Tips: Remove yellowed fronds. Rejuvenate tired plants by pruning to soil level and repotting.

Brake fern (*Pteris ensiformis* 'Silver Lace') has variegated divided fronds.

Ficus
FY-kus

Ficus

- ■ **Light: Medium to bright**
- ■ **Water: Let dry slightly between waterings**
- ■ **Humidity: Average to high**
- ■ **Temperature: Average**
- ■ **Fertilizer: All-purpose**
- ■ **Size: 1-12'H×1-8'W**

Creeping fig *(Ficus pumila)* can be trained to a standard.

Figs make up a diverse genus of more than 800 tropical trees, shrubs, and vines. It includes not only the edible fig but also a number of ornamental plants for indoor gardening.

■ **Shrubby figs** naturally form compact plants. Some make excellent indoor bonsai.

■ **Mistletoe fig** (*F. deltoidea*, syn. *F. diversifolia*) bears spreading branches covered with small, rounded to wedge-shaped leaves and many tiny (but inedible) green figs that turn red in bright sun.

■ **Triangleleaf fig** (*F. triangularis*) has larger leaves with a distinctly triangular outline and rounded edges. It also produces numerous tiny but inedible figs.

■ **Tree-size figs** are forest giants in the wild but can be kept at 3 to 8 feet or so indoors. Some are sold with braided trunks, giving them extra ornamental value. Prune the smaller-leaved varieties for use indoors.

■ **Weeping fig** (*F. benjamina*) is a popular container plant. It has pale brown bark and graceful, arching branches loaded with glossy pointed leaves. It grows to 18 feet tall. Several variegated forms, with leaves speckled or splotched in white or yellow and others with dark green, nearly black leaves, also are available. This plant often loses most of its leaves when moved to a new location. It requires a period of adjustment, but with care, will flourish again.

■ **Rubber tree** (*F. elastica*) has bold, deep green leaves and grows to 10 feet tall. When a rubber plant becomes too lanky, cut off the top and select a side branch to form a new main shoot, or air layer the plant. This species needs bright light to thrive.

■ **Fiddle-leaf fig** (*F. lyrata*, syn. *F. pandurata*) makes a striking container plant. It has durable, papery, deep green leaves shaped like fiddles and adapts well to moderate light. The plant grows 5 to 10 feet tall or more.

■ **Alii fig** (*F. binnendijkii* 'Alii') is a more recent introduction, with long narrow pointed leaves that give it a bamboo appearance. It is more tolerant of being moved than weeping fig.

■ **Indian laurel** (*F. microcarpa*, often listed as *F. retusa* or *F. retusa nitida*) is similar to weeping fig

F. benjamina 'Too Little' (left) and fiddle-leaf fig (F. lyrata) at right

but has a slightly larger leaf and a more upright habit. Indian laurels are commonly seen in commercial interiors or as bonsai.

■ **Climbing figs** rarely produce the clinging aerial roots that allow them to climb unless they are in a humid greenhouse. However,

India rubber tree (left) and F. binnendijkii 'Alii' (right)

they can be trained up trellises, used as groundcovers, or grown as hanging plants. Their thin leaves are more sensitive to dry air than those of other figs.

■ **Creeping fig** (*F. pumila*) has tiny, heart-shaped leaves. It's a fast-growing trailer that looks especially attractive in a hanging basket or cascading from a shelf.

Repotting: Infrequently.

Propagation: Stem cuttings (use rooting hormone) or air layering.

Problems: Figs are sensitive to excess mineral salts, which cause brown leaf tips and leaf drop, so leach their pots frequently. Protect against cold drafts, dry heat, and any sudden changes in environment, which may cause massive leaf drop. Spider mites, mealybugs, thrips, and scale insects are possible pests.

Tips: Prune to maintain shape and size. Wear gloves when handling figs, as the sap irritates the skin and eyes and can cause allergies. Keep plants out of the reach of children.

Fittonia verschaffeltii
fit-TOHN-ee-uh vair-shaf-FELT-ee-eye

Fittonia, nerve plant, mosaic plant

- **Light: Medium**
- **Water: Keep continuously moist**
- **Humidity: High**
- **Temperature: Average**
- **Fertilizer: All-purpose, not a heavy feeder**
- **Size: 6"H×unlimited spread**

Pinch out fittonia's flower spikes to encourage new leaf growth.

The intricately veined, oval leaves of fittonia grow semiupright, then spread over the soil surface and trail over the sides of the container. They bear small green spikes of tiny white to reddish white flowers that are scarcely noticed against the plant's striking green leaves with contrasting veins.

Numerous clones all feature red, pink, or white veins. Some have large leaves, 2 to 4 inches long, while others, such as *F. v. argyroneura* 'Minima', with white veins, have especially small ones. 'Minima' tolerates average humidity levels.

Fittonias, especially the smaller-leaved varieties, are wonderful terrarium plants.
Repotting: As needed.
Propagation: Stem cuttings.
Problems: Aphids, mealybugs, and scale insects are possible pests.
Tips: Prune occasionally to stimulate even growth.

Gardenia augusta
gar-DEEN-ee-uh aw-GUS-tuh

Gardenia

- **Light: Bright to intense**
- **Water: Keep evenly moist**
- **Humidity: High**
- **Temperature: Cool**
- **Fertilizer: Acid-based with added trace elements**
- **Size: 1-5'H×1-3'W**

The common gardenia (*G. augusta*, formerly *G. jasminoides*) has large glossy dark green leaves and produces large fragrant creamy white flowers. Most cultivars have double flowers. The plants bloom from spring through fall and sometimes throughout the year.

Gardenias can be difficult to grow indoors because the plants will not set flower buds when it's warmer than 65°F at night. Plants kept indoors also need high humidity and plenty of sunlight but never searing heat. They are best suited to a cool greenhouse.
Repotting: Infrequently, in an acid growing mix.
Propagation: Stem cuttings.
Problems: Bud drop is caused by high temperatures, overly dry air, or a sudden change in environment. Whiteflies, mealybugs, and mildew are possible pests.
Tips: Prune in early spring and pinch back anytime, but be careful not to remove flower buds.

Gardenias bloom indoors if nighttime temperatures are cool.

Gynura aurantiaca
gy-NYEW-ruh aw-ran-tee-AH-kuh

Velvet plant, purple passion plant

- **Light: Bright**
- **Water: Keep evenly moist**
- **Humidity: Average**
- **Temperature: Average**
- **Fertilizer: All-purpose**
- **Size: 10-24"H×10-48"W**

Pick off velvet plant's foul-smelling flowers and keep the stems pruned.

Velvet plant (formerly sold as *G. sarmentosa*) is a trailing species with lobed leaves densely coated in purple hairs. New leaves are particularly colorful.

'Purple Passion' is easy to grow and attractive in a hanging basket if pruned. With enough light the plant produces clusters of tiny flowers with dingy white petals and orange-yellow centers. Pick these off quickly because they have an unpleasant odor and will produce a mess of dropping petals and seedpods.

There also is a variegated form, 'Aureo-variegata'; it appears pink and purple from a distance, although the actual leaf variegation is yellowish.
Repotting: As needed.
Propagation: Stem cuttings.
Problems: Spider mites, whiteflies, and aphids are possible pests.
Tips: Start anew when plants become woody and unproductive.

Hedera
HED-er-uh

English ivy, Algerian ivy

- **Light: Medium to bright, tolerates low**
- **Water: Keep evenly moist**
- **Humidity: Average**
- **Temperature: Cold to cool, tolerates average**
- **Fertilizer: All-purpose**
- **Size: Unlimited height and spread (trailing)**

English ivy comes in many varieties that all climb and trail.

The eight to 12 species of ivy are among the most popular houseplants in the world. The two most commonly grown indoors offer hundreds of varieties to choose from. Combine that with a general ease of culture and good adaptability to home conditions, and ivy comes out a winner.

Ivies are climbers with three- to five-lobed evergreen leaves. In the wild they use clinging aerial roots to climb up walls, trunks, and rocks. Indoors they are typically used as trailing plants for hanging baskets, although you can train them to climb a trellis. You can also use ivy in a large planter as a groundcover. The plants never bloom indoors.

■ **Algerian ivy** (*H. canariensis*), also called Canary Island ivy, is a fast-growing plant with large brilliantly glossy leaves. 'Variegata' (also known as 'Gloire-de-Marengo') has green leaves with white variegation. Canary Island ivy differs from other ivies in that it needs some warmth. Of subtropical origin, it does best with average temperatures year-round.

■ **English ivy** (*H. helix*) is the original ivy. Countless varieties of this trailing and climbing plant are available. 'Merion Beauty' has small leaves in the characteristic shape. 'Itsy Bitsy' is a tiny variety. Others have leaves that are curled, waved, or crinkled ('Curlilocks' is an example). Still others have color variegation, such as the yellow-gold 'Gold Dust' and white-marked 'Glacier'.

Older cultivars rarely branch, producing long stems with well-spaced leaves instead. As these trail downward, they take on a light, airy look. Many modern cultivars produce full stems with numerous secondary branches, giving them a naturally fuller appearance. Both forms make attractive houseplants.

Repotting: As needed.
Propagation: Stem cuttings.
Problems: Spider mites can be a major problem, especially in dry air, which also causes brown leaf tips. Aphids, mealybugs, and scale insects also are possible pests.
Tips: Prune to control and direct growth. Pinch branch tips on cultivars that don't self-branch to make them denser.

Variegated Algerian ivy tolerates warm rooms better than English ivies.

Hedychium coronarium
heh-DEE-kee-um kor-oh-NAIR-ee-um

Ginger lily

- **Light: Bright**
- **Water: Keep continuously moist, even wet, but let dry during dormancy**
- **Humidity: High**
- **Temperature: Average to high, but cool when dormant, avoid cold drafts**
- **Fertilizer: All-purpose**
- **Size: 4-6'H×3'W**

Ginger lily blooms in late summer, so enjoy it outdoors on a deck or balcony.

Ginger lily is a tall plant with long lance-shaped glossy green leaves on either side of a slightly arching, slender reedlike stem. The white flowers with yellow markings are produced in clusters in late summer to fall and may last for several weeks.

You can put ginger lily outside for the summer, but be sure to bring it indoors before evenings become cool. When the stems start to deteriorate, usually in December, stop watering, then cut them back to near ground level and store the rhizomes nearly dry in a cool spot until new sprouts appear in spring.

Repotting: In late winter or early spring as new growth begins.
Propagation: Division (rhizomes).
Problems: Spider mites and aphids are possible pests.
Tips: Ginger lily may bloom in winter in bright light, even warmth, and high humidity.

Heliconia
hel-ih-KOHN-ee-uh
Lobster claw

- ◼ **Light: Intense**
- ◼ **Water: Keep evenly moist**
- ◼ **Humidity: High**
- ◼ **Temperature: Average to high, avoid cold drafts**
- ◼ **Fertilizer: All-purpose**
- ◼ **Size: 2-10'H×3'W**

Add a few stems of lobster claw to cut arrangements for a tropical touch.

Lobster claws are creeping, rhizomatous plants. Their upright green or bronze leaves are paddlelike or spoon-shape, rising directly from the ground.

Upright or pendent flower stalks bear brilliantly colored boat-shape bracts in two opposite rows (or sometimes in a spiral) usually in the summer but also sporadically throughout the year. The red, pink, orange, and yellow bracts can remain in shape for months. The flowers poke up from the bracts and can be green, red, orange, yellow, or white.

Most lobster claws are far too large for pot culture. Look for the new dwarfs, mostly hybrids of parrot's flower *(H. psittacorum)*. Keeping them underpotted helps maintain a smaller size.

Repotting: As needed.
Propagation: Division (rhizomes).
Problems: Spider mites can be a problem when the air is too dry.
Tips: Lobster claw rhizomes will dry out and die if exposed to the air for more than a day or so.

Heliotropium arborescens
hee-lee-oh-TROH-pee-um ar-bor-ES-enz
Heliotrope

- ◼ **Light: Intense**
- ◼ **Water: Keep evenly moist**
- ◼ **Humidity: High**
- ◼ **Temperature: Average, but cool in winter**
- ◼ **Fertilizer: All-purpose**
- ◼ **Size: 10-18"H×10-18"W**

Heliotrope is a bushy, woody shrub that grows from seed to bloom in only a few months. Most modern types are dwarfs, and many remain under 12 inches tall even without pruning.

The rough, wrinkled, dark green oval leaves of heliotrope often have a purple tinge and seem to beg to be touched, but some people find the sap irritating to the skin and eyes. Instead, just bring your nose to within smelling range of the dense clusters of tiny flowers. Many hybrids have purple, blue, or white flowers. Paler shades seem to be the most highly scented.

Where light is low, heliotrope may bloom only sporadically, but where there is plenty of light, expect bloom from spring through fall.

Repotting: As needed.
Propagation: Stem cuttings or seed.
Problems: Whiteflies are often a serious pest.
Tips: Heliotrope is slightly toxic, so keep it away from children.

Heliotrope's sap can be toxic, so step back and enjoy its fragrant flowers.

Hemigraphis alternata
hem-ih-GRAF-iss al-ter-NAH-tuh
Red flame ivy

- ◼ **Light: Medium to bright**
- ◼ **Water: Let dry slightly between waterings**
- ◼ **Humidity: High**
- ◼ **Temperature: Average, avoid cold drafts**
- ◼ **Fertilizer: All-purpose, not a heavy feeder**
- ◼ **Size: 6"H×6-18"W**

Purple waffle plant (*Hemigraphis* 'Exotica') has shiny puckered leaves.

Red flame ivy *(Hemigraphis alternata*, syn. *H. colorata)* is a creeping plant with oval to heart-shape scalloped leaves that are metallic violet above and wine red underneath. The plant looks best in a hanging basket where its stems arch downward and hide the container.

Short-lived but numerous tubular five-lobed white flower spikes appear during spring and summer, showing up beautifully against the purple background.

Purple waffle plant (*H.* 'Exotica') produces larger, puckered leaves with a purple sheen.
Repotting: As needed.
Propagation: Stem cuttings.
Problems: Low light causes spindly, pale growth. Overwatering leads to crown rot. Whiteflies are possible pests.
Tips: Prune regularly for a full well-balanced appearance.

Hibiscus rosa-sinensis
hih-BIS-kus RO-zuh-sih-NEN-sis
Chinese hibiscus

- **Light: Bright to intense**
- **Water: Keep evenly moist**
- **Humidity: High**
- **Temperature: Average to high**
- **Fertilizer: High phosphorus**
- **Size: 2-5'H×2-5'W**

Chinese hibiscus produces flowers year-round in bright light.

A woody shrub, Chinese hibiscus bears huge saucer-shaped single or double blooms in pink, red, yellow, orange, or white. Each flower lasts only one day (two for double types), but the plant may bloom throughout the year. The shiny dark green leaves vary from heart shaped to deeply lobed and maple shaped.

The more sun the plant gets, especially in winter, the better it blooms. Water regularly; hot sun leads to desiccation. Fertilize regularly for best bloom.
Repotting: As needed.
Propagation: Stem cuttings (use rooting hormone).
Problems: Spider mites are a serious problem in dry air, causing leaves and buds to yellow and drop off. Whiteflies, aphids, mealybugs, and scale insects are possible pests.
Tips: This plant is usually treated with a growth retardant before it's sold to keep it dense and compact. When the effect wears off, the plant becomes more open and requires trimming.

Hippeastrum
hip-ee-AS-trum
Amaryllis

- **Light: Bright**
- **Water: Keep evenly moist, but let dry during fall dormancy**
- **Humidity: Average**
- **Temperature: Average**
- **Fertilizer: Rich in potassium when plant is in leaf**
- **Size: 12-24"H×12-24"W**

The 1- to 2-foot stems of amaryllis bear clusters of trumpet flowers 8 to 10 inches wide. They come in single and double blooms and many colors.

Pot the bulb in autumn, leaving the top third exposed. When a flower stem appears, move the plant to a bright spot. When flowering ends, the foliage will grow for several months. Keep watering and fertilizing during this period when the bulb stores up the energy it needs to flower the following winter. In late summer allow the plant to dry out and become dormant, then cut off the yellowed leaves. Start watering again when new flower buds appear.
Repotting: Every three or four years; blooms best when pot-bound.
Propagation: Division, offsets (bulblets), or seed.
Problems: Rotting, hollow bulbs indicate narcissus fly infestation.
Tips: Amaryllis is toxic, so keep out of reach of children.

Amaryllis flowers come in many colors and color combinations.

Homalomena rubescens
ho-mah-lo-MEE-nuh roo-BES-enz
Heart-leaf homalomena

- **Light: Low to medium**
- **Water: Keep evenly moist**
- **Humidity: Average**
- **Temperature: Average to high**
- **Fertilizer: All-purpose, not a heavy feeder**
- **Size: 18"H×24"W**

Heart-leaf homalomena tolerates low light and warm drafts.

This philodendron relative is native to deep shade in the forests of South America, a situation much like a north window in a home, and has shown itself amenable to indoor growing. It even survives in dark corners indoors, although it grows better in moderate light.

The plant has 4- to 6-inch heart-shaped leaves on sturdy leafstalks. The foliage is dark green and has a waxy appearance. Blooms come readily indoors, but the greenish spathes are of little interest. 'Emerald Gem' has dark green leaves and is perhaps the most widely grown cultivar. 'Queen of Hearts' has leaves with a distinct reddish tinge, and 'King of Spades' has nearly black-green leaves.
Repotting: As needed.
Propagation: Offsets.
Problems: Generally problem free, although thrips and whiteflies are possible pests.
Tips: Buy a plant large enough for your immediate needs.

Hoya carnosa
HOY-uh kar-NO-suh

Hoya, wax plant

- Light: Medium to bright
- Water: Allow to dry between waterings
- Humidity: Average
- Temperature: Average to high
- Fertilizer: High phosphorus
- Size: 6-12"H×12-60"W (trailing)

Hindu rope plant is a hoya with twisted, trailing foliage.

Hoyas are slow-growing, vining plants with thick leaves. It has given rise to numerous cultivars with variously variegated or even crinkled leaves. Hoya produces clusters of extremely fragrant, waxy, star-shaped pinkish-white flowers with red centers in summer or fall, depending on the cultivar. Most hoyas are perfumed only at night. The flowers form on the same spur year after year, so be careful not to prune off these leafless vine extensions. Train a plant on a trellis or use it in a hanging basket.

H. bella is a popular small-leaved species. Rather than climbing, its branches hang down, making it attractive in a hanging basket.

Repotting: Infrequently; it blooms best when pot-bound.
Propagation: Stem cuttings.
Problems: Mealybugs and scale insects are possible pests.
Tips: Hoya becomes straggly with time. Prune leafy vining stems occasionally for a bushier look.

Hymenocallis narcissiflora
hy-men-oh-KAL-liss nar-sis-ih-FLOR-uh

Peruvian daffodil, spider flower, basket flower

- Light: Bright
- Water: Keep evenly moist except during rest cycles
- Humidity: Average to high
- Temperature: Average
- Fertilizer: All-purpose
- Size: 18-30"H×8-15"W

You may purchase a pot of Peruvian daffodils in bloom, with only leaves sprouted, or as bulbs ready to grow. Long strappy leaves maintain their bright green color and pert silhouette for several months before and after flowering. The ornate, fragrant flowers are 4 inches across, each centered with a daffodil-type white and green trumpet surrounded by a halo of long curly petals. Plant new bulbs with necks just above soil level in rich potting mix. Like amaryllis and other lilies, Peruvian daffodils require ample water and fertilizer to bloom, and after a brief rest period, can bloom repeatedly for years indoors.

Repotting: When pot is crowded.
Propagation: Division (bulbs).
Problems: Leaves may not be attractive in winter.
Tips: Rest plants after blooming by reducing water and fertilizer until new growth starts.

Peruvian daffodils are actually lilies and are grown like amaryllis.

Hypoestes phyllostachya
hy-po-ES-teez fyl-lo-STAK-ee-uh

Polka-dot plant, freckle-face

- Light: Bright
- Water: Keep evenly moist
- Humidity: High
- Temperature: Average
- Fertilizer: All-purpose
- Size: 9-18"H×9-12"W

Common names for *Hypoestes* come from the speckled foliage.

It's hard to believe the beautifully marbled leaves of the modern polka-dot plant were once only medium-green leaves modestly spotted with tiny specks of the palest pink. Recent hybrids have bold splashes of bright pink, red, or white, sometimes covering more than half of the leaf's surface. Even the rangy, open habit of the wild plant has been tamed: Today's cultivars are dense, thick plants covered with attractive foliage, and they grow rapidly in good light.

Spikes of tiny magenta to lilac flowers appear from late summer to winter but are of little interest and can simply be pinched off.

Repotting: As needed.
Propagation: Stem cuttings or seed.
Problems: Plants are short-lived. Dry air causes powdery mildew.
Tips: Prune regularly to keep the plant dense. Older plants tend to become weak and unattractive; start over with fresh cuttings or new seed.

Iresine herbstii
ee-reh-SEE-nay HERBST-ee-eye
Bloodleaf

- ■ **Light:** Bright to intense
- ■ **Water:** Keep evenly moist
- ■ **Humidity:** High
- ■ **Temperature:** Average
- ■ **Fertilizer:** All-purpose
- ■ **Size:** 10-36"H×8-30"W

Bloodleaf *(Iresine herbstii)* has rich dark red leaves veined in cherry red.

The ornamental foliage of this spectacular plant is an intense, full-bodied red, as its common name suggests. The leaves could be called reverse heart-shaped: they're curiously pinched at the tips. *(I. lindenii,* also called bloodleaf, has the same coloration but its leaves are pointed at the tips.) The leaves are deep purple with red veins, and the stems are pinkish red; when sunlight shines through, the plants appear to be fluorescent cherry red. 'Aureo-reticulata' has the same leaf shape but produces green leaves lined with yellow veins and occasional patches of brilliant red. 'Purple Lady' is a newer introduction with almost black leaves. The plants do not bloom indoors.
Repotting: As needed.
Propagation: Stem cuttings or seeds.
Problems: Spider mites and aphids are possible pests.
Tips: Bloodleaf looks better when pinched or pruned regularly.

Ixora
iks-OH-ruh
Ixora

- ■ **Light:** Intense
- ■ **Water:** Keep evenly moist
- ■ **Humidity:** High
- ■ **Temperature:** Average
- ■ **Fertilizer:** All-purpose
- ■ **Size:** 2-4'H×2-3'W

Ixoras are woody shrubs with untoothed dark green leaves. They produce dense rounded clusters of flowers at the stem tips. The individual flowers are actually a trumpet shape, with a narrow tube spreading into four lobes. The most common species is *I. coccinea,* which has bright red flowers, but modern cultivars are often hybrids and come in a full range of reds, yellows, oranges, and white. Unlike many brightly colored flowers, they are often scented. Many dwarf cultivars are available.
   Ixora blooms from a young age. Barely rooted cuttings are often already in flower. Pruning the stems after they bloom stimulates denser growth and more flowers. Unpruned shrubs tend to become leggy and may need staking.
Repotting: As needed.
Propagation: Stem cuttings.
Problems: Low light causes poor growth and blooms. Aphids and scale insects are possible pests.
Tips: Tall types must be pruned regularly to be used indoors.

Ixora flowers come in many colors and are often scented.

Jasminum
jas-MY-num
Jasmine

- ■ **Light:** Intense
- ■ **Water:** Keep evenly moist, sparingly in winter
- ■ **Humidity:** Average
- ■ **Temperature:** Average, cold to cool in winter
- ■ **Fertilizer:** High phosphorus
- ■ **Size:** 1-6'H×1-6'W

You can train true jasmine *(Jasminum polyanthum)* to a trellis or a frame.

True jasmines are shrubs or climbing plants that bear numerous white or yellow flowers. Most are highly scented, especially at night. The feathery foliage is often shiny.
   Most jasmines are twining and viny, requiring staking and regular pinching. Even the shrubby types have long branches that need support. Twining *J. polyanthum* is a winter bloomer, bearing dozens of scented, star-shaped, narrow-petaled white flowers at a time, even when young. *J. officinale affine* (syn. *J. grandiflorum),* another twining jasmine, bears highly fragrant pink-tinged white flowers from spring through fall.
Repotting: As needed.
Propagation: Stem cuttings or soil layering.
Problems: Spider mites, aphids, mealybugs, and scale insects are possible pests.
Tips: Prune after flowering, being careful not to remove flower buds.

Jatropha podagrica
ja-TRO-fuh pohd-AG-rik-uh
Bottle plant

- Light: Bright
- Water: Let dry between waterings, and reduce when leaves drop
- Humidity: Average
- Temperature: Average to high
- Fertilizer: All-purpose
- Size: 12-48"H×4-15"W

Bottle plant's vivid flowers are followed by bursting seedpods.

Grow a flowering conversation piece in bottle plant, also called Buddha belly. A sleek, squat gray bulb rises into a bottleneck-shaped stem to 4 feet tall. The stem stores ample water, reducing the plant's need for irrigation and tolerance for soggy soils. Large coarse-textured leaves with deeply rounded lobes emerge at the top of the tapering stem. The leaves drop in winter, but the "drinking straw" in the bottle, its flower stem, stands tall with twinkling red flowers in marked contrast to the swollen bulb. The flowers bloom most of the year in bright light, followed by attractive seedpods that pop open and fling seed several feet away.
Repotting: When it gets top-heavy.
Propagation: Seed and cuttings.
Problems: Overwatering causes rot.
Tips: Put bottle plant outdoors for the summer to attract butterflies.

Justicia brandegeeana
jus-TEE-shuh bran-dee-gee-AH-nuh
Shrimp plant

- Light: Bright
- Water: Keep evenly moist
- Humidity: Average to high
- Temperature: Average
- Fertilizer: All-purpose
- Size: 1-3'H×1-3'W

Shrimp plant (*J. brandegeeana,* syn. *Beloperone guttata*) is a woody, branching evergreen shrub with elliptic dark green leaves. It is easily maintained under 3 feet tall by regular pruning and pinching. The main attraction is the long-lasting pendent inflorescence, 3 to 4 inches long and covered with scale-shaped bracts in salmon pink. The true flowers are white and stick out from the bracts. 'Chartreuse' has lime-green bracts, and 'Yellow Queen' has yellow ones. 'Variegata' bears shrimp pink bracts and leaves sprinkled with snowy white.

Blooms usually appear in spring, but if the plant is regularly deadheaded, it will repeat bloom until late fall.
Repotting: As needed.
Propagation: Stem cuttings or seed.
Problems: Low light causes spindly growth and poor bloom. Spider mites and whiteflies can be pests.
Tips: Prune shrimp plant carefully, because it produces flower buds year-round.

Shrimp plant is named and grown for its showy flowers.

Laurus nobilis
LOR-rus NO-bih-lus
Sweet bay

- Light: Intense
- Water: Let dry slightly between waterings
- Humidity: Average
- Temperature: Cool to average, but cold to cool in winter
- Fertilizer: All-purpose, not a heavy feeder
- Size: 1-4'H×1-4'W

Sweet bay can be pruned as a shrub or trained as a small tree.

Sweet bay appears in ancient artwork that depicts people wearing leafy crowns. The leaves are just as decorative today and are also used in cooking. It is one of the few herbs that truly make good long-term houseplants.

Sweet bay is a slow-growing tree in its native Mediterranean region but is easily pruned for indoor use. It is generally sold as a dense shrub with thick foliage and can even be trained as a topiary. The elliptic leaves are somewhat wavy, dark green, and leathery. It rarely blooms indoors.
Repotting: Infrequently.
Propagation: Stem cuttings in summer (use rooting hormone).
Problems: Mealybugs and scale insects are possible pests.
Tips: Buy a large plant, since it will take several years to develop its bushy form. Sap sometimes irritates the skin; wear gloves when pruning.

Leea guineensis
LEE-ee-uh guin-ee-EN-sis
West Indian holly

- Light: Medium to bright
- Water: Let dry slightly between waterings
- Humidity: High
- Temperature: Average, avoid cold drafts
- Fertilizer: All-purpose
- Size: 2-5'H×2-4'W

West Indian holly is grown indoors for its foliage but may also bloom.

This stalwart foliage plant, also known as *L. coccinea*, is a medium-size shrub in the wild but tends to branch very little indoors, giving it an upright appearance.

It produces shiny deep green leaves with irregularly toothed leaflets. New leaves usually have an attractive reddish tinge.

Mature specimens occasionally bloom indoors. Small but long-lasting berries follow the flattened clusters of pink flowers.

West Indian holly is generally kept pruned to 2 or 3 feet. Because pruning stimulates branching, plants become rounder and fuller as they age.

A purplish-leaved cultivar is sold under the name 'Rubra', 'Burgundy', or *L. rubra*.
Repotting: As needed.
Propagation: Stem cuttings or seed.
Problems: Spider mites and mealybugs are possible pests.
Tips: Black sap spots may form on the undersides of leaves due to guttation and can be wiped off.

Liriope muscari
leer-EYE-oh-pee mus-KAR-ee
Lilyturf

- Light: Bright
- Water: Let dry slightly between waterings
- Humidity: Average
- Temperature: Average, cold to cool in winter
- Fertilizer: All-purpose, not a heavy feeder
- Size: 10-12"H×12"W

Although well-known as a groundcover, lilyturf also makes an attractive houseplant. It is grown for its graceful dark green grassy leaves and is popular in dish gardens and terrariums as well as on windowsills.

Under very good conditions, lilyturf may bloom indoors, with narrow spikes of dark blue to purple flowers. Dwarf and variegated cultivars are all suitable for indoor growing. Big blue lilyturf (*L. muscari*) is the most widely available. The species has dark green leaves; its blue flowers, similar to grape hyacinths, bloom in autumn. Some cultivars have white flowers.
Repotting: Infrequently, looks best when pot-bound.
Propagation: Division.
Problems: Dry air causes leaf dieback. Thrips are possible pests.
Tips: Prune the whole plant back to the soil in late winter and it will put out a flush of new growth.

A common landscape perennial, lilyturf also blooms indoors in bright light.

Mandevilla
man-duh-VIL-luh
Mandevilla

- Light: Bright
- Water: Keep evenly moist
- Humidity: Average
- Temperature: Average
- Fertilizer: All-purpose
- Size: 2-10'H×2-10'W (vining)

You can train mandevilla up a trellis or other support, or prune it into a shrub.

Long known as *Dipladenia*, mandevilla is a woody-stemmed climber with twining stems and elliptic lustrous bright green leaves. Up to 3 inches across, the trumpet-shaped, five-petaled flowers are pink, red, rose, or white with orange to yellow throats. Most are single, but a few double-flowered cultivars are available. Several species exist, including *M. sanderi* and *M. speciosa*, but most plants grown today are hybrids. The flowers bloom spring through autumn.

Flowers appear on new growth, so heavy pruning helps stimulate new blooms.
Repotting: Annually, in spring.
Propagation: Stem cuttings (use a rooting hormone), which might need bottom heat.
Problems: Spider mites, whiteflies, mealybugs, and scale insects are possible pests.
Tips: All parts of this plant are toxic. Keep out of reach of children. Wear gloves when handling; the milky sap can cause skin irritation.

Maranta leuconeura
ma-RAN-tuh loo-ko-NUR-uh
Prayer plant

- Light: Medium to bright
- Water: Keep evenly moist
- Humidity: High
- Temperature: Average, avoid cold drafts
- Fertilizer: All-purpose, not a heavy feeder
- Size: 12H"×12-18"W

Prayer plant's unusual leaves turn upward at night, like praying hands.

The name prayer plant comes from this plant's curious growth habit. In the daytime its satiny foliage lies flat, but at night the leaves turn upward like praying hands.

Prayer plant is closely related to calathea and shares the same leaf shape and coloration. It grows outward and somewhat downward, and so looks good in a hanging basket. It blooms quite readily indoors, but the flowers are of only minor interest.

'Erythroneura', 'Kerchoveana', 'Kerchoveana Variegata', and 'Massangeana' are commonly grown cultivars.

Repotting: Infrequently.
Propagation: Division.
Problems: Spider mites and mealybugs are possible pests.
Tips: This plant must have a semidormant period. Discard yellowed leaves. Start new plants to replace old specimens when they get weak.

Mikania ternata
mih-KAY-nee-uh ter-NAH-tuh
Plush vine, purple plush

- Light: Medium to bright
- Water: Let dry slightly between waterings
- Humidity: High
- Temperature: Average
- Fertilizer: All-purpose during growing period
- Size: 1'H×4'W (vining)

Lovers of purple foliage will adore this rapidly growing plant. It produces long trailing stems covered with felty hairs and 1½-inch maple-shaped, five-lobed leaves that are deep purple underneath, dark copper green above, and covered with fuzzy white hairs on the top. Insignificant flowers are rarely seen on houseplants.

Indoors plush vine is primarily used in hanging baskets, where its trailing stems are put to best use. It can be used to decorate trellises but will need a helping hand, as it does not climb readily on its own.

Repotting: As needed.
Propagation: Stem cuttings; self-layers in soil.
Problems: Avoid spraying leaves to prevent leaf spots. Aphids, mealybugs, and scale insects are possible pests.
Tips: Older plants tend to decline; restart from new cuttings.

Plush vine grows well in hanging baskets indoors and out.

Mimosa pudica
mih-MO-suh puh-DEE-kuh
Sensitive plant

- Light: Bright, direct sun in winter
- Water: Keep evenly moist
- Humidity: Average
- Temperature: Average to high
- Fertilizer: All-purpose
- Size: 12-30"H×16-36"W

Children enjoy stroking sensitive plant's leaves, which quickly fold up.

Here's one plant that is grown simply for the sheer fun of stroking it. It is not particularly pretty and rarely survives more than a year, but its fascinating habit of folding together its finely divided leaflets within a few seconds of being touched makes it a pleasure to own.

Sensitive plant is often sold as a small plant in nurseries but is easily and rapidly grown from seed. For faster germination, pour boiling water over the flat seeds or singe them with a match. The plants will be at their peak size in only three or four months. Sensitive plant flowers readily, with small pink, fuzzy flowers.

Repotting: Rarely required. Pot seedlings as they increase in size.
Propagation: Seed.
Problems: Drafts and dry air cause leaf scorch. Spider mites are possible pests.
Tips: When your sensitive plant begins to fade, compost it and start new plants from seed.

Monstera deliciosa
mon-STAIR-uh deh-lih-see-OH-suh
Split-leaf philodendron, Swiss-cheese plant

- **Light:** Medium to bright
- **Water:** Let dry slightly between waterings
- **Humidity:** Average
- **Temperature:** Average
- **Fertilizer:** All-purpose
- **Size:** 3-6'H×2-5'W

Bright light increases the size and edge cuts of split-leaf philodendron.

A mature split-leaf philodendron produces dark green, leathery, heart-shaped leaves 3 feet across with multiple perforations and deep slashes. Its aerial roots attach to supports to help it climb.

Most plants are sold with relatively small leaves only lightly cut along the edges, and they become even smaller and less deeply cut in the home if grown in low light. At full maturity, the plant may produce large white spathes followed by corncob-like fruits that turn red at maturity and taste like pineapple.
Repotting: Repot infrequently.
Propagation: Stem cuttings, air layering, or seed (but takes years to mature).
Problems: Spider mites and mealybugs are possible pests.
Tips: All parts of this plant are toxic except the ripe fruit; even the sap causes dermatitis.

Murraya paniculata
mur-RAY-uh pan-ih-kyew-LAY-tuh
Orange-jasmine, Mock orange

- **Light:** Medium to bright, tolerates low but will not bloom
- **Water:** Keep evenly moist
- **Humidity:** Average
- **Temperature:** Average, cold to cool in winter
- **Fertilizer:** All-purpose
- **Size:** 3-6'H×3-4'W

This close relative of citrus makes a fine foliage plant, forming a dense bush covered with shiny dark green leaves. You also can grow it as a small tree if you remove the lower branches.

Mock orange bears waxy white five-petaled flowers that are not only attractive and long-lasting but also intensely fragrant, smelling of orange blossoms with just a hint of jasmine. It flowers in late summer and fall and often again in spring. Mature specimens produce attractive red berries. Few other houseplants have so much to offer and can accomplish so much in household conditions.
Repotting: Annually in late winter or early spring for best growth.
Propagation: Stem cuttings.
Problems: Spider mites, mealybugs, and scale insects are possible pests.
Tips: Remove yellowed leaves. Prune as needed after flowering.

Mock orange thrives in average indoor conditions and bears fragrant blooms.

Musa acuminata
MYEW-suh ak-yew-mih-NAY-tuh
Dwarf banana

- **Light:** Medium to bright
- **Water:** Moist at all times
- **Humidity:** High
- **Temperature:** Average to high, avoid cold drafts
- **Fertilizer:** All-purpose
- **Size:** 3-10'H×3-6'W

Compact varieties of the common banana are unlikely to fruit indoors.

You can successfully grow a few banana plants of moderate size indoors. Their huge paddle-shaped leaves make quite an impact. Fruits, though, are unlikely to develop indoors, where average temperatures are too cool and the air too dry. Bananas are tall, treelike herbaceous plants. The "trunk" is actually composed of leaf bases wrapped tightly together like a cigar. Once a banana has fruited, it dies and is replaced by one of its offsets.

'Novak', sold as Super Dwarf Banana, rarely attains more than 4 to 5 feet tall. Its foliage may be green or bear red spots, especially under strong light. It can produce yellow, seedless, edible bananas.
Repotting: As needed.
Propagation: Division or offsets.
Problems: Spider mites, aphids, and mealybugs are possible pests.
Tips: Grow dwarf banana for the pleasure and challenge without expectation of fruit.

Nandina domestica
NAN-dee-nuh do-MES-tik-uh

Heavenly bamboo

- **Light: Medium to bright**
- **Water: Let dry out briefly before watering again**
- **Humidity: Average to high**
- **Temperature: Average**
- **Fertilizer: All-purpose**
- **Size: 12-36"H×6-15"W**

Careful pruning of heavenly bamboo shows off its form to best advantage.

Heavenly bamboo's poetic name suits this carefree woody plant, calling attention to its jointed stems and exotic leaflets colored in intricate patterns. Each leaf is made up of several leaflets geometrically arranged in triangles on thin leafstalks. The airy compound leaves are held primly erect at right angles from the canes. Many cultivars are sold, including dwarfs.

To show this plant's best form, clip off the lower leaves to expose the bamboo-like stems. Creamy flower clusters appear in spring, followed by red berries.

Repotting: When pot is crowded.
Propagation: Division (canes).
Problems: Low light produces sparse growth and few or no flowers or berries.
Tips: Set the plant outside in early spring to feed the birds.

Nematanthus
nem-uh-TAN-thus

Guppy plant

- **Light: Bright**
- **Water: Keep evenly moist**
- **Humidity: Average**
- **Temperature: Average**
- **Fertilizer: High phosphorus**
- **Size: 8-24"H×8-36"W**

Guppy plant gets its name from its tubular flowers. The tiny opening at the tip of each bloom resembles a fish's mouth.

The orange, red, or yellow flowers, sometimes striped in contrasting colors, are carried tight near the stem or in long hanging stalks like dangling fishing lines. Guppy plant blooms sporadically throughout the year, sometimes massively in summer.

The leaves are generally thick, waxy, and shiny, often with a bright red patch underneath. Some have purple tints and others are variegated. The stems usually arch upward and outward, eventually becoming trailing, and so look good in hanging baskets. A few species and hybrids have a more upright rounded habit.

Repotting: Infrequently.
Propagation: Stem cuttings.
Problems: Guppy plant is sensitive to excess mineral salts, so leach frequently. Spider mites and aphids are possible pests.
Tips: Prune in early spring. Be careful not to remove flower buds.

Guppy plant's unusual flowers often bloom off and on through the year.

Neomarica gracilis
nee-oh-MAIR-ih-kuh grah-SIL-us

Apostle plant, walking iris

- **Light: Bright**
- **Water: Keep evenly moist**
- **Humidity: Average**
- **Temperature: Average to cool, cool in winter**
- **Fertilizer: All-purpose**
- **Size: 16"H×24"W**

The name walking iris comes from the way the plant reproduces.

Apostle plant is essentially a tropical iris and has the same fan of flattened, elongated, lance-shaped leaves. It is called apostle plant because it was once believed each fan had to have 12 leaves before it would bloom.

Plantlets form at the tops of the flower stems, which then bend to the ground and take root. The plantlets also can be layered into neighboring pots or cut off and rooted separately.

The plant produces attractive, scented irislike flowers in winter. The blooms are white with a brown center and curling blue petals. Flowers open in the morning and bloom for only one day but are replaced by others.

Repotting: Infrequently.
Propagation: Division, offsets, or layering.
Problems: None significant.
Tips: Keep the plant somewhat pot-bound, as it blooms best when its roots are compressed.

Orchids

- **Light: Medium to intense**
- **Water: Moisten thoroughly, then allow to dry**
- **Humidity: High**
- **Temperature: Average, cool at night**
- **Fertilizer: All-purpose, but higher in phosphorus and potassium during winter; high in nitrogen for those in bark**
- **Size: 5-36"H×3-24"W**

Cattleya skinneri

Some species of orchids grow so well indoors they require less routine care than many other houseplants. Improved breeding and propagation techniques have significantly increased the availability and lowered the cost of many orchid cultivars.

Orchids may have striking flowers, but their foliage is generally unattractive. They often have wrinkled, lumpy pseudobulbs at the base of the leaves and bear thick aerial roots. Grow orchids among other houseplants, where their less attractive features are not so noticeable, and then move them to a more visible spot when they are in bloom.

Always check on the cultural needs of an orchid before purchasing it. Orchids are an extremely varied group of plants, and their cultural requirements vary not only from one genus to another but also among species.

This diversity makes it hard to give a general summary of orchid care but also means there is an orchid suitable for just about every indoor environment. See "Orchids" on page 44 for more information. Expanded cultural details are provided here.

Light: Most orchids fall into one of two categories: those requiring intense light and those preferring medium to bright light. Give the first group full sun throughout the winter months, preferably in a south-facing window, with some shading from direct midday sun in summer. If they take on a yellowish tinge, all is well; if their foliage is bright green, they need more light. This group may need supplemental artificial light during the winter. The orchids that prefer medium to bright light are suited to either east or west windows or curtain-filtered bright windows year-round. They also do well under fluorescent lights.

Water: Water varieties with thick leaves and large pseudobulbs thoroughly, then allow them to dry out before the next watering. Those with thin roots and no pseudobulbs generally need water as soon as the potting mix starts to dry. Most orchids need a short period of dry conditions in autumn to stimulate new flowers.

Humidity: Although some orchids tolerate average humidity, it's best to offer them high humidity

Comet orchid (Angraecum eburneum)

indoors. A humidity tray or humidifier (see page 20) may be necessary during winter.

Temperature: Average indoor temperatures are generally acceptable throughout much of the year. Cool night temperatures are best. An annual period of

Cymbidium King Arthur

cool temperatures (down to 50°F) and reduced watering induces flowering in many orchids.

Fertilizer: Fertilize year-round, more heavily in summer. In general, orchids grown in bark mixtures need fertilizers rich in nitrogen. Those grown on more stable media, such as osmunda fiber, need balanced fertilizers.

Some of the orchids that grow well under average indoor conditions are listed here.

- **Foxtail orchid** *(Aerides)* is a summer-flowering mid-sized epiphyte, a plant that takes moisture and nutrients from the air. Given intense sun, this orchid blooms profusely with fragrant flowers in red, pink, or white on long stalks that arch outward from the plant.
- **Comet orchids** *(Angraecum)* are small plants well suited to indoor gardens. *A. eburneum* (syn. *A. superbum*), which is larger than most comet orchids, bears waxy, greenish white flowers in winter that are fragrant at night.

■ **Lady of the night** (*Brassavola*) blooms readily even under adverse conditions. The flowers are large for the size of the plant and greenish. They are intensely fragrant but only at night.

■ **Spider orchid** (*Brassia*) bears flowers with long, narrow sepals

Brassia 'Data Cooo Day'

that give rise to their common name. The plants are fairly large, with 15-inch flower spikes and leaves that grow to 10 inches long. They generally bloom in fall or winter if given sufficient sunlight.

■ *Bulbophyllum* is the largest and most varied genus in the orchid family. Some are large plants with equally large flowers, but the most popular are dwarf or even miniature plants, which fit easily on a narrow windowsill. Cultural requirements vary widely according to their native habitats, but most need average temperatures, some shade from direct sun, and regular waterings while they are growing actively.

■ *Cattleya* is not nearly as popular as the numerous hybrids derived from crosses between it and related orchids, such as *Rhyncholaelia*, *Laelia*, and *Sophronitis*. These breeder-made groups are called cattleyas or "catts" by orchid fanciers. The genus includes both the old-fashioned corsage orchids and an increasing range of miniature hybrids with smaller blooms. The vigorous plants produce

gorgeous flowers when they receive plenty of sun.

■ *Cymbidium* "miniature" orchids are especially well suited for many indoor gardens. Give the plants cool nights to promote flowering, which usually occurs in winter or spring. The blooms are long-lasting, even as cut flowers.

■ *Dendrobium* is a genus of mostly epiphytic orchids; both evergreen and deciduous types are available. Large flowers bloom in clusters or in a row along the stem. They last between a week and several months, depending on the species. The plants need plenty of bright light.

■ **Clamshell orchids** (*Encyclia*) are often compact in size and have plump, squat pseudobulbs. Many have curious flowers with a shell-shaped lip and modified leaves called sepals that look like long, dangling streamers.

■ **Buttonhole orchids** (*Epidendrum*) have lengthened, cane-shaped pseudobulbs. Many species are too tall for home conditions, but there are plenty of medium-size and dwarf hybrids that fit. Most are suitable indoors on windowsills warmed by the winter sun, where some species may bloom continuously.

■ **Jewel orchid** (*Ludisia discolor*, syn. *Haemaria discolor dawsoniana*), is one of several orchids grown more for its exceptional foliage than for its

Epidendrum Rene Marques Flame Thrower

bloom. This plant grows best in regular potting soil. It may reach a height of 8 inches or so on somewhat trailing stems. Its leaves are a velvety purplish green, nearly black, with a prominent network of red and white veins. Small white or pinkish flowers grow on long spikes in winter.

Jewel orchid (Ludisia discolor)

■ **Tailed orchids** (*Masdevallia*) are grown in cooler temperatures and have curiously unorchidlike flowers with broad sepals partially joined at the base and pointed at the tips, like a moustache with downturned tips. They like bright light with little direct sun.

■ **Pansy orchid** (*Miltonia*) gets its common name from its flat-faced, heavily marbled flowers. The original genus has been subdivided into *Miltonia* and *Miltoniopsis*. The former, which has two-leaved pseudobulbs, needs warm temperatures year round. The latter, which has one-leaved pseudobulbs, needs cooler temperatures. Both types require filtered light.

■ *Odontoglossum* needs moist air and stable growing conditions. It does best in greenhouses with direct sunlight in winter and filtered light in summer. Numerous species and hybrids are available, most bearing long-lasting, fragrant, large flowers. Many bloom twice a year.

(continued)

Orchids *(continued)*

Dendrobium atroviolaceum
Pygmy × Little Elf

■ **Dancing lady** *(Oncidium)* is a large group of epiphytic orchids that generally produce stalks of abundant yellow flowers speckled with brown. Flower size depends on the species but is usually quite small. Dancing lady requires bright light with protection from direct summer sunlight.

■ **Slipper orchid** *(Paphiopedilum)* has long-lasting flowers with a distinctive pouch. Mostly terrestrial, the plants need a more humid, less airy growing mix than other orchids. Simply add extra sphagnum moss to a typical orchid mix. Two main groups exist: those with green leaves, which need cool growing conditions, and those with variegated leaves, which adapt well to average growing conditions. All prefer filtered light.

■ **Moth orchid** *(Phalaenopsis)* is probably the best choice for beginners. It adapts well to average indoor temperatures, does not require high humidity, and is generally well suited to the average home. Unlike many orchids grown solely for their blooms, moth orchid often has attractively marbled foliage. It produces sprays of 2- to 3-inch flowers in a wide range of colors.

Modern hybrids may bloom throughout much of the year. After blooming, cut back the flower stems to the green joint just below the last faded flower, and it often will bloom again.

■ *Rodriguezia* is a genus of mostly miniatures, less than a foot tall. The plants bloom abundantly, producing large clusters of small fragrant flowers, usually white or pinkish. Keep these plants moist and in high humidity.

■ *Vanda* is usually too large for most homes; miniature hybrids are available that are better suited to home culture. The plant needs sunlight from a south window or a greenhouse.

Repotting: Allow roots to extend beyond the pot as long as the plant continues to grow well. When growth slows, repot into a larger container using an appropriate orchid potting mix (see page 22), generally a mixture of bark, perlite, sphagnum moss, and other bulky products. Many orchids also grow on bark or on pieces of osmunda fiber. Tie them solidly to the support until they are well rooted.

Moth orchid *(Phalaenopsis* **Asian Elegance)**

Paphiopedilum **St. Swithin**

Propagation: You can divide most orchids every few years, but leave at least three pseudobulbs in each pot. Some orchids also produce keikis, or plantlets, at the base of or on the flower stalks. You can remove and pot these once they have produced roots.

Problems: Limp leaves or flowers are caused mainly by insufficient light but also can be due to improper watering (usually overwatering). If leaves are old or the plant is deciduous, you can expect yellowing leaves. Otherwise, yellowing results from overwatering or sunburn. Brown spots are due to too much sun or leaf spot disease. Orchids are sensitive to excess mineral salts that cause leaf tip burn and stunted growth, so leach frequently. Spider mites, aphids, mealybugs, and scale insects are possible pests.

Tips: Remove yellowed leaves, and cut back flower stalks to the nearest green joint after blooming. Purchase mature, blooming orchids because young plants often take years to flower.

Ornithogalum caudatum
or-nih-THOG-uh-lum caw-DAY-tum

Pregnant onion, false sea-onion

- ■ **Light: Bright**
- ■ **Water: Let dry slightly between waterings**
- ■ **Humidity: Average**
- ■ **Temperature: Average**
- ■ **Fertilizer: All-purpose**
- ■ **Size: 6-36"H×6-12"W**

Pregnant onion is for display only: All parts of the plant are fragile and toxic.

This pass-along plant (also sold as *O. longibracteatum*) has been shared among friends and family since the Victorian era.

Its aboveground opalescent, pale green, onionlike bulb produces offsets under its semitransparent skin, causing it to bulge outward. Peel off a few layers of skin, break the offsets loose, and pot them.

The leaves are bright green and straplike but tend to be fragile. The plant produces a tall, weak-stemmed flower stalk with numerous star-shaped white flowers with greenish stripes.

Repotting: After flowering; cover only the base of the bulb.

Propagation: Seed or offsets (bulblets).

Problems: Spider mites, whiteflies, mealybugs, and scale insects are possible pests.

Tips: All parts of this plant are toxic, so keep it out of the reach of children.

Osmanthus heterophyllus
oz-MAN-thus het-er-oh-FY-lus

False holly

- ■ **Light: Bright**
- ■ **Water: Let dry slightly botween waterings**
- ■ **Humidity: High**
- ■ **Temperature: Average, cold to cool in winter**
- ■ **Fertilizer: All-purpose**
- ■ **Size: 1-4'H×1-4'W**

Although true holly *(Ilex)* is offered as potted plants in December, few of them survive more than a few months indoors. An excellent alternative is this holly look-alike that can live indoors for decades. All it lacks are bright red berries, but you can always attach artificial ones.

The spine-edged shiny evergreen leaves of false holly even have the leathery texture of true holly. The same plant may have both spiny and spineless leaves but juvenile plants tend to bear only spiny ones. False holly rarely blooms indoors.

Variegated types include sweet olive *(O. fragrans)*, a shrub with narrow, toothless leaves. Tiny fragrant blossoms may appear in cool, humid conditions.

Repotting: Infrequently.

Propagation: Stem cuttings (use rooting hormone).

Problems: Watch for scale insects.

Tips: Pinch new growth regularly to obtain a bushy form.

Unlike true holly, false holly can live a long time indoors.

Oxalis regnellii
oks-AL-is reg-NEL-ee-eye

Oxalis, wood sorrel

- ■ **Light: Medium to bright**
- ■ **Water: Keep evenly moist**
- ■ **Humidity: Average**
- ■ **Temperature: Cool to average**
- ■ **Fertilizer: All-purpose, not a heavy feeder**
- ■ **Size: 8"H×6-18"W**

Wood sorrel *(Oxalis regnellii atropurpurea)* has deep purple leaves.

Oxalis is essentially always in bloom. Even young plants with few leaves bloom steadily.

The most striking characteristic is its three distinctly triangular leaflets. The dull green leaves are borne on weak pink to pale green leafstalks that stand up for a few days, then bend over, giving the plant a mounded appearance. The flowers are white or pale pink and shaped like an open funnel. *O. regnellii atropurpurea* has become more popular than the species. Its leaves are a deep purple, highlighted in some plants by a metallic pink splotch in the center of each leaflet. Its blooms are pink.

Repotting: As needed.

Propagation: Division (tubers).

Problems: Spider mites, whiteflies, thrips, mealybugs, and scale insects are possible pests.

Tips: Needs regular grooming. Or simply shear messy plants to the ground; they'll resprout within two weeks.

Pachira aquatica
puh-KY-ruh uh-KWAH-tih-kuh

Money tree, Malabar chestnut

- ■ **Light:** Medium to bright
- ■ **Water:** Keep evenly moist
- ■ **Humidity:** Average to high
- ■ **Temperature:** Average
- ■ **Fertilizer:** All-purpose
- ■ **Size:** 1-6'H×1-2'W

Grow money tree in a container to control its height.

Money trees grace tropical resorts in the Western Hemisphere and can bring the same vacation ambience to your home every day. Height is greatly limited by container growing, but not the allure of the tree's hand-sized shiny emerald green leaves and mottled gray trunk. Plants are often potted in multiples with their trunks braided. Maintain soil moisture by adding mulch to the soil surface: shells and stones, pea gravel, or sphagnum moss. Although money trees seldom flower indoors, mature ones can, if given a fertilizer for blooming plants and a warm, sunny place outdoors from late spring through summer.

Repotting: Annually until desired height is reached.
Propagation: Stem cuttings or seed.
Problems: Not drought tolerant.
Tips: Root prune, replenish potting mix, and return mature plants to their container to control height.

Pachystachys lutea
pak-ee-STAK-is LOO-tee-uh

Lollipop-plant

- ■ **Light:** Bright
- ■ **Water:** Keep evenly moist
- ■ **Humidity:** High
- ■ **Temperature:** Average to high
- ■ **Fertilizer:** All-purpose
- ■ **Size:** 1-3'H×1-3'W

Lollipop-plant is a fast-growing shrub with puckered, lance-shaped dark green leaves that can reach 6 inches long. Its principal attraction, though, is its decorative and long-lasting 4- to 6-inch flowerheads that appear at the ends of the branches. They are composed of bright, very long-lived yellow bracts from among which peep the tubular, two-lipped true flowers. Most dependable in summer, blooming can occur sporadically throughout the year in good light.

The plant's fast growth rate and tendency to rapidly lose its lower leaves means regular pruning is necessary. Fortunately, the more you prune, the more stems and flowers it produces. Prune right after the bracts fade to ensure you don't clip off unopened flowers.
Repotting: As needed.
Propagation: Stem cuttings.
Problems: Spider mites and whiteflies are possible pests.
Tips: Rejuvenate aging or neglected specimens by cutting to within 6 inches of the soil.

Fast-growing lollipop-plant produces more flowers when pruned.

Palms

- ■ **Light:** Bright, some tolerate medium or even low
- ■ **Water:** Keep evenly moist
- ■ **Humidity:** Average to high
- ■ **Temperature:** Average to high, but cool for a few species
- ■ **Fertilizer:** All-purpose, not heavy feeders
- ■ **Size:** 1-8'H×1-5'W

Chinese fan palm *(Livistona chinensis)*

Palms adapt well to the limited light and controlled temperatures of the indoors, often flourishing for decades.

Palm fronds are fan-shape or pinnate (feathery). Most palms grown indoors have a trunk, albeit sometimes a narrow one, but others are stemless. They can be clumping or single stemmed. Most palms do not bloom indoors and therefore do not bear fruit.

During the spring and summer growing season, water plants regularly and fertilize them lightly. Reduce water and stop feeding them in winter. Protect palms from dry air and direct sunlight, especially if you move them outdoors.

To prune a palm, cut off dead or damaged fronds; never cut off its top. Unlike most plants, palms produce new growth only from the tip, so removing the growing point kills the stem—and the whole plant, if it's single trunked.

Fishtail palm (Caryota mitis)

■ **Fishtail palm** (*Caryota mitis*) becomes large over time. The ribbed texture of the leaflets and their wedge shape account for the common name.

■ **Parlor palm** (*Chamaedorea elegans*, syn. *Neanthe bella*) is small and has light green fronds. It tolerates low light, but given enough light, it will bear open clusters of yellow flowers.

■ **European fan palm** (*Chamaerops humilis*) has fan-shaped leaves about a foot wide. The multiple trunks, reaching 4 feet or taller, are rough and black and grow at an angle.

■ **Areca palm** or butterfly palm (*Dypsis lutescens*) is a cluster of thin yellow canes with arching fronds and strap-shaped, shiny green leaflets. It is medium size and slow growing.

Areca palm (Dypsis lutescens)

■ **Kentia palm** (*Howea forsteriana*) rarely exceeds 7 or 8 feet indoors. Feather-shaped fronds arch outward from a sturdy base and eventually from the trunk, creating a full appearance. It is tolerant of low light.

■ **Chinese fan palm** (*Livistona chinensis*) is a large plant with deeply lobed leaves to 2 feet across. Older plants produce a rough trunk. The plants grow to 10 feet if given enough room and a large enough container.

■ **Majesty palm** (*Ravenea rivularis*) produces a crown of arching, feathery, bright green fronds around a base that keeps increasing in size, eventually forming an upright trunk. It may grow beyond a useful size.

■ **Pygmy date palm** (*Phoenix roebelenii*) is a dwarf, rarely reaching more than 4 feet tall indoors. Its arching, narrow-leaved, feathery fronds at the top of an upright trunk give it the stereotypical palm silhouette.

■ **Lady palm** (*Rhapis excelsa*) features a hairy trunk and 6- to 12-inch-wide fans of thick, shiny leaflets that look like they were clipped with pinking shears.

Repotting: Repot infrequently.

Propagation: Seed (easy for most) or division (some species).

Problems: Spider mites, whiteflies, mealybugs, and scale insects are possible pests.

Tips: Buy a palm the size you need because growth is often slow.

Parlor palm (Chamaedorea elegans)

Pandanus
pan-DAN-us

Screw pine

■ **Light: Medium to bright**
■ **Water: Keep evenly moist**
■ **Humidity: Average to high**
■ **Temperature: Average**
■ **Fertilizer: All-purpose**
■ **Size: 1-10'H×1-7'W**

Screw pine is easy to grow indoors but most types have spiny leaves.

Screw pine's leaves spiral upward, corkscrew fashion, forming a rosette. The long, sword-shaped leaves resemble corn leaves but have prickly edges and a row of spines underneath. Even young plants soon develop a distinct trunk, often dotted with offsets. Thick aerial roots grow downward. Most screw pines become large trees and have to be cut back or started anew.

P. veitchii has leaves striped yellow and green. The new growth of its cultivar 'Verde' is entirely milky white, then lime green, and finally dark green. *P. sanderii* is striped yellow; *P. utilis* has burgundy edges; and *P. baptistii*, with blue-green leaves lightly striped yellow, has smooth leaf edges.

Repotting: As needed.

Propagation: Offsets or seed.

Problems: It is usually trouble free, although spider mites and scale insects are possible pests.

Tips: Keep spiny-leaved plants out of the reach of children.

Passiflora
pas-ih-FLOR-uh

Passionflower

- **Light:** Intense
- **Water:** Keep evenly moist
- **Humidity:** High
- **Temperature:** Average
- **Fertilizer:** All-purpose
- **Size:** 4-10'H×1-4'W

Passiflora caerulea 'Blue Crown' blooms in summer and fall.

Passionflowers are big, rapidly growing vines that cling with long tendrils. The large flowers (4 to 6 inches wide) are complex and quite striking. All types produce abundant three-lobed leaflets. You'll need a trellis or other support to grow these vigorous plants. Give them plenty of space for maximum bloom.

P. caerulea has purple, white, and blue flowers; *P. coccinea* has showy crimson flowers with protruding bright yellow stamens; *P. vitifolia* produces larger, bright red flowers; and *P. 'Incense'* has fragrant, wavy royal purple flowers. *P. quadrangularis* is the popular passionfruit. It flowers but does not bear fruit indoors.

Propagation: Stem cuttings or seed.
Repotting: As needed.
Problems: Plants will not bloom in inadequate light. Spider mites, whiteflies, and scale insects are possible pests.
Tips: Prune just before the plant blooms, being careful not to remove flower buds.

Pelargonium
pel-ar-GO-nee-um

Geranium

- **Light:** Bright to intense
- **Water:** Let dry slightly between waterings
- **Humidity:** Average
- **Temperature:** Average, some prefer cold to cool in winter
- **Fertilizer:** All-purpose in spring, high potassium when in bloom
- **Size:** 6-36"H×6-36"W

A sunny windowsill where it is never above 75°F is ideal for geraniums. They bloom in every season but are most appreciated in winter, when little else is in flower. Many get quite large but the most popular types come in miniature and dwarf varieties. Fancy-leaf cultivars have varicolored leaves, often in bronze, scarlet, yellow, and white.

Zonal geraniums (*P. ×hortorum*) often have a dark green or blackish ring on each leaf. Cultivars can have single flowers, double flowers, cactus flowers, and many other forms in red, salmon, apricot, tangerine, pink, or white. They bloom all year long indoors under good conditions.

Martha Washington or regal geranium (*P. ×domesticum*) grows to about 30 inches. It is most famous for its large colorful flowers which devolop in cool conditions. Leaves are dark green with crinkled edges, and often lemon scented.

Zonal geraniums (*P. ×hortorum*) have dark markings on the leaves.

Ivy geraniums, hybrids of *P. peltatum*, bear leathery leaves with a shape similar to English ivy and sport many clusters of showy

Staghorn peppermint geranium has finely cut leaves with a familiar scent.

flowers, often veined with a darker shade of the overall color. They have weak, spreading stems and are excellent in hanging baskets.

Scented-leaf geraniums are grown primarily for the sharp, evocative fragrances of their leaves. For example, *P. crispum* smells like lemon; *P. graveolens*, like rose; *P. ×nervosum*, like lime; and *P. odoratissimum*, like apple. Blooms are not showy.

Repotting: As needed. Transplant seedlings as they grow.
Propagation: Stem cuttings or seed.
Problems: Whiteflies are potential pests. Botrytis may affect blooms.
Tips: Pinch stem tips to improve form, and remove faded blossoms.

Ivy geranium grows well in a basket where its stems can trail.

Pentas lanceolata
PEN-tas lan-see-oh-LAH-tuh
Star flower, Egyptian star cluster

- **Light: Intense**
- **Water: Keep evenly moist**
- **Humidity: Average**
- **Temperature: Average, avoid cold drafts**
- **Fertilizer: All-purpose**
- **Size: 1-3'H×1-3'W**

When the light is right, star flower blooms year-round.

Star flower is a shrubby plant with elliptic or lance-shape green leaves, slightly hairy and with sunken veins. It bears rounded clusters of small flowers at the stem tips and, under intense or supplemental light, may bloom at least sporadically all year, generally most abundantly in spring and summer.

The main species, *P. lanceolata*, has been mostly superseded by a series of denser, dwarf hybrids in shades of white, pink, magenta, purple, lilac, and red, most of which stay below 3 feet tall and wide (some only 1 foot) and require no staking. If you can't find this plant in the houseplant section of your garden center, look among the outdoor annuals.
Repotting: As needed.
Propagation: Stem cuttings or seed.
Problems: Spider mites and aphids are possible pests.
Tips: Prune to maintain shape.

Peperomia
pep-er-OH-mee-uh
Peperomia

- **Light: Medium to bright**
- **Water: Let dry slightly between waterings**
- **Humidity: Average to high**
- **Temperature: Average**
- **Fertilizer: All-purpose**
- **Size: 5-15"H×6-24"W**

A houseplant with high style, peperomia offers dazzling foliage and flowers in a breathtaking range of shapes, textures, and colors. Some grow upright, others trail; some leaves are flat and shiny, while a few look pleated; and except for similarities in their oddly elongated creamy white blooms, you'd never know they were related. Admire the flowers for a week or so, then remove them to keep plants tidy.
Clumping peperomias grow a rosette of stems that erupt in a dense mass of leaves. The two best known are watermelon (*P. argyreia*), named for its stripes, and ripple (*P. caperata* 'Emerald Ripple'). Silverleaf peperomia (*P. griseoargentea*) shares the corrugated leaf texture of 'Emerald Ripple' but is silvery gray instead of green and sometimes edged in cream and red, like *P. clusifolia*, the red-edged peperomia. *P.* 'Jayde' peperomia has fat, rounded leaves that come to pert points with a silver dot in their centers.
Upright peperomia (*P. obtusifolia*, syn. *P. magnoliifolia*) is called pepper face or baby rubber tree. Its waxy green leaves are bubble-shape and speckled or

Red-edged peperomia *(P. clusifolia)*

splashed with cream or yellow. 'Variegata' has red leaf margins.
Trailing peperomia (*P. scandens*) has thinner stems and heart-shaped leaves that drape gracefully over a pot's edge. Lighter green or edged in cream,

'Emerald Ripple' peperomia sends up pencil-like blooms.

it is also called false philodendron. Creeping buttons (*P. rotundifolia pilosior*) has zigzagging stems with tiny green and silver leaves.
Repotting: Annually until fully grown; replenish the soil and root-prune annually after that.
Propagation: Division (clumping types) or stem cuttings (trailing and upright types).
Problems: Overwatering leads to crown rot. Low light produces pale, spindly growth. Mealybugs, scale, and spider mites are potential pests.
Tips: Remove yellowed leaves. Pinch upright and trailing types to keep growth compact.

Variegated baby rubber plant (left) and P. 'Jayde' (right)

Philodendron
fil-oh-DEN-dron

Philodendron

- **Light: Medium to bright, some tolerate low**
- **Water: Keep evenly moist**
- **Humidity: Average, high for climbers**
- **Temperature: Average**
- **Fertilizer: All-purpose, but do not fertilize plants in low light**
- **Size: 1-10'H×1-8'W**

Red-leaf philodendron (P. erubescens)

No other group of plants is as widely used indoors as philodendrons. The great variety of sizes and growth habits, as well as the uniquely shaped glossy leaves, give the indoor gardener many choices for almost any situation. Philodendrons are tough, tolerant plants that don't need a lot of sunlight. They are classified according to their growth habit.

■ **Climbing philodendrons** are the ones most commonly grown indoors. Under humid conditions, they can attach themselves to a support, especially if it has a rough surface, such as a bark slab or osmunda pole. Otherwise, tie them to their support as they grow. Many of the climbing species also make great trailing plants for hanging baskets.

■ **Spade-leaf philodendron** (*P. domesticum*, also sold as *P. hastatum*) is a lush, evergreen climber with aerial roots. Deeply veined, bright green leaves take the shape of giant spearheads, 8 to 12 inches long. Keep the plant out of cold drafts.

■ **Split-leaf philodendron** (*P. pertusum*) is now classified as *Monstera deliciosa*. See page 94 for more information.

■ **Red-leaf philodendron** (*P. erubescens*) has red stems topped with maroon spear-shape leaves. It's a climber.

■ **Heart-leaf philodendron** (*P. scandens oxycardium*, syn. *P. cordatum*) is a vigorous climber. This plant does fine in the shade and is one of the easiest of all houseplants to grow.

■ **Tree philodendrons** can become large plants, 6 to 8 feet tall. Their leaves, of varying shapes, extend from self-supporting "trunks." Most produce aerial roots that reach down to the soil and help anchor the plant.

■ **Lacy-tree philodendron** (*P. bipinnatifidum*) is a nonclimbing, cut-leaf species with a distinct trunk. It tends to outgrow its allotted space quickly.

■ **Clump-forming philodendrons** form ground-hugging rosettes that are often wider than tall. They rarely need staking and don't usually produce aerial roots. Some get lanky over time; just cut them back and they'll return to their original dense form. They make perfect floor or table plants for locations with medium light.

■ **Hybrid philodendrons** are usually clump-forming plants

Lacy-tree philodendron
(P. bipinnatifidum selloum)

P. 'Prince of Orange' (left) and 'Moonlight' (right) hybrids

with attractive, glossy foliage. Many have some climbing genes in their background and will eventually produce stems that begin to clamber. 'Moonlight' has pointed spade-shaped leaves in bright chartreuse green, darkening to lime green. 'Prince of Orange' has coppery orange new leaves that fade to pale green. Coloration fades to green in low light. 'Xanadu' has arrow-shape, medium-green lobed leaves

Repotting: As needed.

Propagation: Stem cuttings, soil layering, or air layering.

Problems: Climbers eventually become barren at the base. Spider mites, mealybugs, and scale insects are possible, but usually philodendrons are pest free.

Tips: Prune to keep climbing types to the desired height and shape. Direct aerial roots to soil or remove them. Clean the leaves periodically. All parts of the plant are toxic, and the sap irritates the skin, so keep plants out of the reach of children.

Heart-leaf philodendron
(P. scandens oxycardium)

Pilea
py-LEE-uh
Pilea

- **Light:** Medium to bright
- **Water:** Keep evenly moist
- **Humidity:** High
- **Temperature:** Average to high, avoid cold drafts
- **Fertilizer:** All-purpose, not a heavy feeder
- **Size:** 6-12"H×6-24"W

Aluminum plant (*Pilea cadierei* 'Minima') is a compact cultivar.

Most of the *Pilea* species suitable for indoor gardening are small plants, rarely more than a foot tall. They often have leaves with depressed veins, giving them a quilted appearance. The dark green leaves of many species are tinged with red, silver, or copper. Still others have a creeping or trailing habit that makes them particularly useful in hanging baskets. Some species produce inconspicuous flowers in summer.

■ **Aluminum plant** (*P. cadierei*) is one of the most popular species. Its puckered green leaves look like they have been brushed with silver paint. *P. cadierei* 'Silver Tree' is similar but has bronze leaves flushed silver.

■ **Creeping charlie** (*P. depressa* and *P. nummulariifolia*) is a low plant with trailing stems that look best in hanging baskets.

■ **Friendship plant** (*P. spruceana* and *P. involucrata*) has thick, velvety clusters of broad yellow-

Friendship plant (*P. spruceana* 'Norfolk') has a velvety texture.

green leaves with a coppery sheen on the upper surface.

■ **Artillery plant** (*P. microphylla*) bears upright then arching green stems and tiny fleshy apple-green leaves. It gets its common name from its tiny flowers that shoot out pollen within seconds of being watered. It self-sows abundantly when it is healthy and can even become an indoor weed.

Repotting: Annually in late winter or early spring.

Propagation: Stem cuttings; *P. microphylla* self-sows.

Problems: Low light causes spindly growth. Overwatering leads to crown rot. Cold air or cold water damages leaves; keep plants warm at all times. Spider mites and mealybugs are possible pests.

Tips: Start new plants to replace old specimens as they get weak. Prune to maintain desired size.

The flowers of artillery plant (*P. microphylla*) shoot pollen.

Pittosporum tobira
pit-TOS-por-um toh-BY-ruh
Japanese pittosporum, Japanese mock orange

- **Light:** Bright, or medium if flowering is not a priority
- **Water:** Let dry slightly between waterings
- **Humidity:** Average
- **Temperature:** Cold to cool, tolerates average but may fail to bloom
- **Fertilizer:** All-purpose, not a heavy feeder
- **Size:** 1-3'H×1-3'W

P. tobira 'Variegata' produces flowers that smell like orange blossoms.

Japanese pittosporum is a slow-growing woody shrub with whorls of leathery, glossy dark green leaves that resemble those of a rhododendron. In late winter or early spring it produces creamy white flowers that smell like orange blossoms.

'Variegata' is the cultivar most commonly sold as a houseplant. Its leaves are grayish green with variable white edges.

Repotting: As needed.

Propagation: Stem cuttings (use rooting hormone) or air layering.

Problems: Spider mites, mealybugs, and scale insects are possible pests.

Tips: Prune after flowering to maintain the desired size and shape. Because it grows so slowly, always purchase a large enough specimen for your current needs.

Plectranthus
plek-TRANTH-us

Swedish ivy, Cuban oregano

- **Light: Medium to bright**
- **Water: Keep evenly moist**
- **Humidity: Average**
- **Temperature: Average, but cooler at night**
- **Fertilizer: All-purpose**
- **Size: 10-15"H×24-48"W**

Swedish ivy *(Plectranthus verticillatus)* needs little care.

The Swedish ivies are excellent houseplants, tolerant of most home microclimates and needing minimal care. Most have square stems that respond well to occasional tip pinching by producing new leaves year-round. For each set of leaves you remove, two will emerge to thicken the dense foliage. If you don't pinch, tiny spikes of flowers will appear; remove them right away to keep the leaves healthy.

■ **Swedish ivy**, *P. verticillatus* (formerly *P. australis*), may be the ideal hanging basket plant. Shiny, quarter-sized, scalloped leaves and square stems are strong enough to grow up, out, and over a pot's edge. Swedish ivy does not wilt easily and is slow to bloom unless grown in direct sun and fertilized with a fertilizer formulated for blooming plants.

■ **Cuban oregano** (*P. amboinicus*) has an excellent culinary reputation in the American tropics, where its thyme-oregano flavor strikes a good balance with cilantro in black bean and meat

Cuban oregano *(P. amboinicus)* is as tasty as it is attractive.

dishes. Also known as Mexican mint and Spanish thyme, the plant has thick, hairy, aromatic leaves. Both solid green and boldly variegated selections are available. They grow easily from cuttings and quickly cover the top of a pot to spill over its edges.

■ *P. forsteri* '**Marginatus**', as its name implies, has white leaf edges on soft-looking, hairy leaves that are sharply scalloped, or toothed. It is shrubby and does not begin to trail until mature.

Repotting: When the pot is crowded.

Propagation: Stem cuttings root easily in water or potting soil.

Problems: Overwatering stresses the plants, leading to stem rot. Drought stress creates ideal conditions for spider mites and mealybugs. Leaves turn yellow when given excess light.

Tips: For smaller, more manageable Swedish ivies, start a new pot from stem cuttings each fall.

P. forsteri 'Marginatus'

Plumbago auriculata
plum-BAY-go aw-rik-yew-LAH-tuh

Plumbago, cape leadwort

Light: Intense
Water: Keep evenly moist
Humidity: High
Temperature: Average, but cool in winter
Fertilizer: All-purpose
Size: 1-3'H×1-3'W

***Plumbago auriculata* offers abundant flowers on a slow-growing plant.**

Plumbago (also known as *P. capensis*) is grown for its abundant pale blue flowers that can appear nonstop from spring through fall. Although a climber in the wild, in pots it is usually grown as a shrub or a trailer.

The spoon-shaped leaves are medium green or sometimes grayish. The flowers are trumpet-shape, with five flaring petals and a distinctive sunken midvein. Buy a large plant if you want flowers the first year, because plumbago is slow growing.

P. auriculata alba, with pure white flowers, is a popular variety, as is the cobalt blue 'Royal Cape'.

Repotting: As needed.

Propagation: Stem cuttings or seed.

Problems: Yellow leaves indicate a lack of manganese. Spider mites, whiteflies, and mealybugs are possible pests.

Tips: Prune as needed to maintain desired size and shape.

Podocarpus macrophyllus 'Maki'
po-do-KAR-pus mak-ro-FYL-lus MAH-kee

Buddhist pine, southern yew

- **Light:** Medium to intense
- **Water:** Let dry slightly between waterings
- **Humidity:** Average
- **Temperature:** Average, but cold to cool in winter
- **Fertilizer:** All-purpose, not a heavy feeder
- **Size:** 1-10'H×1-5'W

Pruning is the key to growing Buddhist pine as a houseplant.

Indoors this coniferous tree must be maintained as a shrub. Fortunately, pinching the tips encourages branching and bushiness. It can even be maintained as a bonsai. The flowers and purple fruit are almost never produced indoors. 'Maki' has a denser habit and shorter leaves than the species. It's a slow grower that does best with cool winters.

Repotting: As needed.

Propagation: Stem cuttings (from upright shoots) or seed.

Problems: Overwatering leads to stem rot. Leaves die back in dry air. Spider mites, whiteflies, mealybugs, and scale insects are possible pests.

Tips: Because it grows so slowly, always purchase a large enough specimen for your current needs.

Pogonatherum paniceum
po-go-NATH-er-um pan-ih-SEE-um

House bamboo

- **Light:** Bright
- **Water:** Keep evenly moist
- **Humidity:** Average to high
- **Temperature:** Cool to average
- **Fertilizer:** All-purpose
- **Size:** 12-24"H×8-18"W

House bamboo's fine-textured, grassy stems explode in all directions like a feathery crown above its container. Despite its appearance, this plant, also known as baby bamboo and dwarf bamboo, is actually a diminutive relative of perennial landscape grasses. Its stems are thin and reedy, with wide, short, bamboo-like leaves crowded near the tips. The stars in the crown are flowers: flat little light brown spikes that hold slender grass awns above the leaves. Its botanic name means "flowing beard," which aptly describes its soothing resilience. When a soft breeze or your hand brushes house bamboo, it rustles gently in return.

Repotting: When the pot is crowded.

Propagation: Division.

Problems: Low light, dry air or dry soil may cause sections to brown; prune to rejuvenate.

Tips: After the flowers have bloomed, cut the plant down completely to restart new growth.

House bamboo is related to perennial landscape grasses.

Polyscias
po-LEE-see-us

Aralia

- **Light:** Medium to bright
- **Water:** Let dry slightly between waterings
- **Humidity:** High
- **Temperature:** Average
- **Fertilizer:** All-purpose, not a heavy feeder
- **Size:** 1-10'H×1-3'W

Balfour aralia (left) and ming aralia (right)

Aralias are woody shrubs frequently grown indoors for their lacy, often variegated foliage and treelike appearance even when small. The leaves of some cultivars are aromatic when crushed or bruised.

Ming aralia (*P. fruticosa*) is often grown as a bonsai. Fern-leaf aralia (*P. filicifolia*) bears deeply cut olive-green leaves with purple midribs. Pot several plants together for a fuller look. Roseleaf aralia (*P. guilfoylei*) gets its name from its deeply cut leaves. Balfour aralia (*P. scutellaria*) has rounded leaflets that are leathery and glossy dark green, with sunken veins.

Give aralias plenty of room, and prune them frequently to achieve good form. Most require pinching to maintain in the home. None of them is likely to bloom indoors.

Repotting: As needed.

Propagation: Stem or root cuttings.

Problems: Spider mites, mealybugs, and scale insects are possible pests.

Tips: Prune as needed to maintain desired size and shape.

Primula
PRIM-yew-luh
Primrose

- **Light:** Bright, intense in winter
- **Water:** Keep evenly moist
- **Humidity:** High
- **Temperature:** Cold to cool
- **Fertilizer:** None
- **Size:** 6-18"H×6-20"W

Polyanthus primrose is a garden perennial often sold as a gift plant.

Primroses are difficult to maintain outside a greenhouse, so choose healthy-looking specimens with medium-green leaves and plenty of buds with only a few flowers open.

Fairy primrose (*P. malacoides*) bears star-shaped, scented flowers, single or double, usually in shades of white, lilac, pink, or red, in tiers on tall stalks to 18 inches high.

German primrose (*P. obconica*), sometimes sold as *P. sinensis*, reaches 12 inches and blooms in white, lilac, crimson, or salmon. The leaves contain primin, a skin-irritating substance, so try primin-free strains, such as 'Libre'.

Colorful polyanthus primrose (*P. ×polyantha*) can recuperate after blooming. Plant it in the garden in moist soil and partial shade.
Repotting: Not required.
Propagation: *P. ×polyantha* by division; seed (in a greenhouse).
Problems: Spider mites are a potential pest in dry air.
Tips: Buy plants in bloom and compost them when they fade.

Punica granatum nana
PYEW-nih-kuh grah-NAH-tum NAH-nuh
Dwarf pomegranate

- **Light:** Intense
- **Water:** Keep evenly moist
- **Humidity:** High
- **Temperature:** Average, but cold to cool in winter
- **Fertilizer:** All-purpose
- **Size:** 12-40"H×12-40"W

This plant is a natural dwarf. It can grow to 6 feet outdoors but with minimal pruning is easily kept at half that height indoors. It is popular as a bonsai because of its flowers and fruits that grow in proportion to the size of the plant.

Dwarf pomegranate has small, narrow, shiny dark green leaves. In early summer, but also sporadically throughout the year, it produces showy scarlet flowers. They form edible 2 inch reddish fruits. Stake any branches heavily laden with fruit.

Several cultivars are available with various flower colors or double blooms. The plant is surprisingly easy to grow indoors.
Repotting: Infrequently; blooms best when pot-bound.
Propagation: Stem cuttings or seed (single varieties).
Problems: Spider mites, whiteflies, mealybugs, and scale insects are possible pests.
Tips: Leave faded flowers on the plant to produce fruit.

Dwarf pomegranate bears fruit indoors in bright light and high humidity.

Radermachera sinica
rad-er-mah-KER-uh SIN-ih-kuh
China doll

- **Light:** Medium to bright
- **Water:** Keep evenly moist
- **Humidity:** Average to high
- **Temperature:** Average
- **Fertilizer:** All-purpose
- **Size:** 1-5'H×1-4'W

China doll is really a tree, so it needs regular pinching and pruning.

The shiny bright green leaves of China doll have a delicate fernlike appearance. Each mature leaf measures up to 2 feet long and nearly as wide, with innumerable pointed leaflets.

Although it is actually a tree, the plants usually sold are barely more than seedlings and don't even yet have woody stems, let alone branches. For a fuller appearance in the nursery, China doll is usually planted three or more to a pot. It is also treated with a growth retardant, which decreases the distance between the leaves, making the plant more compact. When the effect wears off, you'll have to begin pinching and pruning to stimulate branching. China doll does not bloom indoors.
Repotting: As needed.
Propagation: Seed, stem cuttings, or air layering.
Problems: Whiteflies, mealybugs and scale insects are possible pests.
Tips: Remove yellowed leaves. Pinch to maintain compact shape.

Rhododendron Indica hybrids
ro-do-DEN-dron IN-dih-kuh
Pot azalea

- **Light: Bright; place temporary plants in any location**
- **Water: Keep evenly moist**
- **Humidity: High**
- **Temperature: Average; cooler in winter. Avoid cold drafts**
- **Fertilizer: Acid-based with added trace elements**
- **Size: 6-36"H×6-36"W**

Move pot azalea outdoors in fall to encourage rebloom.

Pot azaleas are usually sold in full bloom in white, pink, salmon, red, and bicolors. Their funnel-shaped flowers are usually semidouble or double. Unlike other azaleas, they are evergreen, holding on to their small thin dark green leaves all year.

After they flower, some people simply discard pot azaleas, but you can get them to bloom again. Put them outside in fall, bringing them indoors only when frost threatens. They will bloom again through winter and perhaps sporadically throughout the year.

Repotting: Infrequently; does best if slightly pot-bound. Use a lime-free potting mix.
Propagation: Stem cuttings (use rooting hormone).
Problems: Spider mites, aphids, mealybugs, and scale insects are possible pests.
Tips: All plant parts are toxic, so keep plants away from children.

Rosa
RO-zuh
Miniature rose

- **Light: Intense**
- **Water: Let dry slightly between waterings**
- **Humidity: High**
- **Temperature: Cool, but cold in winter, tolerates average**
- **Fertilizer: All-purpose**
- **Size: 6-24"H×6-18"W**

Usually thought of as outdoor plants, miniature roses also make an appealing tabletop display grown as small bushes, climbers, or standards. The delicate 1- to 1½-inch blooms are available in a wide range of colors.

Miniature roses are sold as gift plants, designed to be discarded after blooming or planted outdoors in the garden. But it is possible to grow and bloom miniature roses indoors. To succeed, give them the same care you would give them outdoors: abundant light; cool, well-circulated air; and cold temperatures during the winter.
Repotting: In any season.
Propagation: Stem cuttings.
Problems: Highly susceptible to spider mites, especially in dry air. Whiteflies, aphids, mealybugs, and scale insects are also common pests. Several leaf diseases are possible but not likely.
Tips: Clip off yellow leaves and faded flowers. Plant outdoors after blooms fade.

Grow miniature roses in bright light indoors, just as you would outside.

Ruellia makoyana
roo-EL-ee-uh ma-koy-AH-nuh
Monkey plant, trailing velvet plant

- **Light: Bright**
- **Water: Keep evenly moist**
- **Humidity: High**
- **Temperature: Average**
- **Fertilizer: All-purpose**
- **Size: 10-24"H×10-18"W**

Show off monkey plant's foliage by placing the plant on a low table.

The most commonly grown *Ruellia* for indoor use is *R. makoyana,* the monkey plant. It is enjoyed as much for its colorful foliage as for its bloom. This plant remains attractive throughout the year because of its thin, ovate leaves, which are silver-veined and velvety, olive green above and purple underneath. Blooms are numerous trumpet-shaped rose red flowers up to 2 inches in diameter, appearing during fall and winter. You can form the plant into a small shrub or accentuate its trailing habit for use in a hanging basket.

Monkey plant thrives indoors but does best in high humidity. Use a humidifier or a humidity tray if your house is dry.
Repotting: Annually.
Propagation: Stem cuttings.
Problems: Spider mites, whiteflies, mealybugs, and scale insects are possible pests.
Tips: Pinch often for new growth.

Saintpaulia ionantha
saynt-PAWL-ee-uh eye-oh-NAN-thuh

African violet

■ **Light:** Bright
■ **Water:** Keep evenly moist, avoid wetting foliage
■ **Humidity:** High
■ **Temperature:** Average, avoid sudden changes
■ **Fertilizer:** All-purpose
■ **Size:** 2-10"H×2-24"W

Water African violets from below to avoid damaging the leaves.

African violets produce a single rosette of velvety smooth or hairy dark green leaves on short leafstalks and bear clusters of single, semidouble, or double flowers in white or shades of pink, red, violet, purple, or blue, and even lime green, pale yellow, and bicolors. The star- or bell-shape flowers have ruffled, rounded, or fringed petals. Trailing African violets bear numerous stems that arch outward and hang down. They look best in hanging baskets.
Repotting: Keep slightly pot-bound.
Propagation: Leaf cuttings, offsets, or seed.
Problems: Susceptible to viruses and fungal infections. Cold water that touches foliage causes yellow rings on leaf surfaces. Thrips, aphids, cyclamen mites, and mealybugs are possible pests.
Tips: Remove all dead leaves and flowers promptly. Shape by removing side shoots, except on trailing cultivars.

Sanchezia speciosa
san-KEE-zee-uh spee-see-OH-suh

Sanchezia, shrubby whitevein

■ **Light:** Bright
■ **Water:** Keep evenly moist
■ **Humidity:** High
■ **Temperature:** Average
■ **Fertilizer:** All-purpose
■ **Size:** 2-5'H×2-5'W

This sanchezia (syn. *S. spectabilis, S. glaucophylla,* and *S. nobilis*) is grown especially for its dramatic foliage. The smooth, bright green stems bear large elliptic glossy dark green leaves to 12 inches long, with spectacular veining. Both the midrib and the main veins are brilliantly colored. The flowers are stunning terminal spikes consisting of small red bracts from among which shoot bright yellow blooms. They appear in summer and can last more than a month.

Sanchezia needs occasional pruning. You can keep it under 3 feet tall and wide by pinching and trimming it. Prune anytime after flowering until late winter. Any later and you risk removing the summer's flower buds.
Repotting: As needed.
Propagation: Stem cuttings.
Problems: Spider mites and scale insects are possible pests.
Tips: Remove faded flowers. Give the plant an occasional shower.

Sanchezia is grown for its foliage but the flower spikes are stunning too.

Sansevieria
san-seh-VAIR-ee-uh

Snake plant

■ **Light:** Low to bright
■ **Water:** Let dry slightly between waterings
■ **Humidity:** Low to average
■ **Temperature:** Average
■ **Fertilizer:** All-purpose once during growing season, not a heavy feeder
■ **Size:** 6-60"H×6-36"W

Gold bands edging the leaves of 'Laurentii' accentuate its upright form.

Legendary for its ability to tolerate low light, burning heat, and even months of total neglect, snake plant grows much better in a bright location with regular watering as soon as the soil becomes dry.
■ **Snake plant,** *S. trifasciata* produces erect, leathery, strap-shape leaves, horizontally banded dark and light green in a snakeskin pattern. Colonies of separate plants accumulate in the original pot. Under bright light, the plant eventually produces a tall stalk of tubular greenish flowers that give off a heavenly scent at night.

'Laurentii', with yellow stripes along the leaf edges, is a popular cultivar. 'Hahnii' is a dwarf plant that forms dense rosettes of broad, dark green leaves less than 10 inches tall. 'Golden Hahnii' has creamy yellow stripes.

Low-growing 'Hahnii' makes a sturdy tabletop plant for low-light areas.

■ **Spear sansevieria** (*S. cylindrica*) which is also related to dracaenas and agaves, is an unusually showy species. It has rigid, upright, round succulent leaves that taper toward the sharp tips. The spikes are banded in dark green and grow straight up or arch like outstretched fingers, depending on the cultivar. The plant can grow to 5 feet tall and may send up tall stalks of fragrant, night-blooming pink flowers if growing conditions are optimal.
Repotting: Repot infrequently in a well-drained growing mix.
Propagation: Division (rhizomes) or leaf or leaf section cuttings of nonvariegated types.
Problems: Leaves become floppy under low light. Leaves break easily. Overwatering leads to root rot. Spider mites and mealybugs are possible pests.
Tips: Remove flower stalks after blooming has stopped.

Spear sansevieria has round succulent leaves tapered like fingers.

Saxifraga stolonifera
saks-ih-FRAG-uh sto-lon-IF-er-uh
Strawberry begonia

■ **Light:** Bright
■ **Water:** Let dry slightly between waterings
■ **Humidity:** Average, but high for 'Tricolor'
■ **Temperature:** Cold to cool, tolerates average
■ **Fertilizer:** All-purpose, not a heavy feeder
■ **Size:** 6-12"H×6-12"W

Strawberry begonia is a ground-hugging, rosette-forming plant. The rounded dark green leaves have silver along the veins and reddish hairs underneath.

Strawberry begonia's real draw is its numerous thin and stringy runners. They produce plantlets at their tips, exactly as strawberries outdoors do. Thus the plant looks best indoors displayed in a hanging basket.

A variegated cultivar, 'Tricolor', with an attractive pink to white leaf margin, is popular and does best in a terrarium.
Repotting: Annually, when flowering ceases.
Propagation: Division, layering, or plantlets.
Problems: Spider mites, whiteflies, mealybugs, and scale insects are possible pests.
Tips: Remove flower stalks to improve the plant's appearance.

Let strawberry begonia's runners hang downward from the pot.

Scadoxus multiflorus
skuh-DAHKS-us mul-tih-FLOR-us
Blood lily, blood flower

■ **Light:** Bright, but keep in darkness when dormant
■ **Water:** Keep evenly moist, but keep dry during dormancy
■ **Humidity:** High
■ **Temperature:** Cool to average; cold to cool when dormant
■ **Fertilizer:** All-purpose
■ **Size:** 18-24"H×12-18"W

After dormancy, blood lily produces huge flowers in bright light.

Blood lily (also known as *Haemanthus multiflorus*) sends up broad lance-shaped to oval, nearly stemless leaves that form an arching rosette, followed by a thick leafless flower stalk often marbled with maroon spots. At the tip forms a large ball of bright red flowers to 6 inches across. Although each bloom has six colorful petals, long scarlet stamens dominate the flower, giving the entire flowerhead the appearance of a giant red powderpuff.

After blooming, cut off the faded foliage and store the bulbs, still in their pots, in a cool basement or other similar spot.
Repotting: Infrequently; pot-bound plants bloom more profusely. Plant with the tip of the bulb protruding from the soil.
Propagation: From offsets or seed.
Problems: None significant.
Tips: Give plants plenty of room.

Schefflera
shef-LAIR-uh
Schefflera, false aralia

- **Light:** Medium to bright, tolerates low for short periods
- **Water:** Let dry slightly between waterings
- **Humidity:** Average
- **Temperature:** Average
- **Fertilizer:** All-purpose, not a heavy feeder
- **Size:** 1–10'H×1–4'W

Common schefflera *(Schefflera actinophylla)*

Several treelike or shrubby plants are commonly known as schefflera.

- **Common schefflera** (*S. actinophylla,* syn. *Brassaia actinophylla*) is often sold several small seedlings to a pot, each with only three to five pointed, toothed, bright green leaflets and thin stems. It matures rapidly into a plant with much larger, darker green leaves a foot or more across, made up of 7 to 16 smooth-edge leaflets spreading out like the sections of an umbrella on thick, sturdy stems.

Common schefflera grows upright indoors and is not inclined to branch, so it is better to buy a pot with several stems: they guarantee a fuller appearance over time. The plant is normally susceptible to spider mites, but some cultivars, such as 'Amate', with particularly shiny leaves, were chosen for mite resistance. Common schefflera is slow to root from cuttings and is usually propagated by seed or, for cultivars, by air layering.

- **Dwarf or miniature schefflera** (*S. arboricola* syn. *Heptapleurum arboricola*) is only smaller than the common schefflera in leaf size; it can easily reach over 6 feet in height and diameter. Fortunately, unlike the common schefflera, it branches readily and you can keep it in check by pruning regularly. The compound leaves are up to 7 inches across and dark green. Several cultivars exist, including some with yellow variegation or notched leaves, such as 'Gold Capella', which has creamy yellow leaflets surrounded by green margins, and 'Trinette', which has more irregular gold variegation. This species is easy to root from stem cuttings.
- ***S. elegantissima*** is far better known by its old name, *Dizygotheca elegantissima*. Even its

False aralia *(S. elegantissima)*

Dwarf schefflera *(S. arboricola)*

common name reflects no link with the schefflera clan: It's called false aralia. In its youth, it doesn't look at all like a schefflera, with thin, dark brownish green leaves with lighter veins that spread into nine fingers with saw-toothed edges. However, at maturity it changes its appearance completely and produces bigger leaves with broad, medium-green leaflets that better show its schefflera nature. Like the common schefflera, this species is difficult to propagate from cuttings but air layering works well.

Several cultivars of false aralia are available, such as 'Galaxy', with broader and less numerous segments than the species, and 'Galaxy Variegated', which has similar leaves edged in cream.

Repotting: Infrequently.
Propagation: By air layering, seed, or stem cuttings (use rooting hormone).
Problems: Low light causes spindly growth. Overwatering leads to root rot or leaf loss. Leaves may also drop if the air is too dry. Spider mites, thrips, mealybugs, and scale insects are possible pests.
Tips: Remove yellow leaves promptly. Prune as needed to maintain the size and shape you desire.

Selaginella
seh-laj-ih-NEL-luh

Moss-fern, spike-moss, sweat-plant, spreading club-moss

- **Light:** Medium to bright
- **Water:** Keep evenly moist
- **Humidity:** High to very high
- **Temperature:** Average, keep plants out of cold drafts
- **Fertilizer:** All-purpose, not a heavy feeder
- **Size:** 2-6"H×4-8"W

Trailing spike-moss thrives in high humidity and moist conditions.

This group of primitive, mosslike plants related to ferns are popular terrarium plants.

Bright green trailing spike-moss (*S. kraussiana*) is the most popular species. It forms spreading mats of trailing stems with feathery foliage. Its cultivar 'Aurea' is similar, but is chartreuse green. Tiny 'Brownii' forms a dense cushion of green only 2 inches tall but to 6 inches wide.

The most unusual species is the so-called resurrection fern (*S. lepidophylla*). It is usually sold as a rolled-up ball of apparently dead foliage. Soak it in water, though, and the ball unfurls to reveal a flattened rosette of green, scale-covered stems.
Repotting: As needed.
Propagation: Stem cuttings or division (most self-layer).
Problems: Dry air causes leaf dieback and browning.
Tips: Trim any overgrown sections.

Senecio macroglossus 'Variegatus'
seh-NEE-see-o mak-ro-GLOS-us

Cape ivy, wax vine

- **Light:** Medium to bright
- **Water:** Allow to dry between waterings
- **Humidity:** Medium
- **Temperature:** Average
- **Fertilizer:** High phosphorus in winter and spring, all-purpose in summer and fall
- **Size:** 1'H×1'W

Like most plants that store water in stems or leaves, wax vine thrives on benign neglect. The key to maintaining this unusual vining plant is simply to let it dry out between waterings. Also called Cape ivy for its origins in South Africa, the leaves look like fat and waxy soaps in the shape of ivy foliage. The thick, olive green wedges have creamy edges and an intriguing, almost holographic, dusty patina. In a bright sunny window, cheerful yellow daisylike blooms appear in surreal contrast to the dense foliage. Leave plenty of space around natal ivy for good air circulation and to avoid breaking its sometimes brittle trailing stems.
Repotting: Only when pot-bound.
Propagation: Stem cuttings.
Problems: None significant.
Tips: Maintain healthy new growth by clipping several inches off each stem twice a year.

Variegated natal ivy combines vining foliage with daisylike flowers.

Serissa foetida
suh-RIS-uh FET-ih-duh

Serissa, snow-rose

- **Light:** Bright to intense
- **Water:** Keep evenly moist
- **Humidity:** Average
- **Temperature:** Cold to average, avoid cold drafts
- **Fertilizer:** All-purpose
- **Size:** 10-24"H×10-30"W

Often grown as bonsai, serissa also makes a good small shrub indoors.

Serissa makes an attractive miniature tree or shrub, rarely reaching over 2 feet tall and easily maintained at half that.

The tiny leathery leaves are elliptic and dark green, sometimes variegated with cream or yellow. The flowers, barely ¼ inch and borne most heavily in spring and summer, can be pink or white and single or double, depending on the cultivar. Plants with green leaves tend to flower more heavily than those with variegated leaves.

Popular cultivars include 'Flore Pleno', with smaller, fully double white flowers, and 'Variegated Pink', with cream-edged green leaves and pink flowers.
Repotting: Annually in late winter or early spring.
Propagation: Stem cuttings or air layering.
Problems: Spider mites and scale insects are possible pests.
Tips: Serissa can be pruned into topiary or bonsai forms.

Sinningia
sih-NING-gee-uh
Sinningia, gloxinia

- **Light:** Bright, miniatures tolerate medium, no light needed during dormancy
- **Water:** Keep evenly moist, withhold water to induce dormancy
- **Humidity:** Average to high, very high for microminiatures
- **Temperature:** Average, cool during dormancy
- **Fertilizer:** High in phosphorus
- **Size:** 1-24"H×1-12"W

Florist's gloxinia *(Sinningia speciosa)* blooms repeatedly before dormancy.

Sinningias usually have hairy, elliptical leaves and tubular or bell-shape flowers, but their tubers help distinguish them from other gesneriads, most of which have fibrous roots or rhizomes.

Miniature sinningias have short-stemmed rosettes rarely more than 8 inches in diameter and often less than 2 inches. The flowers come in purple, pink, red, salmon, white, and bicolors. The plants produce new shoots even before the previous ones have faded. *S. pusilla* is a 1- by 1-inch microminiature that produces tiny tubular lilac flowers with white throats throughout the year and rarely goes dormant. Miniatures tolerate medium light and do best on a humidity tray (see page 20). Microminiatures

need very high humidity and are best grown in a terrarium.

Cardinal flower *(S. cardinalis)* is an upright grower that produces one or more stems of bright green hairy leaves from a large woody tuber that is usually left partly exposed. The plant grows 12 to 24 inches tall and 12 inches wide. It produces brilliant red or white tubular flowers over a long period, usually in fall or winter.

Brazilian edelweiss *(S. canescens)* grows to 12 inches tall and wide. The stem and the leaves are covered with silvery white hairs. Tubular red flowers are so covered with silvery hairs that they appear pink. When the leaves dry up, stop watering and store the plant dry until new growth appears.

Florist's gloxinia *(S. speciosa)* is commonly sold in full bloom as a gift plant, about 12 inches tall and wide. To grow well and last for many years, it needs humidity and bright light. If fading foliage is removed, it can bloom three or four times in succession before requiring dormancy.

Repotting: After dormancy, when growth resumes.
Propagation: Seed or leaf or stem cuttings.
Problems: Flower buds fail to open when the air is too dry. Cyclamen mites, thrips, aphids, whiteflies, and mealybugs are possible pests.
Tips: Remove faded blooms after flowers die back.

Brazilian edelweiss is so covered with hairs that the whole plant looks silver.

Solanum pseudocapsicum
so-LAY-num soo-doh-KAP-si-kum
Jerusalem cherry

- **Light:** Bright to intense
- **Water:** Keep evenly moist
- **Humidity:** High
- **Temperature:** Average
- **Fertilizer:** All-purpose
- **Size:** 12-18"H×12-18"W

Move Jerusalem cherry outdoors in summer to encourage pollination.

Often confused with ornamental pepper *(Capsicum annuum)*, Jerusalem cherry derives its common name from its round, orange-red fruits that usually mature in December and continue through much of the winter. It's an erect, bushy evergreen shrub with small white flowers.

The plant is usually treated as an annual and discarded after blooming but can be kept from year to year if trimmed back harshly and kept in bright light.
Repotting: As needed.
Propagation: Seed.
Problems: Overwatering leads to stem rot. Flowers must be pollinated to set fruit. Spider mites, whiteflies, aphids, and mealybugs are possible pests.
Tips: Pollinate blooms indoors by gently shaking the plant daily when it is in flower. Be careful not to remove flower buds when pruning. Fruits and leaves are somewhat toxic; keep the plant away from children and pets.

Soleirolia soleirolii
so-leh-ROL-ee-uh so-leh-ROL-ee-eye
Baby's tears

- ◼ **Light:** Medium to bright
- ◼ **Water:** Keep moist at all times, can stand in water
- ◼ **Humidity:** High to very high
- ◼ **Temperature:** Cold to cool, tolerates average
- ◼ **Fertilizer:** All-purpose
- ◼ **Size:** 2"H×indefinite width

Keep baby's tears moist at all times, even letting it sit in water.

Baby's tears is a tiny creeping groundcover with thin stems and tiny round leaves. It can spread indefinitely as long as it finds open moist soil, rooting as it grows.

It makes a good terrarium plant because it thrives in high humidity but it is highly invasive and requires pruning every few weeks or so. The species also makes an interesting trailing plant for a small hanging basket; its stems cascade beautifully over the edges of a pot.

The green form is most common, but you'll also find 'Aurea', with golden green leaves, and 'Variegata', with silver variegated leaves.
Repotting: In any season.
Propagation: Division or stem cuttings.
Problems: Aphids are possible pests.
Tips: Keep the pot in a saucer of water to ensure constant moisture.

Solenostemon scutellarioides
so-len-AH-steh-muhn skoo-tel-air-ee-OY-deez
Coleus

- ◼ **Light:** Bright to intense
- ◼ **Water:** Keep evenly moist
- ◼ **Humidity:** Average
- ◼ **Temperature:** Average
- ◼ **Fertilizer:** All-purpose
- ◼ **Size:** 10-36"H×10-36"W

Coleus is a fast-growing, tropical shrub with square stems that are usually upright but sometimes creeping or trailing. Old-fashioned cultivars tended to produce a single stem unless pinched regularly, but most modern selections are self-branching.

To train a coleus as an indoor tree, pinch out side branches until it reaches the desired "trunk" height, then pinch the upper stems to encourage masses of foliage-covered stems at the top of the trunk. Make sure you stake it, as the stem can be fragile.

The velvety, oval, scalloped leaves come in a multitude of colors, with toothed or fringed margins, depending on the variety. Prune out the narrow flower spikes when they appear.
Repotting: Annually, in any season.
Propagation: Stem cuttings or seed (not all varieties grow true).
Problems: The plant declines in beauty and vigor after blooming. Whiteflies, mealybugs, and scale insects are possible pests.
Tips: Prune at any season.

Thousands of cultivars of coleus are available in an array of colors.

Spathiphyllum wallisii
spath-ih-FYL-um wah-LIS-ee-eye
Peace lily

- ◼ **Light:** Medium to bright, survives in low but probably won't bloom
- ◼ **Water:** Keep very moist during growth and bloom, let dry slightly between waterings at other times
- ◼ **Humidity:** Average
- ◼ **Temperature:** Average to high, avoid cold drafts
- ◼ **Fertilizer:** All-purpose, not a heavy feeder
- ◼ **Size:** 6-48"H×6-48"W

Peace lily blooms in medium light throughout the year.

Peace lily gets its common name from its distinctive flower. A pure white bract (spathe) forms a softly curved backdrop for the central column (spadix) of tiny, closely set true flowers. The blooms are often scented but sometimes only at night.

Broad but pointed to lance-shaped leaves on arching stems form a rosette around the flower. With time, a single plant slowly produces offsets, creating an attractive full pot of foliage.
Repotting: Infrequently.
Propagation: Offsets.
Problems: Spider mites, whiteflies, mealybugs, and scale insects are possible pests.
Tips: Pot multiple stems for a fuller effect. Remove yellowed leaves. Wash the foliage occasionally.

Streptocarpus ×hybridus
strep-to-KAR-pus HY-brid-us
Cape primrose

- **Light:** Bright
- **Water:** Keep evenly moist during growth and bloom; let dry between waterings at other times
- **Humidity:** High
- **Temperature:** Average, but cool in winter
- **Fertilizer:** All-purpose
- **Size:** 8-14"H×10-30"W

Cape primrose is a close relative of African violet.

Cape primrose produces arching flower stalks directly from the stemless narrow leaves, which grow to 12 inches long. Colorful flowers bloom in white, pink, red, violet, or blue, often with contrasting veins and a yellow throat. Plants sold as *Streptocarpella* produce arching stems of small, thick leaves. Pale lavender to deep purple flowers are small but numerous, especially during the summer months.
Repotting: As needed.
Propagation: Cape primrose by division, seed, leaf or leaf section cuttings; *Streptocarpella* by division, seed, or stem cuttings.
Problems: Aphids, thrips, and mealybugs are possible pests.
Tips: Remove yellowed leaves and trim back those with brown tips. Remove flower stalks after blooming. If the leaves go limp but the potting mix is still moist, move the plant to a dry shady spot until it has recovered.

Strobilanthes dyerianus
stro-bih-LANTH-eez dye-er-ee-AN-us
Persian shield

- **Light:** Bright
- **Water:** Let dry slightly between waterings
- **Humidity:** High
- **Temperature:** Average
- **Fertilizer:** All-purpose, not a heavy feeder
- **Size:** 1-4'H×1-3'W

The narrow, lance-shape, quilted leaves of Persian shield are heavily marbled with rich purple and highlighted with iridescent silvery pink markings above and deep wine-red below.

Persian shield is a fast-growing shrub; it may need pinching or pruning to prevent lankiness. Leaves are less colorful in early autumn, a sign that the plant is mature. It produces long-lasting, funnel-shape pale blue flowers just before it goes into decline. To prevent this, pinch off the flower buds before they open.
Repotting: As needed.
Propagation: Stem cuttings.
Problems: Dry air causes leaf dieback. Spider mites are possible pests.
Tips: When older specimens become weak, start over with fresh cuttings.

The foliage of Persian shield glistens with purple and silver tones.

Stromanthe sanguinea 'Triostar'
stro-MAN-thuh san-GWIN-ee-uh
Stromanthe

- **Light:** Medium
- **Water:** Keep evenly moist
- **Humidity:** Average to high
- **Temperature:** Medium, protect from strong fluctuations
- **Fertilizer:** All-purpose
- **Size:** 8-12"H×8-24"W

The unusual shape and color of 'Triostar' leaves stand out.

Deep colors and natural animation give this plant a special appeal for the indoor garden. Like its relative, prayer plant (*Maranta*), 'Triostar' folds its leaves at night to reveal rosy pink undersides. Amusing to see, this habit evolved to befuddle insects. But the daytime view is grand too. Each leaf is rich emerald green, stroked with warm white, spaced 1 to 2 inches apart on dark green stems rising from a tight clump that fans out just above the soil surface. Mature plants may send up stalks of white panicles with orange-red sepals and red bracts. 'Triostar' is not the easiest plant to grow, but well worth your efforts.
Repotting: When the pot is crowded.
Propagation: Division.
Problems: Dry plants invite insect infestations, particularly mealybugs. Overwatering causes stems and leaves to collapse or become diseased.
Tips: Direct sun scalds leaves.

Succulents

- Light: Bright to intense
- Water: Let dry slightly between waterings
- Humidity: Average
- Temperature: Average to high, but cold to cool in winter
- Fertilizer: All-purpose
- Size: 3-96"H×3-60"W

Burro's tail *(Sedum morganianum)* and rosary vine *(Ceropegia woodii)*

Succulents store water in their stems, leaves, or thick roots in order to thrive in arid climates. They also have evolved into unique and wonderful shapes, colors, and textures.

Succulents are generally easy to care for. They need a porous, fast-draining soil, plenty of sunlight and water, and good air circulation. During the winter, growth slows and they prefer a cool, dry environment. Many succulents need this rest time in order to bloom the following season. In summer revitalize the plants by moving them outdoors. See page 45 for more information on succulents.

■ *Adenium* takes rather strange forms, each one creating its own sculptural design. The fleshy stem varies from gray to pale brown; the leaves are a shiny green but not produced in abundance. They generally drop off during dormancy. The flowers are brilliant red to pink with pale centers and appear in clusters at the branch tips during summer. Desert-rose (*A. obesum*) is a popular species with pink flowers.

■ *Adromischus*—called pretty-pebbles, sea-shells, plover-eggs, leopard's-spots, and crinkleleaf,

among other common names—are stout-stemmed succulents that grow in clumps and look best in a shallow, broad container. Many have crinkled or egg-shaped leaves with speckles or spots. The plants grow in indirect light but develop better leaf color in bright light.

■ **Pinwheel plants** *(Aeonium)* produce rosettes, some on tall stems, others hugging the ground. The spoon-shaped leaves vary from apple green to a deep maroon-tinged red. The flowers are usually small and yellow and bloom in profusion. The stems die after blooming.

■ **Agave** or century plant is a large plant with thick, pointed leaves. Several of the smaller types, such as painted century plant (*A. victoriae-reginae*), are particularly suitable for indoor gardening, although *A. americana* and its variegated cultivars are also popular indoor plants, despite their large size. After a plant matures it may produce a tall flower spike but will die after producing seed. Offsets produced at the base of the plant continue to grow.

■ **Aloe** is another genus of great diversity, but all species produce rosettes of spiny leaves. *A. vera* (also known as *A. barbadensis*) is the best known. It is commonly called medicine-plant or burn aloe, since it is most widely known for the healing properties of its sap.

■ **Rosary vine** *(Ceropegia)*, also called hearts-entangled, produces long purple runners with tiny heart-shaped leaves. The leaves, borne in pairs at regular intervals along the vine, are patterned with silver on top and purple beneath.

■ **Silver-crown** *(Cotyledon)* is a large and diverse genus. The plants are shrubby, and their mature size ranges from a few inches to several feet. Most species have persistent succulent leaves in varying colors from yellow-green to blue-gray and bell-shape yellow to red flowers on long stems held above the leaves during spring and summer.

Crown-of-thorns *(Euphorbia milii)* and jade plant *(Crassula ovata)*

■ **Jade plant** *(Crassula)* species are characterized by unusual and varied leaf forms, arrangements, and colors. Most types are easy to grow. Common names include airplane-plant, baby jade, moss crassula, rattail crassula, rattlesnake, scarlet-paintbrush, and silver jade plant.

■ *Echeveria* species, also called hen and chicks, all have in common a rosette form. Their greatly varied leaf color ranges from pale green through deep purple. The plants can be smooth-leaf or hairy and have stemless rosettes, or the rosettes can grow on a stalk.

■ *Euphorbia* is a diverse genus. Common names include African milk bush, corkscrew, cow's-horn, crown-of-thorns, and living-baseball. All species have a toxic or at least irritating milky sap.

■ **Mother-of-pearl plant** *(Graptopetalum)* bears rosettes of thick leaves on long stems. The

Silver squill *(Ledebouria socialis)* and variegated devil's backbone *(Pedilanthes tithymaloides)*

foliage is a luminous white with pink-purple tones. Mature rosettes measure approximately 3 inches across. The bell-shape flowers

(continued)

Succulents *(continued)*

Grow string-of-beads *(Senecio rowleyanthus)* in a hanging basket.

are straw color with maroon markings. Plants are easy to grow and especially suited for growing in hanging baskets.

■ *Haworthia* comes in many forms, and all are excellent indoors. Although they grow in moderate light, bright indirect light improves their foliage color and texture. The leaves of most species are thick and form rosettes on stemless plants. They flower at different times, depending on the species. The flowers are small and borne in clusters on long stems. After flowering, the plants may go dormant and will need repotting.

■ *Kalanchoe* is a popular genus grown for both its colorful flowers and succulent foliage. Christmas kalanchoe *(K. blossfeldiana)* produces heads of brilliant scarlet, orange, or yellow flowers on thin stems 15 inches tall. Its shiny, oval green leaves are tinged with red. It blooms only if it receives short days (nights exceeding 14 hours) in winter. Panda plant *(K. tomentosa)* grows to 15 inches tall and has plump leaves branching from a central stem. The pointed leaves are covered with silvery hairs and tipped with rusty brown bumps. *K. daigremontiana,* like some other species, has plantlets on its leaves.

■ Silver squill *(Ledebouria socialis),* usually sold under its old name,

Scilla violacea, is a small plant ideally suited for windowsills. Its fleshy, pointed olive green leaves are splotched silvery gray, with wine red undersides. The leaves are 2 to 4 inches long. The purple bulb grows above the soil. The plant produces clusters of tiny green flowers in spring.

■ Living stones *(Conophytum, Dinteranthus, Fenestraria, Lapidaria, Lithops, Pleiospilos,* and others) are perhaps the most interesting of all succulents. As the name implies, these plants resemble small rocks. Because their cultural needs can be complex, living stones are recommended only for advanced gardeners. They need minimal watering during their nonflowering periods, which for some occur in summer months. They are usually best propagated from seed.

■ *Pachyphytum,* known as thick-plant, has fat, rounded leaves that form rosettes on long stems. Leaf color varies from a dusty gray-pink to a bluish gray. Rosettes can be up to 8 inches across, depending on the species. Small bell-shaped flowers range from white to orange to red or pink. The plants need plenty of bright, but not too hot, light to bring out their leaf color. They are a good choice for hanging baskets.

■ Madagascar palm *(Pachypodium)* includes plants that are shrubby and ones that are columnar and covered with thorns. Most species have long, thick, leathery dark green foliage. The flowers range from white to yellow to red. The star-shaped blooms are borne at the tips

Kalanchoe tomentosa and *Aeonium arboreum*

Carrion-flower *(Stapelia gigantea)* may have foul-smelling blooms.

of the branches in spring. The plants go through a leafless winter dormancy, during which water should be withheld.

■ Variegated devil's backbone *(Pedilanthes tithymaloides 'Variegatus')* gets its name from its fleshy gray-green stems that zigzag upward. They bear waxy, pale green leaves that are beautifully variegated and edged white with a carmine red tinge. The spurred, bracted inflorescences are red and look like birds' heads.

■ Elephant-bush *(Portulacaria)* is a shrub with a reddish brown trunk and stems and small green leaves. This plant is easy to grow. The attractive stems and shrubby habit make it ideal for bonsai.

■ *Sedum* is another varied genus that includes easy-to-grow indoor species. Donkey's tail, or burro's-tail *(S. morganianum),* is a trailing, slow-growing succulent. Its light gray to blue-green leaves are ½ to 1 inch long, oval, and plump. The 3- to 4-foot trailing stems, densely covered with leaves, create a braid or rope effect. This plant is ideal for hanging containers.

■ *Senecio* is a large and widely varied genus that includes small succulents, hanging or climbing vines, and large shrubs. The stems of all the succulent species are spineless, supporting leaves that are spherical and thick, or flat

Combine succulents to make an attractive dish garden.

and elongated. The flowers are daisylike but not as interesting as the foliage. String-of-beads plant (*S. rowleyanus*) has ropelike hanging stems that bear unusual, ½-inch, spherical leaves. The leaves look like light green beads with pointed tips and a single translucent band across them.

■ **Carrion-flowers** (*Stapelia*) have leafless green stems and large star-shaped flowers that are notable for their lurid colors, odor of rotting meat, and size. The flowers are generally in shades of yellow or red with maroon spotting and are borne along the stems in late summer and fall.

Repotting: Annually for young plants. Mature plants do better when pot-bound. Use a shallow pot and a very porous soil mix (see page 22).

Propagation: Stem cuttings, offsets, or leaf cuttings (some species).

Problems: Overwatering leads to root rot. Stem and leaf rot are caused by cool, damp air. Leaves wilt and discolor from too much water, especially in winter. Underwatering causes brown, dry spots. Mealybugs and scale insects are possible pests.

Tips: Cut off flower stalks as the blooms age. Keep plants warm in summer but cool in winter.

Syngonium podophyllum
sin-GO-nee-um po-do-FYL-um
Arrowhead vine

■ **Light: Medium to bright, can tolerate low but won't thrive**
■ **Water: Keep evenly moist**
■ **Humidity: Average**
■ **Temperature: Average, keep out of cold drafts**
■ **Fertilizer: All-purpose**
■ **Size: 6-96"H×6-48"W**

Arrowhead vine is unusual because of a change that occurs as the plant ages. Young plants are stemless and compact, producing arrow-shaped leaves at the ends of erect stalks. They are usually dark green and may have bold silvery white variegation. With age the leaves become lobed and the stems begin to climb. Eventually the variegation disappears, and each leaf fans into many leaflets.

To retain the juvenile leaf form and variegation, prune back the climbing stems as they appear. New growth will appear at the plant's base having the compact habit and arrow-shaped leaves of young plants. Older climbing stems require support.

Popular cultivars include 'Emerald Gem', with green leaves attractively quilted; 'White Butterfly', with a white overlay on a green background; and 'Pink Allusion', with attractive metallic pink highlights.

Repotting: As needed.

Propagation: Stem cuttings.

Problems: Spider mites, aphids, mealybugs, and scale insects are possible pests.

Tips: The plant is toxic; keep it away from children and pets.

Arrowhead vine (left) and 'Pink Allusion' (right)

Tolmeia menziesii
tol-MEE-uh men-ZEES-ee-eye
Piggyback plant

■ **Light: Bright**
■ **Water: Keep evenly moist**
■ **Humidity: High**
■ **Temperature: Cool, but cold in winter**
■ **Fertilizer: All-purpose**
■ **Repotting: Annually in any season**
■ **Size: 1-2'H×1-3'W**

Piggyback plant readily produces new plants to replace fading ones.

Piggyback plant is popular with indoor gardeners because of its plantlets, which sprout on top of the foliage, causing the leaves to arch downward. The trailing leaves quickly produce a large plant suitable for a hanging basket or a plant pedestal.

The plant forms a clump of hairy, lobed, medium-green foliage that looks much like maple leaves. Upright, open stalks of tiny brownish flowers follow, but they are of little ornamental value and are usually cut off.

A variegated form, 'Taff's Gold' (*T. menziesii* 'Maculata'), has paler green leaves mottled with cream and pale yellow.

Repotting: As needed.

Propagation: Offsets or soil layering.

Problems: Spider mites and mealybugs are possible pests.

Tips: Older plants do not age gracefully, so start new ones from plantlets every year or two.

Tradescantia
trad-es-KANT-shee-uh

Spiderwort, inch plant, wandering Jew

- **Light: Bright**
- **Water: Keep evenly moist**
- **Humidity: Average to high**
- **Temperature: Average**
- **Fertilizer: All-purpose, not heavy feeders**
- **Size: 8-16"H×10-36"W (trailing)**

The trailing stems of 'Albovitata' are best displayed in a hanging basket.

Typically spiderworts have boat-shaped leaves of varying lengths borne alternately along trailing stems. All of them have small seasonal blooms, but most are grown strictly for their colorful or variegated foliage. They are used as groundcovers, in hanging baskets, or as trailing plants on shelves. They are renowned for their ease of care; in fact, many are pass-along plants that have been shared among family and friends for generations.

■ **Flowering inch plant** (*Tradescantia cerinthoides,* syn. *T. blossfeldiana*) has larger leaves than most spiderworts, to 6 inches long, green and hairless above and purple with fuzzy white hairs below. It produces white flowers intermittently throughout the year. 'Variegata' has creamy stripes and is purplish below.

■ **Striped inch plant**, or wandering Jew (*T. fluminensis*), is a trailing plant with variegated light green over purple leaves. It occasionally produces white flowers. Silver wandering Jew (*T. pendula,* now *T. zebrina*) is a long-popular trailing plant with shiny green leaves with broad, iridescent silver bands and purple undersides.

■ **White velvet** (*T. sillamontana*) is one of the hairiest spiderworts. Its green leaves are densely covered in woolly white hair. It has shorter, more densely covered stems than most others in its group and tends to grow upright at first but does become trailing. The magenta flowers are spectacular in summer.

■ **Boat-lily** and Moses-in-the-cradle, the common names for *T. spathacea,* come from the odd way it bears flowers. At the base of the terminal leaves on the shoots, small white blooms appear within cupped bracts like a small boat or a swaddled baby.

■ **Striped inch-plant** (*Callisia elegans,* syn. *Setcreasea elegans*) is very similar to *Tradescantia* and shares the same common name. The leaves are olive green with white lengthwise stripes, purple underneath, and silky to the touch. The flowers are white and appear in clusters at the stem ends in winter.

■ **Teddy-bear plant** (*Cyanotis kewensis*) is a smaller creeper

Silver wandering Jew

with a fleshy brown stem and triangular, somewhat succulent leaves that are olive green above and reddish below. It is entirely covered with fuzzy brown hair. It may produce pink-purple flowers in summer.

■ **Seersucker plant** (*Geogenanthus poeppigii*) is a prostrate plant that creeps but doesn't trail. The plant's main attraction is the beautiful quilting of the leaves.

Boat-lily

■ **Tahitian bridal veil** (*Gibasis geniculata*) is a hanging plant with small, pointed leaves—green above, purple below—borne opposite each other along trailing stems. Given enough light, the plant bears a profusion of tiny delicate white flowers on thin stalks above the foliage.

■ **Brown spiderwort** or bear ears (*Siderasis fuscata*) forms clustering rosettes of broad, oblong, olive green leaves with a silvery central band and a purple underside. The whole plant is covered with coppery brown hairs. It bears large, lavender-blue flowers in clusters from the center of the plant. Because it produces no visible stems, it is multiplied only by division.

Repotting: As needed.

Propagation: Stem cuttings.

Problems: Variegated leaves sometimes revert to an all-green form; remove these. Spider mites and aphids are possible pests.

Tips: Cut back overly long stems to stimulate regrowth from the base. Remove dried leaves.

Yucca elephantipes
YUK-ka el-eh-fan-TIP-eez
Spineless yucca

- **Light: Medium to bright light**
- **Water: Let dry between waterings**
- **Humidity: Average to high**
- **Temperature: Average**
- **Fertilizer: All-purpose, year- round until mature**
- **Size: 1-10'H×1-2'W**

Spineless yucca is a softer relative of the popular outdoor plant.

Spineless yucca's bold form deserves a nightlight to cast its strong silhouette on your wall. Its narrow green leaves are a foot long and clustered in sharply pointed crowns along and on top of distinctive brown-gray trunks.

The plant is soft-tipped and lush compared to the desert yuccas, with more and larger leaves on a faster-growing plant. Mature and juvenile forms are both excellent houseplants: one to three trunks 3 feet to 5 feet tall with several crowns and plenty of trunk exposed, or a 6-inch pot with one crown of leaves. Offsets called pups soon form at the soil surface and, when removed, create a palmlike effect with a tuft of foliage at the tip of a trunk.
Repotting: Annually until mature.
Propagation: Offsets.
Problems: The plant tolerates dry conditions but not drought.
Tips: Root-prune and repot in original pot to control size.

Zamioculcas zamiifolia
zam-ee-o-KUL-kas zam-ee-ih-FO-lee-uh
Aroid palm, aroid fern, zeezee plant

- **Light: Medium to bright, tolerates low for long periods**
- **Water: Let dry slightly between waterings, tolerates long periods of drought**
- **Humidity: Average**
- **Temperature: Average**
- **Fertilizer: All-purpose, not a heavy feeder**
- **Size: 1-4'H×1-4'W**

Aroid palm forms a rosette of thick, fleshy leafstalks that radiate upward and outward. They bear glossy, elliptic leaflets in a feather shape, creating the effect of a palm leaf. The whole plant is dark green. With time, it produces offsets and fills its pot with foliage.

The plant can go for long periods without any water at all, eventually losing its leaflets. Eventually the leafstalks will dry out too, but not before producing small tubers along their length, where the leaflets used to be.
Repotting: As needed.
Propagation: Division (suckers) or bulblets from leaves.
Problems: Mealybugs and scale insects are possible pests.
Tips: Purchase a large enough specimen for your current indoor needs. The plant is toxic, so keep it away from children and pets.

Aroid palm tolerates average home conditions and even some neglect.

Zantedeschia
zan-teh-DEE-shee-uh
Calla lily

- **Light: Bright**
- **Water: Keep continuously moist**
- **Humidity: High**
- **Temperature: Average, but cold to cool during dormancy**
- **Fertilizer: All-purpose**
- **Size: 12-36"H×6-24"W**

Hybrid calla lilies are a colorful change from the original white.

The elegant flower of the calla lily, actually a colored leaf called a spathe that curls around a fragrant yellow column of true flowers, needs no introduction. Besides being a popular cut flower, calla lily is a good houseplant.

The best-known calla lily is the largest: *Z. aethiopica*. It bears creamy white spathes, 5 to 10 inches long, on top of wide, glossy, arrow- or heart-shaped leaves. It can reach 3 feet or more in height when in flower. Smaller hybrid callas in shades of white, pink, yellow, orange, and red are increasingly popular.

When blooms fade, reduce watering. During dormancy, keep the rhizome nearly dry, watering it only enough to keep it from shriveling.
Repotting: At the end of dormancy.
Propagation: Division (rhizomes).
Problems: Spider mites are possible pests in dry air.
Tips: Pick off yellowed leaves and cut faded flower stalks.

RESOURCES

Please call greenhouses and nurseries before planning a visit; some are open by appointment only and many are not open to the public every day of the week.

Plants and seeds

Epie Acres
247 Wilson Ave.
Placentia, CA 92870 USA
714/524-0994
www.epies.net
Epiphyllum plants

Florida Plants Online
www.floridaplants.com/interior.htm
Tropical plants and supplies

Glasshouse Works
Church St. P.O. Box 97
Stewart, OH 45778 USA
800/837-2142 (orders only)
740/662-2142
www.glasshouseworks.com
Tropical and rare plants

Kartuz Greenhouses
Sunset Island Exotics
1408 Sunset Dr.
Vista, CA 92081 USA
760/941-3613
www.kartuz.com
Gesneriads, begonias, flowering tropicals, subtropicals, vines

Lauray of Salisbury
432 Undermountain Rd., Rte. 41
Salisbury, CT 06068 USA
860/435-2263
www.lauray.com
Cacti, orchids, begonias, gesneriads, succulents

Logee's Greenhouses, Ltd.
141 North St.
Danielson, CT 06239 USA
888/330-8038
www.logees.com
Tropical and subtropical plants

Lyndon Lyon Greenhouses, Inc.
P.O. Box 249
14 Mutchler St.
Dolgeville, NY 13329 USA
315/429-8291
www.lyndonlyon.com
African violets, orchids, gesneriads, and rare tropical plants

New Leaf Nurseries
2456 Foothill Dr.
Vista, CA 92084 USA
760/726-9269
www.newleafnurseries.com
Pelargonium and coleus plants

Oak Hill Gardens
P.O. Box 25
37W550 Binnie Rd.
Dundee, IL 60118 USA
847/428-8500
www.oakhillgardens.com
Orchids and supplies

P & J Greenhouses
20265 82nd Ave.
Langley, BC V2Y 2A9 Canada
604/888-3274
www.geranium-greenhouses.com
Geraniums

Plant Delights Nursery, Inc.
9241 Sauls Road
Raleigh, NC 27603 USA
919/772-4794
www.plantdelights.com
Flowering maples, sedums, and rare plants

Rhapis Gardens
P.O. Box 287
Gregory, TX 78359 USA
361/643-2061
www.rhapisgardens.com
Rhapis palms, sago palms, aralias

Russell's Bromeliads
1690 Beardall Ave.
Sanford, FL 32771 USA
407/322-0864
www.russellsairplants.com
Tillandsias and other bromeliads

Stokes Tropicals
4806 E. Old Spanish Trail
Jeanerette, LA 70544 USA
866/478-2502
www.stokestropicals.com
Bananas, cannas, gingers, and other tropicals

William Dam Seeds
279 Hwy #8 West Flamborough
Box 8400
Dundas, ON L9H 6M1 Canada
905/628-6641
www.damseeds.com
Herb seeds and plants

Supplies

Eco Enterprises
1240 N.E. 175th St., Suite B
Shoreline, WA 98155 USA
800/426-6937
www.ecogrow.com
Growing and lighting supplies

Charley's Greenhouse & Garden
17979 State Rte. 536
Mount Vernon, WA 98273 USA
800/322-4707
www.charleysgreenhouse.com
Greenhouses and growing supplies

Digital Raingardens
5922 Shadow Wood Dr.
Corpus Christi, TX 78415 USA
361/852-5063
www.raingardens.com
Palm and other houseplant seeds

Gardener's Supply Company
128 Intervale Rd.
Burlington, VT 05401 USA
888/833-1412
www.gardeners.com
Seed-starting supplies, organic fertilizers and pest controls, hand tools, watering systems

Hydrofarm
2299 Pine View Way
Petaluma, CA 94954 USA
800/634-9990
www.hydrofarm.com
Hydroponic growing supplies, lighting supplies

Indoor Gardening Supplies
P.O. Box 527
Dexter, MI 48130 USA
800/823-5740
www.indoorgardensupplies.com
Growing and lighting supplies

The Scotts Company
888/270-3714
www.scotts.com
www.ortho.com
www.miracle-gro.com
Fertilizers, mulches, pest controls

Windowbox.com
3821 S. Santa Fe Ave.
Vernon, CA 90058 USA
888/427-3362
www.windowbox.com
Container gardening supplies

INDEX

Note: Page references in bold type refer to Gallery entries and include photographs. Page references in italic type refer to additional photographs. Plants are listed by their common names unless none is given.

METRIC CONVERSIONS

U.S. UNITS TO METRIC EQUIVALENTS			METRIC EQUIVALENTS TO U.S. UNITS		
To Convert From	Multiply by	To Get	To Convert From	Multiply by	To Get
Inches	25.4	Millimeters	Millimeters	0.0394	Inches
Inches	2.54	Centimeters	Centimeters	0.3937	Inches
Feet	30.48	Centimeters	Centimeters	0.0328	Feet
Feet	0.3048	Meters	Meters	3.2808	Feet
Yards	0.9144	Meters	Meters	1.0936	Yards
Square inches	6.4516	Square centimeters	Square centimeters	0.1550	Square inches
Square feet	0.0929	Square meters	Square meters	10.764	Square feet
Square yards	0.8361	Square meters	Square meters	1.1960	Square yards
Acres	0.4047	Hectares	Hectares	2.4711	Acres
Cubic inches	16.387	Cubic centimeters	Cubic centimeters	0.0610	Cubic inches
Cubic feet	0.0283	Cubic meters	Cubic meters	35.315	Cubic feet
Cubic feet	28.316	Liters	Liters	0.0353	Cubic feet
Cubic yards	0.7646	Cubic meters	Cubic meters	1.308	Cubic yards
Cubic yards	764.55	Liters	Liters	0.0013	Cubic yards

To convert from degrees Fahrenheit (F) to degrees Celsius (C), first subtract 32, then multiply by ⁵⁄₉.

To convert from degrees Celsius to degrees Fahrenheit, multiply by ⁹⁄₅, then add 32.

Complete Guide to Vegetables, Fruits & Herbs
ORTHO BOOKS
PLANNING ■ PLANTING ■ GROWING

ORTHO'S All About Bonsai
ORTHO BOOKS
■ Step-by-step growing and training techniques
■ Learn how to choose bonsai styles and tools
■ Comprehensive guide to plant selection

ORTHO'S All About Orchids
ORTHO BOOKS
■ Complete orchid growing information
■ Tips on selecting easy-care orchids
■ Instructions for breeding new orchid varieties

ORTHO ALL ABOUT Perennials
All NEW Edition

ORTHO ALL ABOUT Roses
All NEW Edition
AMERICAN ROSE SOCIETY ENDORSED

Get dramatic results

Purchase these exciting titles from the brands you trust for gardening expertise—wherever books are sold.

Ortho® ALL ABOUT
HOUSEPLANTS

Bring living beauty to your home with houseplants. *All About Houseplants* shows how to select and grow more than 150 blooming and foliage plants that will thrive indoors. This easy-to-follow guide explains how to integrate plants into your decor and outlines steps to make them thrive.

Page 83

Page 88

Page 60

COMPREHENSIVE SELECTION GUIDE

HOW TO GROW HEALTHY PLANTS

Page 51

Page 46

Page 48

SOLUTIONS TO COMMON PROBLEMS

Created, written, and checked by garden experts

ISBN 978-0-696-23218-3

90000

9 780696 232183

$12.95

$16.95 in Canada

Visit us at meredithbooks.com